Lee's Invasion of the North

Lee's Invasion of the North

The Campaign of Antietam (Sharpsburg), 1862, during the American Civil War

ILLUSTRATED

Robert Underwood Johnson
and
Clarence Clough Buel

LEONAUR

Lee's Invasion of the North
The Campaign of Antietam (Sharpsburg), 1862, during the American Civil War
Robert Underwood Johnson
and
Clarence Clough Buel

ILLUSTRATED

FIRST EDITION

Leonaur is an imprint of Oakpast Ltd
Copyright in this form © 2017 Oakpast Ltd

ISBN: 978-1-78282-670-5 (hardcover)
ISBN: 978-1-78282-671-2 (softcover)

http://www.leonaur.com

Publisher's Notes

Contents

From the Peninsula to Antietam

Posthumous Notes by George B. McClellan,
Major-General, U. S. A.

It is not proposed to give in this article a detailed account of the battles of South Mountain and Antietam, but simply a sketch of the general operations of the Maryland campaign of 1862 intended for general readers, especially for those whose memory does not extend back to those exciting days, and whose knowledge is derived from the meagre accounts in so-called histories, too often intended to mislead and pander to party prejudices rather than to seek and record the truth.

★★★★★★

After General McClellan had written the article on the Peninsular Campaign published in *The Century* magazine for May, 1885, he was requested to write an account of the battle of Antietam, which he promised to do at his leisure. He had kept the promise in mind, and as occasion served had sketched introductory portions of the proposed article. In the morning after his sudden death, these manuscript pages were found on his table, with some others freshly written, possibly on the previous day or evening. There was also an unsealed note to one of the editors (in reply to one he had received), in which he said that he would at once proceed with the article and finish it.

It was his custom in writing for the press to make a rapid but complete sketch, often abbreviating words and leaving blanks for matter to be copied from documents, and then to rewrite the entire article for publication. It would seem that in this case he had first in mind the consideration stated in the second paragraph of the article, and had given his attention to the history of the army, from the close of the Seven Days' battles to

THE NATIONAL CEMETERY AT SHARPS-
BURG—OVERLOOKING THE VALLEY
OF THE ANTIETAM.

the advance from Washington toward South Mountain and Antietam. There was no manuscript relating to later events. He had
commenced what appears to be his final copy of this first portion of the article, but had completed only about three pages of
foolscap, which extend in the print below to a place indicated.
It is an interesting fact that in this final copy the paragraph
commencing with the words "So long as life lasts" was apparently the last written, being on a separate page and indicated
by a letter A for insertion where it stands. This tribute of admiration for the army which loved him as he loved them was
among the last thoughts, if it was not the very last, which his
pen committed to paper.

Although this introduction to the account of Antietam is but
his first sketch, and not in the final shape he would have given
it for publication, it is so comprehensive and complete, and
contains so much that is of historical importance, that his literary executor has considered it his duty to allow its publication
in *The Century* in the form in which General McClellan left it,
and thus as far as possible fulfil a promise made in the last hours
of his life.

William C. Prime.

Literary Executor of General McClellan.

★★★★★★

A great battle can never be regarded as "a solitaire," a jewel to be
admired or condemned for itself alone, and without reference to surrounding objects and circumstances. A battle is always one link in a

long chain of events; the culmination of one series of manoeuvres, and the starting-point of another series—therefore it can never be fully understood without reference to preceding and subsequent events.

Restricted as this narrative is intended to be, it is nevertheless necessary to preface it by a brief story of the antecedent circumstances.

In an article already published in *The Century*, May, 1885, I have narrated the events of the Peninsular campaign up to the time when, at the close of the Seven Days' battles, the Army of the Potomac was firmly established on its proper line of operations, the James River.

So long as life lasts the survivors of those glorious days will remember with quickened pulse the attitude of that army when it reached the goal for which it had striven with such transcendent heroism. Exhausted, depleted in numbers, bleeding at every pore, but still proud and defiant, and strong in the consciousness of a great feat of arms heroically accomplished, it stood ready to renew the struggle with undiminished ardour whenever its commander should give the word. It was one of those magnificent episodes which dignify a nation's history, and are fit subjects for the grandest efforts of the poet and the painter.

(Many years ago, it was my good fortune, when in Europe, to make the acquaintance of a charming old Westphalian baron who was *aide-de-camp* to King Jerome in the days of his prosperity. In 1813 my friend was sent by his king with important dispatches to the Emperor, and, as it happened, arrived while the Battle of Lutzen was in progress. He approached from the rear and for miles passed through crowds of stragglers, feeling no doubt that the battle was lost, and that he was about to witness the crushing defeat of the French. Still keeping on and on, he at last found the Emperor at the front, and to his great surprise discovered that the battle was won. Thus, it very often happens in war that there are on each side two armies in the field, one of the fighting men with the colours, the other of stragglers and marauders in the rear; the relative strength of these two armies depends upon the state of discipline and the peculiar circumstances of the time.) The paragraph enclosed by brackets was in the first sketch of the article, but was omitted by General McClellan in the final manuscript. W. C. P.

At the close of such a series of battles and marches the returns of the killed, wounded, and missing by no means fully measure the temporary decrease of strength; there were also many thousands unfitted for duty for some days by illness, demoralisation, and fatigue. The first thing to be done was to issue supplies from the vessels already sent to the James, and to allow the men some little time to rest and recover their strength after the great fatigue and nervous tension they had undergone.

In order to permit a small number to watch over the safety of the whole army, and at the same time to prepare the way for ulterior operations, so that when the army advanced again upon Richmond by either bank of the James its base of supplies might be secure with a small guard, the position was rapidly entrenched, the work being completed about the 10th of July.

Prior to the 10th of July two brigades of Shields's division, numbering about 5300 men, had joined the army, bringing its numbers for duty up to 89,549, officers and men, about the same strength as that with which it entered upon the siege of Yorktown, the reinforcements received in the shape of the divisions of Franklin and McCall, the brigades of Shields, and a few regiments from Fort Monroe having slightly more than made good the losses in battle and by disease. But among these 89,000 for duty on the 10th of July were included all the extra duty men employed as teamsters, and in the various administrative services, and, with the further deductions necessary for camp guards, guards of communications, depots and trains, flank detachments, etc., reduced the numbers actually available for offensive battle to not more than (60,000?)

★★★★★★

According to General McClellan's *Tri-monthly Return*, dated July 10, 1862 (*Official Records*, Vol. XI., Pt. III.), he would appear to be mistaken, above, in saying that the "89,000 for duty" included "all the extra duty men," for in the return he classifies (excluding the forces under Dix) 88,435 as "present for duty, equipped," at Harrison's Landing, and in the next column he accounts for 106,460 as the "aggregate present." Obviously, there is no meaning in the return if the 88,435 "present for duty, equipped," did not exclude the 18,021 (supposably extra duty men like teamsters, etc.) which made the difference between the "present for duty, equipped," and the 106,466 "aggregate present."

★★★★★★

A few days sufficed to give the men the necessary rest, and to renew the supplies exhausted on the march across the Peninsula; the army was once more in condition to undertake any operation justified by its numbers, and was in an excellent position to advance by either bank of the James. (End of finished draft.)

FAC-SIMILE OF A PART OF GENERAL McCLELLAN'S LAST MANUSCRIPT.

It was at last upon its true line of operations, which I had been unable to adopt at an earlier day in consequence of the Secretary of War's peremptory order of the 18th of May requiring the right wing to be extended to the north of Richmond in order to establish communication with General McDowell. General McDowell was then under orders to advance from Fredericksburg, but never came, because, in spite of his earnest protest, these orders were countermanded from Washington, and he was sent upon a fruitless expedition toward the Shenandoah instead of being permitted to join me, as he could have done, at the time of the affair of Hanover Court House.

I urged in vain that the Army of the Potomac should remain on the line of the James, and that it should resume the offensive as soon as re-enforced to the full extent of the means in possession of the Government. Had the Army of the Potomac been permitted to remain on the line of the James, I would have crossed to the south bank of that river, and while engaging Lee's attention in front of Malvern, would have made a rapid movement in force on Petersburg, having gained which, I would have operated against Richmond and its communications from the west, having already gained those from the south.

Subsequent events proved that Lee did not move northward from Richmond with his army until assured that the Army of the Potomac was actually on its way to Fort Monroe; and they also proved that so long as the Army of the Potomac was on the James, Washington and Maryland would have been entirely safe under the protection of the fortifications and a comparatively small part of the troops then in that vicinity; so that Burnside's troops and a large part of the Union Army of Virginia might, with entire propriety, have been sent by water to join the army under my command, which—with detachments from the West—could easily have been brought up to more than 100,000 men disposable on the actual field of battle.

In spite of my most pressing and oft-repeated entreaties, the order was insisted upon for the abandonment of the Peninsula line and the return of the Army of the Potomac to Washington in order to support General Pope, who was in no danger so long as the Army of the Potomac remained on the James. With a heavy heart, I relinquished the position gained at the cost of so much time and blood. As an evidence of my good faith in opposing this movement it should be mentioned that General Halleck had assured me, verbally and in writing, that I was to command all the troops in front of Washington, including those of Generals Burnside and Pope—a promise that was not carried into effect.

As the different divisions of the Army of the Potomac reached Aquia Creek and the vicinity of Washington they were removed from my command, even to my personal escort and camp guard, so that on the 30th of August, in reply to a telegram from him, I telegraphed General Halleck from Alexandria:

> I have no sharpshooters except the guard around my camp. I have sent off every man but those, and will now send them with the train as you direct. I will also send my only remaining squadron of cavalry with General Sumner. I can do no more. You now have every man of the Army of the Potomac who is within my reach.

I had already sent off even my headquarters wagons—so far as landed—with ammunition to the front.

On the same day, I telegraphed to General Halleck, "I cannot express to you, etc."

★★★★★★

The dispatch which General McClellan here indicates, as intending to insert when revising the manuscript, proceeds as follows:

"I cannot express to you the pain and mortification I have experienced today in listening to the distant sound of the firing' of my men. As I can be of no further use here, I respectfully ask that if there is a possibility of the conflict being renewed tomorrow, I may be permitted to go to the scene of battle with my staff, merely to be with my own men, if nothing more; they will fight none the worse for my being with them. If it is not deemed best to intrust me with the command even of my own army, I simply ask to be permitted to share their fate on the field of battle. Please reply to this tonight.

"I have been engaged for the last few hours in doing what I can to make arrangements for the wounded. I have started out all the ambulances now landed. As I have sent my escort to the front, I would be glad to take some of Gregg's cavalry with me, if allowed to go.

"G. B. McClellan, Major-General."

The dispatch was dated "Camp near Alexandria, Aug. 30th, 1862, 10:30 p. m." On the following day, he received this answer:

"Washington, Aug. 31, 1862, 9:18 a. m.

"Major-General McClellan: I have just seen your telegram of 11:05 last night. The substance was stated to me when received, but I did not know that you asked for a reply immediately. I cannot answer without seeing the President, as General Pope is in command, by his orders, of the department.

"I think Couch's division should go forward as rapidly as possible, and find the battlefield.

"H. W. Halleck, General-in-Chief."

★★★★★★

On the 1st of September, I met General Halleck at his office in Washington, who by verbal order directed me to take charge of Washington and its defences, but expressly prohibited me from exercising any control over the active troops under General Pope.

At this interview, I informed General Halleck that from information received through one of my aides I was satisfied that affairs were not progressing favourably at the front, and urged him to go out in person to ascertain the exact state of the case. He declined doing this, but finally sent Colonel Kelton, his adjutant-general.

Next morning while at breakfast at an early hour I received a call from the President, accompanied by General Halleck.

The President informed me that Colonel Kelton had returned and represented the condition of affairs as much worse than I had stated to Halleck on the previous day; that there were thirty thousand stragglers on the roads; that the army was entirely defeated and falling back to Washington in confusion. He then said that he regarded Washington as lost, and asked me if I would, under the circumstances, consent to accept command of all the forces. Without one moment's hesitation and without making any conditions whatever, I at once said that I would accept the command and would stake my life that I would save the city. Both the President and Halleck again asserted that it was impossible to save the city, and I repeated my firm conviction that I could and would save it. They then left, the President verbally placing me in entire command of the city and of the troops falling back upon it from the front.

I at once sent for my staff-officers and dispatched them on various duties; some to the front with orders for the disposition of such corps as they met, others to see to the prompt forwarding of ammunition and supplies to meet the retreating troops. In a very short time I had made all the requisite preparations and was about to start to the front in person to assume command as far out as possible, when a message came to me from General Halleck informing me that it was the President's order that I should not assume command until the troops had reached the immediate vicinity of the fortifications. I therefore waited until the afternoon, when I rode out to Upton's Hill, the most advanced of the detached works covering the capital.

Soon after arriving there the head of Hatch's command of infantry arrived, immediately followed by Generals Pope and McDowell escorted by a regiment, or part of a regiment, of cavalry. I obtained what information I could from General Pope and dispatched the few remaining aides with me to meet the troops on the roads leading in on the left, with final orders to them, when quite a heavy distant artillery firing broke out in the direction of the Chantilly and Vienna road.

Asking General Pope what that was, he replied it was probably an attack on Sumner, who commanded the rear-guard in that direction; in reply to another question he said that he thought it probably a serious affair. He and McDowell then asked if I had any objection to their proceeding to Washington. I said that they might do so, but that I was going to the firing. They then proceeded on with their escort while, with a single *aide* (Colonel Colburn) and three orderlies, I struck across country to intercept the column on our right by the shortest line. It was a little after dark when I reached the column.

I leave to others who were present the description of what then occurred: the frantic cheers of welcome that extended for miles along the column; the breaking of ranks and the wild appeals of the men that I should then and there take them back on the line of retreat and let them snatch victory out of defeat.

★★★★★★

In November, 1887, George Kimball of Boston wrote to the editors:
"Though a quarter of a century has passed since 'those darkest days of the war,' I still retain a vivid remembrance of the sudden and complete change which came upon the face of affairs when General McClellan was restored to command. At the time, I was serving in Company A, 12th Massachusetts Volunteers, attached to Ricketts's division of the First Army Corps. The announcement of McClellan's restoration came to us in the early evening of the 2nd of September, 1862, just after reaching Hall's Hill, weary from long marching and well-nigh disheartened by recent reverses. The men were scattered about

in groups, discussing the events of their ill-starred campaign, and indulging in comments that were decidedly uncomplimentary to those who had been responsible for its mismanagement. We did not know, of course, the exact significance of all that had happened, as we afterward learned it, but being mainly thinking men, we were able to form pretty shrewd guesses as to where the real difficulty lay.

"Suddenly, while these mournful consultations were in full blast, a mounted officer, dashing past our bivouac, reined up enough to shout, "'Little Mac" is back here on the road, boys!' The scene that followed can be more easily imagined than described. From extreme sadness, we passed in a twinkling to a delirium of delight. A Deliverer had come. A real 'rainbow of promise' had appeared suddenly in the dark political, sky. The feeling in our division upon the return of General McClellan had its counterpart in all the others, for the Army of the Potomac loved him as it never loved any other leader.

"In a few days, we started upon that long march into Maryland, and whenever General McClellan appeared among his troops, from the crossing of the Potomac at Washington to the grapple with Lee at Antietam, it was the signal for the most spontaneous and enthusiastic cheering I ever listened to or participated in. Men threw their caps high into the air, and danced and frolicked like schoolboys, so glad were they to get their old commander back again. It is true McClellan had always been fortunate in being able to excite enthusiasm among his troops, but demonstrations at this time took on an added and noticeable emphasis from the fact that he had been recalled to command after what the army believed to be an unwise and unjust suspension.

"The climax seemed to be reached, however, at Middletown, where we first caught sight of the enemy Here, upon our arrival, we found General McClellan sitting upon his horse in the road. The enemy occupied a gap in the South Mountain, a mile or two beyond. Reno and Hatch were fighting, and the smoke of their guns could be seen halfway up the mountain. As each organisation passed the general, the men became apparently forgetful of everything but their love for him. They cheered and cheered again, until they became so hoarse they could cheer no longer. It seemed as if an intermission had been declared in order that a reception might be tendered to the general-in-chief. A great crowd continually surrounded him, and the most extravagant demonstrations were indulged in. Hundreds even hugged the horse's legs and caressed his head and mane.

"While the troops were thus surging by, the general continually pointed with his finger to the gap in the mountain through which our path lay. It was like a great scene in a play, with the roar of the guns for an accompaniment. Another enthusiastic demonstration that I remember occurred in the afternoon of that the 17th at Antietam, when the general rode along our line of battle. The cheers could not have been heartier than they were. General McClellan may have had opponents elsewhere; he had few, if any, among the soldiers whom he commanded."

★★★★★★

Let it suffice to say that before the day broke the troops were all in position to repulse attack, and that Washington was safe.

On the 3rd it was clear that the enemy intended an invasion of Maryland and Pennsylvania by crossing the Upper Potomac; I therefore moved the Second, Ninth, and Twelfth Corps to the Maryland side of the Potomac in position to meet any attack upon the city on that side.

As soon as this was done I reported the fact to General Halleck, who asked what general I had placed in command of those three corps; I replied that I had made no such detail, as I should take command in person if the enemy appeared in that direction. He then said that my command included only the defences of Washington and did not extend to any active column that might be moved out beyond the line of works; that no decision had yet been made as to the commander of the active army. He repeated the same thing on more than one occasion before the final advance to South Mountain and Antietam took place.

I should here state that the only published order ever issued in regard to the extent of my command after my interview with the President on the morning of the 2nd was the following:

War Department, Adjutant-General's Office,
Washington, September 2, 1862.
Major-General McClellan will have command, of the fortifications of Washington and of all the troops for the defence of the capital.

By order of Major-General Halleck.

E. D. Townsend, Assistant Adjutant-General.

★★★★★★

The order is in its original form, as it was first given to the, newspapers and as it appeared in some of them, this order purported to be issued "by order of the Secretary of War."—Original Editors.

On the 3rd the President, by an order in his own handwriting, but signed by the Secretary of War directed General Halleck to "organise an army for active operations . . . independent of the forces he may deem necessary for the defence of Washington, when such active army shall take the field."—Original Editors.

★★★★★★

A few days after this and before I went to the front, Secretary Seward came to my quarters one evening and asked my opinion of the condition of affairs at Harper's Ferry, remarking that he was not at ease on the subject. Harper's Ferry was not at that time in any sense under my control, but I told Mr. Seward that I regarded the arrangements there as exceedingly dangerous; that in my opinion the proper course was to abandon the position and unite the garrison (about ten thousand men) to the main army of operations, for the reason that its presence at Harper's Ferry would not hinder the enemy from crossing the Potomac; that if we were unsuccessful in the approaching battle, Harper's Ferry would be of no use to us and its garrison necessarily would be lost; that if we were successful we would immediately recover the post without any difficulty, while the addition of ten thousand men to the active army would be an important factor in securing success. I added that if it were determined to hold the position the existing arrangements were all wrong, as it would be easy for the enemy to surround and capture the garrison, and that the garrison ought, at least, to be withdrawn to the Maryland Heights, where they could resist attack until relieved.

The Secretary was much impressed by what I said, and asked me to accompany him to General Halleck and repeat my statement to him. I acquiesced, and we went together to General Halleck's quarters, where we found that he had retired for the night. But he received us in his bedroom, when, after a preliminary explanation by the Secretary as to the interview being at his request, I said to Halleck precisely what I had stated to Mr. Seward.

Halleck received my statement with ill-concealed contempt—said that everything was all right as it was; that my views were entirely erroneous, etc, and soon bowed us out, leaving matters at Harper's Ferry precisely as they were. On the 7th of September, in addition to the three corps already mentioned (the Second, Ninth, and Twelfth), the First and Sixth Corps, Sykes's division of the Fifth Corps, and Couch's division of the Fourth Corps, were also on the Maryland side of the river; the First and Ninth Corps at Leesboro; the Second and Twelfth in front of Rockville; the Sixth Corps at Rockville; Couch's division at Offutt's Cross Roads; Sykes's division at Tenallytown.

As the time had now arrived for the army to advance, and I had received no orders to take command of it, but had been expressly told that the assignment of a commander had not been decided, I determined to solve the question for myself, and when I moved out from Washington with my staff and personal escort I left my card with P. P. C. written upon it, at the White House, War Office, and Secretary Seward's house, and went on my way. (General McClellan's orders from the 1st to the 8th of September, inclusive, are dated "Headquarters, Washington." On the 9th he resumed the heading, "Headquarters, Army of the Potomac," at Rockville.—Original Editors).

I was afterward accused of assuming command without authority, for nefarious purposes, and in fact I fought the battles of South Mountain and Antietam with a halter around my neck, for if the Army of the Potomac had been defeated and I had survived I would, no doubt, have been tried for assuming authority without orders, and, in the state of feeling which so unjustly condemned the innocent and most meritorious General F. J. Porter, I would probably have been condemned to death. I was fully aware of the risk I ran, but the path of duty was clear and I tried to follow it. It was absolutely necessary that Lee's army should be met, and in the state of affairs I have briefly described there could be no hesitation on my part as to doing it promptly.

Very few in the Army of the Potomac doubted the favourable result of the next collision with the Confederate army, but in other quarters not a little doubt prevailed, and the desire for very rapid movements, so loudly expressed after the result was gained, did not make itself heard during the movements preceding the battles; quite the contrary was the case, as I was more than once cautioned that I was moving too rashly and exposing the capital to an attack from the Virginia side.

As is well known, the result of General Pope's operations had not

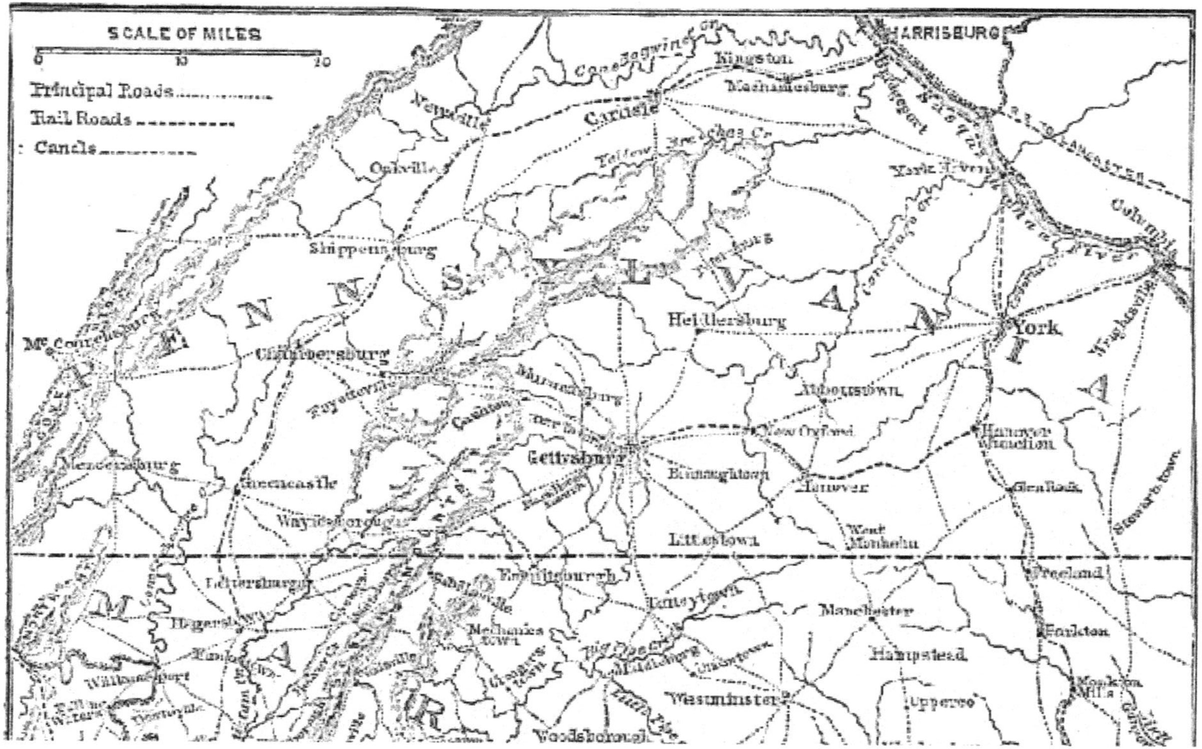

SCALE OF MILES
0
10
20
Principal Roads
Rail Roads
Canals
HARRISBURG
Kingston
Mechanicsburg
Carlisle
Newville
Oakville
Shippensburg
Chambersburg
Greencastle
Waynesborough
Mercersburg
Heidlersburg
York
Gettysburg
Hanover
Abbottstown
New Oxford
Littlestown
Emmittsburgh
Taneytown
Manchester
Hampstead
Westminster
Woodsborough
Hagerstown
Williamsport
Freeland
Columbia
Glen Rock

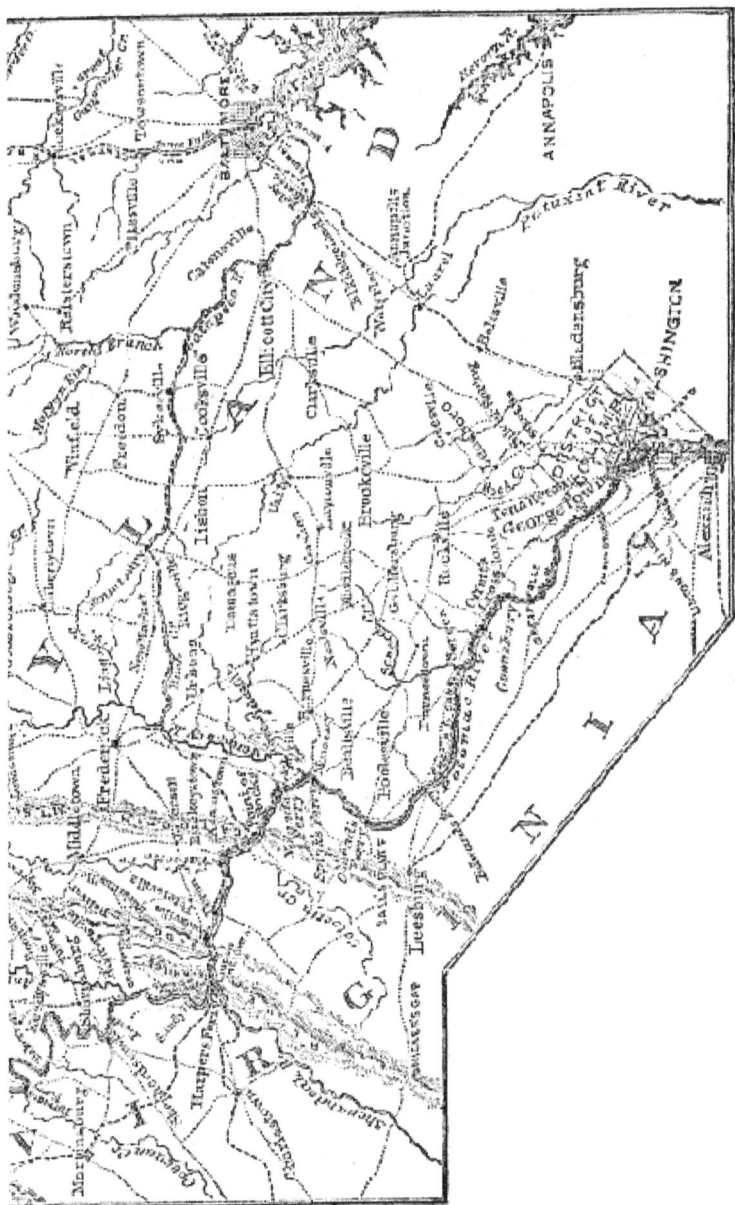

MAP OF THE MARYLAND CAMPAIGN.

been favourable, and when I finally resumed command of the troops in and around Washington they were weary, disheartened, their organisation impaired, their clothing, ammunition, and supplies in a pitiable condition. The Army of the Potomac was thoroughly exhausted and depleted by its desperate fighting and severe marches in the unhealthy regions of the Chickahominy and afterward, during the second Bull Run campaign; its trains, administration services and supplies were disorganised or lacking in consequence of the rapidity and manner of its removal from the Peninsula as well as from the nature of its operations during the second Bull Run campaign.

In the departure from the Peninsula, trains, supplies, cavalry, and artillery in many instances had necessarily been left at Fort Monroe and Yorktown for lack of vessels, as the important point was to remove the infantry divisions rapidly to the support of General Pope. The divisions of the Army of Virginia were also exhausted and weakened, and their trains were disorganised and their supplies deficient by reason of the movements in which they had been engaged.

Had General Lee remained in front of Washington it would have been the part of wisdom to hold our own army quiet until its pressing wants were fully supplied, its organisation was restored, and its ranks were filled with recruits—in brief, until it was prepared for a campaign. But as the enemy maintained the offensive and crossed the Upper Potomac to threaten or invade Pennsylvania, it became necessary to meet him at any cost notwithstanding the condition of the troops, to put a stop to the invasion, save Baltimore and Washington, and throw him back across the Potomac. Nothing but sheer necessity justified the advance of the Army of the Potomac to South Mountain and Antietam in its then condition, and it is to the eternal honour of the brave men who composed it that under such adverse circumstances they gained those victories.

The work of supply and reorganisation was continued as best we might while on the march, and even after the close of the battles (September 14th-17th) so much remained to be done to place the army in condition for a campaign, that the delay which ensued was absolutely unavoidable, and the army could not have entered upon a new campaign one day earlier than it did. It must then be borne constantly in mind that the purpose of advancing from Washington was simply to meet the necessities of the moment by frustrating Lee's invasion of the Northern States, and, when that was accomplished, to push with the utmost rapidity the work of reorganisation and supply so that a new campaign might be promptly inaugurated with the army in condition to prosecute it to a successful termination without intermission.

The advance from Washington was covered by the cavalry, under General Pleasonton, which was pushed as far to the front as possible, and was soon in constant contact with the enemy's cavalry, with whom several well-conducted and successful affairs occurred.

Partly in order to move men freely and rapidly, partly in consequence of the lack of accurate information as to the exact position and intention of Lee's army, the troops advanced by three main roads: that part near the Potomac by Offutt's Cross Roads and the mouth of the Seneca; that by Rockville to Frederick, and that by Brookville and Urbana to New Market. We were then in condition to act according to the development of the enemy's plans and to concentrate rapidly in any position.

If Lee threatened our left flank by moving down the river road, or by crossing the Potomac at any of the fords from Coon's Ferry upward, there were enough troops on the river road to hold him in check until the rest of the army could move over to support them; if Lee took up a position behind the Seneca near Frederick the whole army could be rapidly concentrated in that direction to attack him in force; if he moved upon Baltimore the entire army could rapidly be thrown in his rear and his retreat would be cut off; if he moved by Gettysburg or Chambersburg upon York or Carlisle we were equally in position to throw ourselves in his rear.

The first requisite was to gain accurate information as to Lee's movements, and the second, to push the work of supply and reorganisation as rapidly as possible.

General Lee and I knew each other well. In the days before the war we served together in Mexico, and we had commanded against each other in the Peninsula. I had the highest respect for his ability as a commander, and knew that he was a general not to be trifled with or carelessly afforded an opportunity of striking a fatal blow. Each of us naturally regarded his own army as the better, but each entertained the highest respect for the endurance, courage, and fighting qualities of the opposing army; and this feeling extended to the officers and men. It was perfectly natural under these circumstances that both of us should exercise a certain amount of caution,—I in my endeavours to ascertain Lee's strength, position, and intentions before I struck the fatal blow; he to abstain from any extended movements of invasion, and to hold his army well in hand until he could be satisfied as to the condition of the Army of the Potomac after its second Bull Run campaign, and as to the intentions of its commander.

On Memorial Day, 1885, General McClellan addressed from this rostrum a large assembly of members of the " Grand Army of the Republic."

In the Ranks to the Antietam

By David L. Thompson, Co. G, 9th New York Volunteers.

On the 5th of Septeniber, 1862, Hawkins' Zouaves, as a part of Burnside's corps, from Fredericksburg, landed at Washington to assist in the defence of the capital, then threatened by Lee's first invasion of Maryland, and, as events proved, to join in the pursuit of the invaders. Here, in pursuance of a measure for shortening the baggage train which had lately been decided on, we were deprived of our Sibley tents those cumbersome, conical caravansaries, in which eighteen men lie upon the ground with their feet toward the centre.

Shelter tents came soon to replace the "Sibleys," and with them came marching orders—the army was moving west. At dusk, we set up our new houses. A shelter or dog tent is like a bargain—it takes two to make it. Each man is provided with an oblong piece of thick, unbleached muslin about the length of a man—say six feet—and two-thirds as wide, bordered all round with buttons and button-holes alternately matching respectively the button-holes and buttons of his comrade's piece. To set it up, cut two crotched stakes, each about four feet long, point them at the uncrotched end, and drive them into the ground about six feet apart; cut a slender pole to lie horizontally from one crotch to the other, button the two pieces of muslin together and throw the resulting piece over the pole, drawing out the corners tight and pinning them down to the ground by means of little loops fastened in them. You will thus get a wedge-shaped structure—simply the two slopes of an ordinary roof—about three and a half feet high at its highest point, and open at both ends.

This will accommodate two men, and in warm, pleasant weather is all that is needed. In rainy weather, a third man is admitted. A piece of rope about four feet long is then tied to the top of one of the stakes and stretched out in the line of direction of the ridge pole, the free

A DISORGANIZED PRIVATE.

end being brought down to the ground and pinned there. The third man then buttons his piece of muslin to one slope of the roof, carries the other edge of the piece out around the tightened rope and brings it back to the edge of the other slope, to which it is buttoned. This third piece is shifted from one end of the tent to the other, according to the direction of the wind or storm. You thus get an extension to your tent in which knapsacks can be stored, leaving the rest of the space clear for sleeping purposes. This is large enough to accommodate three men lying side by side.

But will such a structure keep out rain? Certainly, just as your umbrella does—unless you touch it on the inside when it is soaked. If you do, the rain will come in, drop by drop, just where you have touched it. To keep the water from flowing in along the surface of the ground, dig a small trench about three inches deep all around the tent, close up, so that the rain shed from the roof will fall into it. Such a house is always with you potentially, for you carry the materials on your back and can snap your fingers at the baggage wagon. For three-fourths of the year it is all the shelter needed, as it keeps out rain, snow, and wind perfectly, being penetrable only by the cold.

We marched at last, and on the 12th of September entered Frederick, wondering all the way what the enemy meant. We of the ranks little suspected what sheaves he was gathering in at Harper's Ferry, behind the curtain of his main body. We guessed, however, as usual, and toward evening began to get our answer. He was right ahead, his rear-guard skirmishing with our advance. We came up at the close

26

of the fight at Frederick, and, forming line of battle, went at double-quick through cornfields, potato patches, gardens, and backyards—the German washer-women of the 103rd New York regiment going in with us on the run. It was only a measure of precaution, however, the cavalry having done what little there was to do in the way of driving out of the city a Confederate rear-guard not much inclined to stay. We pitched tents at once in the outskirts, and after a hearty supper went to explore the city.

The next morning the feeling of distrust which the night before had seemed to rule the place had disappeared, and a general holiday feeling took its place. The city was abloom with flags, houses were open everywhere, trays of food were set on the window-sills of nearly all the better class of houses, and the streets were filled with women dressed in their best, walking bareheaded, singing, and testifying in every way the general joy. September 13th in Frederick City was a bright one in memory for many a month after—a pleasant topic to discuss over many a camp-fire.

The next day our regiment went on a reconnoissance to a speck of a village, rather overweighted by its name,—Jefferson,—about eight miles from Frederick and on our left. Far up the mountainside ahead of us we could see, in the fields confronting the edge of the woods that crowned the ridge, the scattered line of Rush's Lancers, their bright red pennons fluttering gayly from their spear heads.

We reached camp again about 10 o'clock at night, and found awaiting us marching orders for 2 o'clock the following morning. Late as it was, one of my tent-mates—an enterprising young fellow—started out on a foraging expedition, in pursuance of a vow made several days before to find something with which to vary his monotonous regimen of "hard-tack" and "salt horse." He "ran the guard"—an easy thing to do in the darkness and hubbub—and returned shortly after, struggling with a weight of miscellaneous plunder; a crock of butter, a quantity of apple-butter, some lard, a three-legged skillet weighing several pounds, and a live hen. It was a marvel how he managed to carry so much; but he was a rare gleaner always, with a comprehensive method that covered the ground. That night we had several immense flapjacks, the whole size of the pan; then, tethering the hen to one of the tent pegs, we went to sleep, to be roused an hour or so later by hearing our two-legged prize cackling and fluttering off in the darkness.

Up to the 10th the army had not marched so much as it had drifted, but from this point on our purpose seemed to grow more definite and the interest deepened steadily. There had been sporadic fighting through the day (the 13th), but it was over the hills to the west, and we heard nothing of it beyond those airy echoes that take the shape of rumour. Now, however, the ferment at the front, borne back by galloping orderlies, was swiftly leavening the mass. Occasionally, on our march we would pass a broken gun wheel or the bloated body of a slaughtered horse, and in various ways we knew that we were close upon the enemy, and that we could not now be long delayed. This would have been told us by the burden of our daily orders, always the same, to hold ourselves "in readiness to march at a moment's notice," with the stereotyped addendum, "three days' cooked rations and forty rounds." Everyone lay down to sleep that night with a feeling of impending battle.

By daylight next morning we were in motion again—the whole army. The gathering of such a multitude is a swarm, its march a vast migration. It fills up every road leading in the same direction over a breadth of many miles, with long ammunition and supply trains disposed for safety along the inner roads, infantry and artillery next in order outwardly, feelers of cavalry all along its front and far out on its flanks; while behind, trailing along every road for miles (ravelings from the great square blanket which the enemy's cavalry, if active, snip off with ease), are the rabble of stragglers—laggards through sickness or exhaustion, squads of recruits, convalescents from the hospital, special duty men going up to rejoin their regiments.

Each body has its route laid down for it each day, its time of starting set by watch, its place of bivouac or camp appointed, together with the hour of reaching it. If two roads come together, the corps that reaches the junction first moves on, while the other files out into the fields, stacks arms, builds fires, and boils its coffee. Stand, now, by the roadside while a corps is filing past. They march "route step," as it is called,—that is, not keeping time,—and four abreast, as a country road seldom permits a greater breadth, allowing for the aides and orderlies that gallop in either direction continually along the column. If the march has just begun, you hear the sound of voices everywhere, with roars of laughter in spots, marking the place of the company wag—generally some Irishman, the action of whose tongue bears out his calling.

Later on, when the weight of knapsack and musket begins to tell, these sounds die out; a sense of weariness and labour rises from the toiling masses streaming by, voiced only by the shuffle of a multitude of feet, the rubbing and straining of innumerable straps, and the flop of full canteens. So uniformly does the mass move on that it suggests a great machine, requiring only its directing mind. Yet such a mass, without experience in battle, would go to pieces before a moderately effective fire. Catch up a handful of snow and throw it, it flies to fluff; pack it, it strikes like stone. Here is the secret of organisation—the aim and crown of drill, to make the units one, that when the crisis comes, the missile may be thoroughly compacted. Too much, however, has been claimed for theoretic discipline—not enough for intelligent individual action. No remark was oftener on the lips of officers during the war than this: "Obey orders! *I* do your thinking for you." But that soldier is the best whose good sense tells him when to be merely a part of a machine and when not.

The premonitions of the night were not fulfilled next day. That day—the 14th of September—we crossed the Catoctin range of mountains, reaching the summit about noon, and descended its western slope into the beautiful valley of Middletown. Half-way up the valley's western side we halted for a rest, and turned to look back on the moving host. It was a scene to linger in the memory. The valley in which Middletown lies is four or five miles wide, as I remember it, and runs almost due north and south between the parallel ranges of Catoctin and South Mountains. From where we stood the landscape lay below us, the eye commanding the opposite slope of the valley almost at point-blank.

An hour before, from the same spot, it had been merely a scene of quiet pastoral beauty. All at once, along its eastern edge the heads of the columns began to appear, and grew and grew, pouring over the ridge and descending by every road, filling them completely and scarring the surface of the gentle landscape with the angry welts of war. By the farthest northern road—the farthest we could see—moved the baggage wagons, the line stretching from the bottom of the valley back to the top of the ridge, and beyond, only the canvas covers of the wagons revealing their character. We knew that each dot was a heavily loaded army wagon, drawn by six mules and occupying forty feet of road at least. Now they looked like white beads on a string. So far away were they that no motion was perceptible.

The constant swelling of the end of the line down in the valley, where the teams turned into the fields to park, gave evidence that, in this way, it was being slowly reeled along the way. The troops were marching by two roads farther south. The Confederates fighting on the western summit must have seen them plainly. Half a mile beyond us the column broke abruptly, filing off into line of battle, right and left, across the fields. From that point backward and downward, across the valley and up the farther slope, it stretched with scarcely a gap, every curve and zigzag of the way defined more sharply by its sombre presence. Here, too, on all the distant portions of the line, motion was imperceptible, but could be inferred from the casual glint of sunlight on a musket barrel miles away. It was 3 o'clock when we resumed our march, turning our backs upon the beautiful, impressive picture—each column a monstrous, crawling, blue-black snake, miles long, quilled with the silver slant of muskets at a "shoulder," its sluggish tail writhing slowly up over the distant eastern ridge, its bruised head weltering in the roar and smoke upon the crest above, where was being fought the battle of South Mountain.

We were now getting nearer to the danger line, the rattle of musketry going on incessantly in the edges of the woods and behind the low stone fences that seamed the mountain-side. Then we came upon the fringes of the contest—slightly wounded men scattered along the winding road on their way to the hospital, and now and then a squad of prisoners, wounded and unwounded together, going under guard to the rear.

The brigade was ordered to the left of the road to support a regular battery posted at the top of a steep slope, with a cornfield on the left, and twenty yards or so in front, a thin wood. We formed behind the battery and a little down the slope—the 89th on the left, the 9th next, then the 103rd. We had been in position but a few minutes when a stir in front advised us of something unusual afoot, and the next moment the Confederates burst out of the woods and made a dash at the battery. We had just obeyed a hastily given order to lie down, when the bullets whistled over our heads, and fell far down the slope behind us. Then the guns opened at short range, full-shotted with grape and canister. The force of the charge was easily broken, for though it was vigorously made it was not sustained—perhaps was not intended to be, as the whole day's battle had been merely an effort of the enemy to check our advance till he could concentrate for a general engagement.

As the Confederates came out of the woods their line touched ours on the extreme left only, and there at an acute angle, their men nearly treading on those of the 89th, who were on their faces in the cornfield, before they discovered them. At that instant, the situation just there was ideally, cruelly advantageous to us. The Confederates stood before us not twenty feet away, the full intention of destruction on their faces—but helpless, with empty muskets. The 89th simply rose up and shot them down.

It was in this charge that I first heard the "rebel yell"; not the deep-breasted Northern cheer, given in unison and after a struggle, to signify an advantage gained, but a high shrill yelp, uttered without concert, and kept up continually when the fighting was approaching a climax, as an incentive to further effort. This charge ended the contest for the day on that part of the line. Pickets were set well forward in the woods, and we remained some time in position, waiting. How a trivial thing will often thrust itself upon the attention in a supreme moment was well exemplified here. All about us grew pennyroyal, bruised by the tramping of a hundred feet, and the smell of it has always been associated in my memory with that battle.

Before the sunlight faded, I walked over the narrow field. All around lay the Confederate dead—undersized men mostly, from the coast district of North Carolina, with sallow, hatchet faces, and clad in "butternut"— a colour running all the way from a deep, coffee brown up to the whitish brown of ordinary dust. As I looked down on the poor, pinched faces, worn with marching and scant fare, all enmity died out. There was no "secession" in those rigid forms, nor in those fixed eyes staring blankly at the sky. Clearly it was not "their war." Some of our men primed their muskets afresh with the finer powder from the cartridge-boxes of the dead. With this exception, each remained untouched as he had fallen.

Darkness came on rapidly, and it grew very chilly. As little could be done at that hour in the way of burial, we unrolled the blankets of the dead, spread them over the bodies, and then sat down in line, munching a little on our cooked rations in lieu of supper, and listening to the firing, which was kept up on the right, persistently. By 9 o'clock this ceased entirely. Drawing our blankets over us, we went to sleep, lying upon our arms in line as we had stood, living Yankee and dead Confederate side by side, and indistinguishable.—This was Sunday, the 14th of September.

The next morning, receiving no orders to march, we set to work collecting the arms and equipments scattered about the field, and burying the dead. The weather being fine, bowers were built in the woods—generally in fence corners—for such of the wounded as could not be moved with safety; others, after stimulants had been given, were helped down the mountain to the rude hospitals. Before we left the spot, some of the country people living thereabout, who had been scared away by the firing, ventured back, making big eyes at all they saw, and asking most ridiculous questions. One was, whether we were from Mexico! Those belated echoes, it seemed, were still sounding in the woods of Maryland.

The Battle of South Mountain, Or Boonsboro'

By Daniel H. Hill, Lieutenant-General, C. S. A.

Fighting for Time at Turner's and Fox's Gaps.

The conflict of the 14th of September, 1862, is called at the North the Battle of South Mountain, and at the South the Battle of Boonsboro'. So many battlefields of the Civil War bear double names that we cannot believe the duplication has been accidental. It is the unusual which impresses. The troops of the North came mainly from cities, towns, and villages, and were, therefore, impressed by some natural object near the scene of the conflict and named the battle from it. The soldiers from the South were chiefly from the country and were, therefore, impressed by some artificial object near the field of action.

In one section the naming has been after the handiwork of God; in the other section it has been after the handiwork of man. Thus, the first passage of arms is called the battle of Bull Run at the North,— the name of a little stream. At the South, it takes the name of Manassas, from a railroad station. The second battle on the same ground is called the Second Bull Run by the North, and the Second Manassas by the South. Stone's defeat is the battle of Ball's Bluff with the Federals, and the battle of Leesburg with the Confederates. The battle called by General Grant, Pittsburg Landing, a natural object, was named Shiloh, after a church, by his antagonist. Rosecrans called his first great fight with Bragg, the Battle of Stone River, while Bragg named it after Murfreesboro', a village.

So, McClellan's Battle of the Chickahominy, (Gaines's Mill), a little river, was with Lee the Battle of Cold Harbor, a tavern. The Federals speak of the battle of Pea Ridge, of the Ozark range of mountains, and the Confederates call it after Elk Horn, a country inn. The Union soldiers called the bloody battle three days after South Mountain from the little stream, Antietam, and the Southern troops named it after the village of Sharpsburg. Many instances might be given of this double naming by the opposing forces. According to the same law of the unusual, the war-songs of a people have generally been written by non-combatants. The bards who followed the banners of the feudal lords, sang of their exploits, and stimulated them and their retainers to deeds of high emprise, wore no armour and carried no swords.

So, too, the impassioned orators, who roused our ancestors in 1776 with the thrilling cry, "Liberty or Death," never once put themselves in the way of a death by lead or steel, by musket-ball or bayonet stab. The noisy speakers of 1861, who fired the Northern heart and who fired the Southern heart, never did any other kind of *firing*. (Of the political speakers of 1860 a number might be mentioned who afterward served, in some cases with distinction, in the respective armies; for example, Banks, Baker, Frank P. Blair, Jr., Logan, Garfield, Schurz, on the Union side; and Breckinridge, Toombs, Cobb, Floyd, and Pryor of the Confederates).

The Battle of South Mountain was one of extraordinary illusions and delusions. The Federals were under the self-imposed illusion that there was a very large force opposed to them, whereas there was only one weak division until late in the afternoon. They might have brushed it aside almost without halting, but for this illusion. It was a battle of delusions also, for, by moving about from point to point and meeting the foe wherever he presented himself, the Confederates deluded the Federals into the belief that the whole mountain was swarming with rebels. I will endeavour to explain the singular features of the battle and what caused them.

In the retirement of Lee's army from Frederick to Hagerstown and Boonsboro', my division constituted the rear-guard. It consisted of five brigades (Wise's brigade being left behind), and after the arrival at Boonsboro' was intrusted with guarding the wagon trains and parks of artillery belonging to the whole army. Longstreet's corps went to Hagerstown, thirteen miles from Boonsboro', and I was directed to distribute my five brigades so as not only to protect the wagons and guns, but also to watch, all the roads leading from Harper's Ferry, in order to intercept the Federal forces that might make their escape before Jackson had completed the investment of that place. It required a considerable separation of my small command to accomplish these two objects, and my tent, which was pitched about the centre of the five brigades, was not less than three miles from Turner's Gap on the National road crossing South Mountain.

During the forenoon of the 13th General Stuart, who was in an advance position at the gap in the Catoctin Mountain, east of Middletown, with our cavalry, sent a dispatch to me saying that he was followed by two brigades of Federal infantry, and asking me to send him a brigade to check the pursuit at South Mountain. I sent him the brigades of Colquitt and Garland, and the batteries of Bondurant and Lane, with four guns each. Pleasonton's Federal cavalry division came up to the mountain and pressed on till our infantry forces were displayed, when it returned without fighting.

The Confederates, with more than half of Lee's army at Harper's Ferry, distant a march of two days, and with the remainder divided into two parts, thirteen miles from each other, were in good condition to be beaten in detail, scattered and captured. General Longstreet writes to me that he urged General Lee in the evening of the 13th to unite at Sharpsburg the troops which were then at Hagerstown and Boonsboro'. He said that he could effect more with one-third of his own corps, fresh and rested, than with the whole of it, when exhausted by a forced march to join their comrades. That night, finding that he could not rest, General Longstreet rose and wrote to his commander, presenting his views once more, favouring the abandonment of the defence of the mountain except by Stuart and the concentration at Sharpsburg.

I received a note about midnight of the 13th from General Lee saying that he was not satisfied with the condition of things on the turnpike or National road, and directing me to go in person to Turner's Gap the next morning and assist Stuart in its defence. In his official report, General Lee says:

> Learning that Harper's Ferry had not surrendered and that the enemy was advancing more rapidly than was convenient from Fredericktown, I determined to return with Longstreet's command to the Blue Ridge to strengthen D. H. Hill's and Stuart's divisions engaged in holding the passes of the mountains, lest the enemy should fall upon McLaws's rear, drive him from the Maryland Heights, and thus relieve the garrison at Harper's Ferry.

This report and the note to me show that General Lee expected General Stuart to remain and help defend the pass on the 14th.

RATIONS FROM THE STALK.

But on reaching the Mountain House between daylight and sunrise that morning, I received a message from Stuart that he had gone to Crampton's Gap. (See map). He was too gallant a soldier to leave his post when a battle was imminent, and doubtless he believed that there was but a small Federal force on the National road. (Generals Colquitt and Rosser have both written to me that General Stuart told them he had been followed by only a small Federal force. D. H. H.)

I found Garland's brigade at the Mountain House and learned that Colquitt's was at the foot of the mountain on the east side. I found General Colquitt there without vedettes and without information of the Federals, but believing that they had retired.

General Cox's Federal division was at that very time marching up the old Sharpsburg or Braddock's road, a mile to the south, seizing the heights on our right and establishing those heavy batteries which afterward commanded the pike and all the approaches to it. General Pleasonton, of the Federal cavalry, had learned the ground by the reconnoissance of the day before, and to him was intrusted the posting of the advance troops of Reno's corps on the south side of the pike. He says:

> I directed Scammon's brigade to move up the mountain on the left-hand road, gain the crest, and then move to the right, to the turnpike in the enemy's rear. At the same time, I placed Gibson's battery and the heavy batteries in position to the left, covering the road on that side and obtaining a direct fire on the enemy's position in the gap.

This shows that Pleasonton knew that the Confederate forces were at the foot of the mountain. However, I brought Colquitt's brigade back to a point near the summit and placed the 23rd and 28th Georgia regiments on the north side of the pike behind a stone-wall, which afforded an excellent fire upon the pike. The other three regiments, the 6th and 27th Georgia and the 13th Alabama, were posted on the south side of the pike, a little in advance of the wall and well protected by a dense wood.

This brigade did not lose an inch of ground that day. The skirmishers were driven in, but the line of battle on both sides of the road was the same at 10 o'clock at night as it was at 9 o'clock in the morning. After posting Colquitt's brigade I went with Major Ratchford of my staff on a reconnoissance to our right. About three-fourths of a mile from the Mountain House we discovered, by the voices of command

and the rumbling of wheels, that the old road and heights above it were occupied, and took it for granted that the occupation was by Federal troops. We did not see them, and I suppose we were not seen by them. Colonel T. L. Rosser of the cavalry had been sent that morning with his regiment and Pelham's artillery, by order of General Stuart, to seize Fox's Gap on the Braddock road. Cox had got to the heights first and confronted Rosser with a portion of his command, while the remainder of it could be plainly seen at the foot of the mountain. General Rosser writes to me that he reported the situation of things to Stuart, who was passing by on the east side of the mountain on his way south. He, Rosser, was not directed to report to me, and I did not suspect his presence. I do not know to this hour whether Ratchford and myself came near stumbling upon him or upon the enemy.

Returning through the woods we came upon a cabin, the owner of which was in the yard, surrounded by his children, and evidently expectant of something. The morning being cool, Ratchford was wearing a blue cloak which he had found at Seven Pines. In questioning the mountaineer about the roads, I discovered that he thought we were Federals.

"The road on which *your* battery is," said he, "comes into the valley road near the church."

This satisfied me that the enemy was on our right, and I asked him: "Are there any rebels on the pike?"

"Yes; there are some about the Mountain House."

I asked: "Are there many?"

"Well, there are *several*; I don't know how many."

"Who is in command?"

"I don't know."

Just then a shell came hurtling through the woods, and a little girl began crying. Having a little one at home of about the same age, I could not forbear stopping a moment to say a few soothing words to the frightened child, before hurrying off to the work of death. The firing had aroused that prompt and gallant soldier, General Garland, and his men were under arms when I reached the pike. I explained the situation briefly to him, directed him to sweep through the woods, reach the road, and hold it at all hazards, as the safety of Lee's large train depended upon its being held. He went off in high spirits and I never saw him again. I never knew a truer, better, braver man. Had he lived, his talents, pluck, energy, and purity of character must have put him in the front rank of his profession, whether in civil or military life.

After passing through the first belt of woods Garland found Rosser, and, conferring with him, determined to make his stand close to the junction of the roads, near the summit of the mountain (Fox's Gap). He had with him five regiments of infantry and Bondurant's battery of artillery—his infantry force being a little less than one thousand men, all North Carolinians. The 5th regiment was placed on the right of the road, with the 12th as its support; the 23rd was posted behind a low stone-wall on the left of the 5th; then came the 20th and 13th. From the nature of the ground and the duty to be performed, the regiments were not in contact with each other, and the 13th was 250 yards to the left of the 20th. Fifty skirmishers of the 5th North Carolina soon encountered the 23rd Ohio, deployed as skirmishers under Lieutenant-Colonel R. B. Hayes, afterward President of the United States, and the action began at 9 a.m. between Cox's division and Garland's brigade.

I will delay an account of the fight to give the strength of the forces engaged. (See also Table of Opposing Forces in the Maryland Campaign). The Ninth Corps (Reno's) consisted of four divisions under Cox, Willcox, Sturgis, and Rodman; or eight brigades—Scammon and Crook (Cox); Christ and Welsh (Willcox); Nagle and Ferrero (Sturgis); and Fairchild and Harland (Rodman). It had 29 regiments of infantry, 3 companies of cavalry, and 8 batteries of artillery, 3 of them United States batteries of regulars under Benjamin, Clark, and Muhlenberg. (According to General Cox, until the arrival of Willcox with his division, about 2 o'clock, Cox's division and a portion of Pleasonton's cavalry were, the only Union troops on the field. Sturgis arrived on the field about 3:30).

General Cox, who fought Garland, had six Ohio regiments under Brigadiers Scammon and Crook, and also the batteries of McMullin and Simmonds, and three companies of cavalry. The heavy batteries in position (20-pounder Parrotts) were of service to him also, in commanding the approaches to the scene of the conflict. The strength of the division is not given directly, but Scammon estimates his effectives at 1455. The other brigade was most likely equally strong, and I conclude that Cox's infantry, artillery, and cavalry reached three thousand. (In effect confirmed by General Cox). Garland's brigade is estimated at "scarce a thousand."

Scammon's brigade led the attack with great spirit. The 13th North Carolina, under Lieutenant-Colonel Ruffin, and the 20th, under Colonel Alfred Iverson, were furiously assailed on the left. Both regiments were under tried and true soldiers, and they received the assault calmly. Lieutenant Crome, of McMullin's battery, ran up a section of artillery by hand, and opened with effect upon the 20th North Carolina; but the skirmishers under Captain Atwell of that regiment killed the gallant officer while he was himself serving as a gunner. The section was abandoned, but the Confederates were unable to capture it. The effort seemed to be to turn the 13th; and Colonel Ruffin in vain urged General Garland to go to the other part of his line. But with Garland the post of danger was the post of honour. Judge Ruffin, in a recent letter to me, thus speaks of the fall of the hero:

I said to him: 'General, why do you stay here? you are in great danger.' To which he replied: 'I may as well be here as yourself.' I said: 'No, it is my duty to be here with my regiment, but you could better superintend your brigade from a safer position.'
Just then I was shot in the hip, and as there was no field-officer then with the regiment, other than myself, I told him of my wound, and that it might disable me, and in that case I wished a field-officer to take my place. He turned and gave some order, which I have forgotten. In a moment I heard a groan, and looked and found him mortally wounded and writhing in pain. We continued to occupy this position for some time, when I sent my adjutant to the right to see what was going on (as the furious fighting had ceased in that direction).
He returned and reported that the remainder of the brigade was gone and that the ground was occupied by the enemy. I then attempted to go to the left, hoping to come in contact with some portion of your command, but was again confronted by the enemy. I next tried to retreat to the rear, but to my dismay found myself entirely surrounded. The enemy in front was pressing us, and I saw but one way out, and that was to charge those in my front, repel them, if possible, and then, before they could recover, make a dash at those in my rear and cut my way out. This plan was successfully executed.
I shall never forget the feelings of relief which I experienced when I first caught sight of you. You rode up to me, and, shaking my hand, said that you had given us up for lost and did not see how it was possible for us to have escaped. You then attached us to G. B. Anderson's brigade, which had come up in the meantime. . . . I remember one remark which you made

BRIGADIER-GENERAL SAMUEL GARLAND, JR., C. S. A.,
KILLED AT SOUTH MOUNTAIN

just after congratulating me upon cutting my way out that surprised me very much. You said that you were greatly gratified
to find that McClellan's whole army was in your front. As I
knew how small your force was, I could not understand how
it could be a source of pleasure to you to find yourself assailed
by twenty times your number. In a moment, you made it plain
to me by saying that you had feared at first that McClellan's attack upon you was but a feint, and that with his main army he
would cross the mountain at some of the lower gaps and would
thus cut in between Jackson's corps and the forces under Lee.

A little before this I had seen from the lookout station near the
Mountain House the vast army of McClellan spread out before me.
The marching columns extended back far as eye could see in the distance; but many of the troops had already arrived and were in double
lines of battle, and those advancing were taking up positions as fast as
they arrived. It was a grand and glorious spectacle, and it was impossible to look at it without admiration. I had never seen so tremendous
an army before, and I did not see one like it afterward. For though
we confronted greater forces at Yorktown, Sharpsburg, Fredericksburg,

and about Richmond under Grant, these were only partly seen, at most a corps at a time. But here four corps were in full view, one of which was on the mountain and almost within rifle-range. The sight inspired more satisfaction than discomfort; for though I knew that my little force could be brushed away as readily as the strong man can brush to one side the wasp or the hornet, I felt that General Mc-Clellan had made a mistake, and I hoped to be able to delay him until General Longstreet could come up and our trains could be extricated from their perilous position.

When two distinct roars of artillery were heard south of us that morning, I thought that the nearer one indicated that McClellan was forcing his way across some gap north of Harper's Ferry with a view of cutting Lee's army in two. I suppose that Stuart believed that this would be the movement of the enemy, and for this reason abandoned Turner's Gap and hastened to what he believed to be the point of danger. McClellan was too cautious a man for so daring a venture. (See General Franklin's paper on the engagement at Crampton's Gap,). Had he made it, Jackson could have escaped across the Potomac, but the force under Lee in person (Longstreet's corps and my division) must have been caught. My division was very small and was embarrassed with the wagon trains and artillery of the whole army, save such as Jackson had taken with him.

It must be remembered that the army now before McClellan had been constantly marching and fighting since the 25th of June. It had fought McClellan's army from Richmond to the James, and then had turned about and fought Pope's army, re-enforced by parts of McClellan's, from the Rapidan to the Potomac. The order excusing barefooted men from marching into Maryland had sent thousands to the rear. Divisions had become smaller than brigades were when the fighting first began; brigades had become smaller than regiments, and regiments had become smaller than companies. (Thus the 18th Virginia Regiment, Vol. XIX., of the *Official Records* is put at 120 men; 56th Virginia Regiment at 80; 8th Virginia at 34; Hampton Legion at 77; 17th South Carolina Regiment at 59. D. H. H.)

Dabney, a careful statistician, in his *Life of Jackson*, estimates Lee's forces at Sharpsburg (Antietam) at 33,000 men, including the three arms of service. (According to Thomas White, Chief Clerk in the Adjutant-General's Office at Lee's headquarters, General Lee had 33,000 *infantry* at Sharpsburg, or 41,500 of all arms. Adding 2000 for the previous casualties—only partly given—the total Confederate force on the 14th would appear to be 43,500, of which 15,000 were at Harper's Ferry, on the Virginia side, and 28,500 in Maryland).

Three of Longstreet's twelve brigades had gone to Harper's Ferry with Jackson. He (Longstreet) puts the strength of his nine brigades at Hagerstown on the morning of the 14th of September at thirteen thousand men. Accepting the correctness of his estimate for the present (though I expect to prove it to be too large), I find that Lee had under his immediate command that morning but eighteen thousand men. McClellan gives his force at Sharpsburg at 87,164. Had he made the movement which Stuart and myself thought he was making, it was hardly possible for the little force under Lee in person to have escaped, encumbered as it was with wagon trains and reserve artillery.

Forming his infantry into a solid column of attack, Lee might have cut a way through the five-fold force of his antagonist, but all the trains must have been lost, an irreparable loss to the South. Frederick the Great's campaign against the allies shows what he would have done had he been in command of the Federal Army. But the American soldier preferred to do sure work rather than brilliant work, his natural caution being increased by the carping criticisms of his enemies.

Upon the fall of Garland, Colonel McRae, of the 5th North Carolina regiment, assumed command, and ordered the two regiments on the left to close in to the right. This order either was not received or it was found to be impossible of execution. The main attack was on the 23rd North Carolina behind the stone-wall. The Federals had a plunging fire upon this regiment from the crest of a hill, higher than the wall, and only about fifty yards from it. The 12th North Carolina, a badly trained regiment, on that day under the command of a young captain, deserted the field.

★★★★★★

Mr. R. V. Minor, of Oxford, North Carolina, a member of the 12th North Carolina regiment, writes to the editors that on the morning of the 14th of September his regiment numbered seventy-two men, and that they advanced along the mountain crest until they were in the midst of enemies. The commander, an inexperienced captain, then gave the order to "fire and fall back." The order was obeyed, but the fire was returned so promptly, at close range, that the withdrawal was attended with confusion. However, "thirty or forty" members of the 12th regiment halted on the line of the 13th North Carolina, of their own (Garland's) brigade. Lieutenant -Colonel T. Ruffin, Jr., commander of the 13th regiment, says in his report: "I feel it to be just that I should acknowledge the fact that we were joined by a small party of the 12th North Carolina regiment early in the morning, who continued with us throughout the day and rendered us very efficient aid."

★★★★★★

The 12th Ohio, actuated by a different impulse, made a charge upon Bondurant's battery and drove it off, failing, however, to capture it. The 30th Ohio advanced directly upon the stone-wall in their front, while a regiment moved upon the 23rd North Carolina on each flank. Some of the 30th Ohio forced through a break in the wall, and bayonets and clubbed muskets were used freely for a few moments. Garland's brigade, demoralised by his death and by the furious assault on its centre, now broke in confusion and retreated behind the mountain, leaving some two hundred prisoners of the 5th, 23rd, and 20th North Carolina in the hands of the enemy. The brigade was too roughly handled to be of any further use that day. Rosser retired in better order, not, however, without having some of his men captured, and took up a position from which he could still fire upon the old road, and which he held until 10 o'clock that night.

General Cox, having beaten the force in his front, now showed a disposition to carry out General Pleasonton's instructions, and advance to the Mountain House by the road running south from it on the summit of the mountain. There was nothing to oppose him. My other three brigades had not come up; Colquitt's could not be taken from the pike except in the last extremity. So, two guns were run down from the Mountain House and opened a brisk fire on the advancing foe. A line of dismounted staff-officers, couriers, teamsters, and cooks was formed behind the guns to give the appearance of battery supports. I do not remember ever to have experienced a feeling of greater *loneliness*. It seemed as though we were deserted by "all the world and the rest of mankind." Some of the advancing Federals encountered Colquitt's skirmishers under Captain Arnold, and fell back to their former positions.

General Cox seems not to have suspected that the defeat of Garland had cleared his front of every foe. He says in his report:

"The enemy withdrew their battery to a new position on a ridge more to the front and right, forming their infantry in support and moving columns toward both our flanks."

It was more than half an hour after the utter rout and dispersion of Garland's brigade when G. B. Anderson arrived at the head of his small but fine body of men.

★★★★★★

General Hill in his official report thus describes the posting of his forces after the defeat of Garland:

> There were two mountain roads practicable for artillery on the right of the main turn pike. The defence of the farther one had cost Garland his life. It was now intrusted to Colonel Rosser of the cavalry, who had reported to me, and who had artillery and dismounted sharpshooters. General Anderson was intrusted with the care of the nearest and best road. Bondurant's battery was sent to aid him in its defence. The brigade of Colquitt was disposed on each side of the turnpike, and that with Lane's battery was judged adequate to the task. There was. however, a solitary peak on the left, which, if gained by the Yankees, would give them control of the ridge commanding the turnpike. I had a large number of guns from Cutts's artillery placed upon the hill.... to sweep the approaches.... Rodes and Ripley came up soon after Anderson.

★★★★★★

He made an effort to recover the ground lost by Garland, but failed and met a serious repulse. General Cox says of this attack:

> The enemy made several attempts to retake the crest, advancing with great obstinacy and boldness.

Under the strange illusion that there was a large Confederate force on the mountain, the Federals withdrew to their first position in the morning to await the arrival of the other three divisions of Reno's corps. Willcox's arrived about noon, and Sturgis's and Rodman's between 3 and 4 o'clock, but there was no advance until 5 p. m. The falling back of Cox's division is alluded to by Colonel Ewing of Scammon's brigade and by Major Lyman J. Jackson of Crook's brigade. The former says:

> We fell back to the original position until the general advance at 5 p. m.

Major Jackson, after speaking of fighting the enemy behind a stone-wall with the cooperation of two other regiments, adds:

45

We then fell back to the hillside in the open fields, where we were out of reach of their guns, and remained here *with the rest of our brigade* until an advance was made against the enemy by the Pennsylvania and Rhode Island troops on our right.

After the arrival of his whole corps General Reno arranged his line of battle as follows: Cox's division on the left, resting on the batteries already in position; Willcox's on the right, supported by the division of Sturgis. Rodman's division was divided; Fairchild's brigade was sent to the extreme left to support the batteries, and Harland's was placed on the extreme right.

In the meantime, Rodes and Ripley, of my division, reported to me for orders. Rodes was sent with his brigade of twelve hundred men to a commanding knoll north of the pike or National road. Ripley was directed to attach himself to G. B. Anderson's left. Anderson, being thus strengthened, and finding there was no enemy in his immediate front, sent out the 2nd and 4th North Carolina regiments of his brigade on a reconnoissance to the front, right, and rear. Captain E. A. Osborne, commanding the skirmishers of the 4th North Carolina, discovered a brigade in an old field south of Fox's Gap, facing toward the turnpike and supporting a battery with its guns turned in the same direction.

Captain Osborne hastened back to Colonel Grimes, commanding the regiment, and told him that they could deliver a flank fire upon the brigade before it could change its position to meet them. But a Federal scout had seen the captain, and the brigade was the first to open fire. The fight was, of course, brief, the regiment beating a hasty retreat. The brigade halted at the edge of the woods, probably believing that there was a concealed foe somewhere in the depths of the forest. This Federal brigade was, possibly, Benjamin C. Christ's of Willcox's division—the same which had made the successful flank movement in the previous fight. (This engagement is not mentioned by Cox, Wilcox, or Christ. The Union brigade was more probably that of Colonel H. S. Fairchild, Rodman's division).

About 3: 30 p. m. the advance of Longstreet's command arrived and reported to me—one brigade under Colonel Gr. T. Anderson and one under General Drayton. They were attached to Ripley's left, and a forward movement was ordered. In half an hour or more I received a note from Ripley saying that he was progressing finely; so, he was, to the rear of the mountain on the west side. Before he returned the fighting was over, and his brigade did not fire a shot that day.

★★★★★★

In *The Century* magazine for December, 1886, page 308, was printed a letter from William L. De Rosset, Colonel of the 3rd North Carolina regiment, in which, after stating that General Hill disclaims any intention of reflecting on Ripley's brigade in this statement, the writer says:

The facts are these: He (General Hill) correctly states Ripley's manoeuvres at Boonsboro' until we reached a position at the foot of the mountain,—on the west side,—when General Ripley said to me that we were entirely cut off from the rest of the army, except G. B. Anderson's brigade, which was on our right, and that he assumed the command of the two brigades, directing me to take command of the three regiments (Colonel Doles, with his 4th Georgia, having been detached and sent to a position on the north of the pike), and that he would remain near me, directing me at the same time to advance slowly up the mountain with a strong line of skirmishers in front.

Upon reaching the summit, after toiling through the dense undergrowth of laurel, Captain Thurston, in command of the skirmish line, reported troops in his front, a few minutes later confirming his first impression that they were G. B. Anderson's brigade, presenting their flank and advancing toward his left. This was promptly reported through my adjutant to General Ripley, who directed me to withdraw to my original position, which having been accomplished, I was directed to hold my then position until further orders. After nightfall I moved forward, changing front to the left, a short distance, to the support of General Drayton, remaining there 'without drawing trigger' until we took up the line of march for Sharpsburg, about 10 to 12 at night. While, therefore, we accomplished nothing tangible, we were in position to do any duty for which we might be called.

★★★★★★

The Federal commander intrusted to General Burnside the management of the fight, but under his own eyes; Burnside ordered a general advance on both sides of the pike. The First Corps, under Hooker, was to attack on the north side of the National road, while the Ninth Corps, under Reno, was to move forward, as before, on the south side. Hooker's corps consisted of 3 divisions, 10 brigades, or

42 regiments, with 10 batteries of artillery and a battalion of cavalry. General Meade, a division commander, had under him the brigades of Seymour, Magilton, and Gallagher, containing 13 regiments with 4 batteries attached. General Hatch, division commander, had under him the brigades of Doubleday, Phelps, Patrick, and Gibbon—17 regiments and 4 batteries. General Ricketts, division commander, had under him the brigades of Duryea, Christian, and Hartsuff—12 regiments and 2 batteries. From the nature of the ground, none of the artillery of Hooker's corps could be used, except that which went directly up the pike with Gibbon's brigade and one battery (Cooper's) on the enemy's right.

The hour for the general advance is not specified in the reports. Some of the Federal officers, as we have seen, speak of the general advance at 5 p. m. General Sturgis says that he became engaged on the south side of the pike at 3: 30 p. m. General Meade, on the north side, says that he moved toward the right at 2 p. m., while General Ricketts, who took part in the same movement, says that he did not arrive at the foot of the mountain until 5 p. m.

★★★★★★

2 p.m. is the hour at which General Meade says he received the order to move to the front, from the point where his division was halted beyond Middletown, at Catoctin creek. Meade turned off to the right, followed the old Hagerstown road to Mount Tabor Church, and then formed line at the foot of the mountain for the climb. Cooper's battery opened fire at 3:30. Hatch followed Meade, and. Ricketts moved last.

★★★★★★

If General Meade was not mistaken as to the time of his starting, he must have been long delayed in the thick woods through which the first part of his march was made. Here is probably the best place to explain the extraordinary caution of the Federals, which seemed so mysterious to us on that 14th of September. An order of General Lee, made while at Frederick, directing Jackson to capture Harper's Ferry, and Longstreet and myself to go to Boonsboro', had fallen into the hands of the Federals, and had been carried to General McClellan. This order (known at the South as the Lost Dispatch) was addressed to me, but I proved twenty years ago that it could not have been lost through my neglect or carelessness.

★★★★★★

In a letter to the editors, dated February 24th, 1888, General

Hill says: "I went into Maryland under Jackson's command. I was under his command when Lee's order was issued. It was proper that I should receive that order through Jackson and not through Lee. I have now before me the order, received from Jackson. . . . My adjutant-general made affidavit, twenty years ago, that no order was received at our office from General Lee. But an order from Lee's office, directed to me, was lost and fell into McClellan's hands, Did the courier lose it? Did Lee's own staff officers lose it? I do not know."

★★★★★★

The Federal commander gained two facts from the order, one of which was needless and the other misleading. He learned that Jackson had gone to Harper's Ferry—a truth that he must have learned from his own scouts and spies and the roar of artillery in his own ears: the cannonading could be distinctly heard at Frederick, and it told that *someone* was beleaguering Harper's Ferry. The misleading report was that Longstreet was at Boonsboro'. (*Special Orders No. 191*, which was the "lost order," sent Longstreet to Boonsboro'. It was afterward modified by General Lee so as to place Longstreet at Hagerstown).

The map of the battlefield of South Mountain, prepared in 1872, ten years after the fight, by the United States Bureau of Engineers, represents ten regiments and one battalion under Longstreet at the foot of the mountain on the morning of the 14th of September, 1862. But Longstreet was then an ordinary, day's march from that point. In fact, after the removal of Colquitt's brigade, about 7 a.m., there was not a Southern soldier at the foot of the mountain until 3 p. m., when Captain Park of the 12th Alabama Regiment was sent there with forty men. General McClellan in his report says:

> It is believed that the force opposed to us at Turner's Gap consisted of D. H. Hill's corps (fifteen thousand) and a part if not the whole of Longstreet's, and perhaps a portion of Jackson's,—probably thirty thousand in all. (*Official Records*, Volume XIX., Pt. I., p. 53.)

The mistake of the Federal commander in regard to General Longstreet was natural, since he was misled by the Lost Dispatch. But it seems strange that the United States Engineers should repeat the blunder, with the light of history thrown for ten years upon all the incidents of the battle. It was incomprehensible to us of the losing side that the men who charged us so boldly and repulsed our attacks so

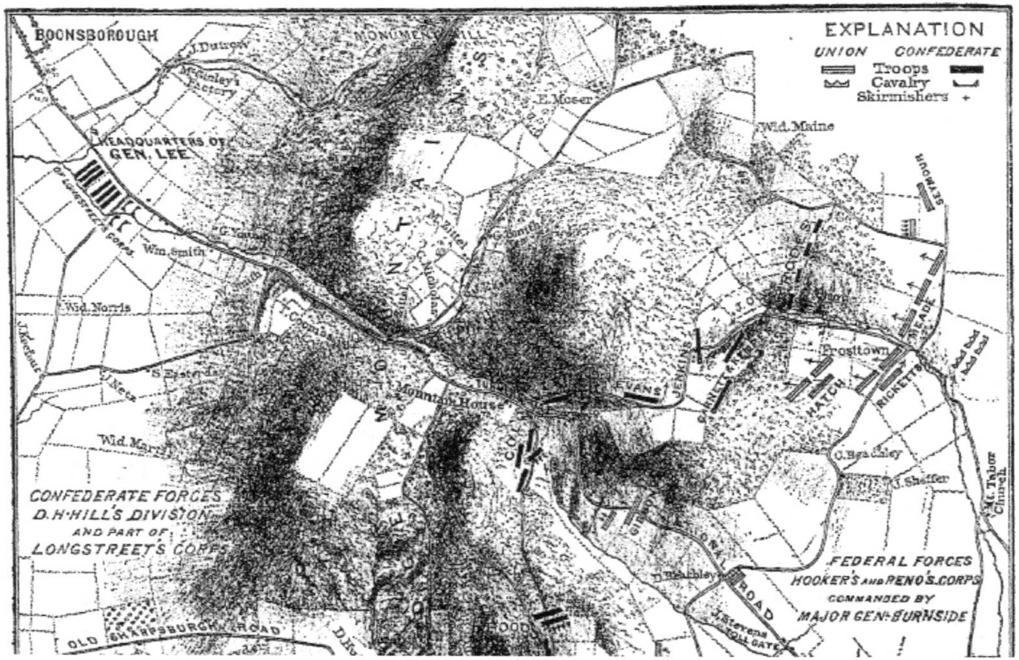

EXPLANATION
UNION CONFEDERATE
Troops
Cavalry
Skirmishers
BOONSBOROUGH
J. Dutrow
McGinley's Factory
E. Moser
Wid. Maine
HEADQUARTERS OF GEN. LEE
OF LONGSTREET'S CORPS
Wm. Smith
Wid. Norris
J. Keefout
S. Easterday
J. Ness
Mountain House
Wid. Martz
SEYMOUR
MEADE
Frostown
RICKETTS
HATCH
EVANS
JENKINS
GARNETT
COLQUITT
O. Beachley
J. Shaffer
Mt. Tabor Church
CONFEDERATE FORCES
D. H. HILL'S DIVISION
AND PART OF
LONGSTREET'S CORPS
FEDERAL FORCES
HOOKER'S AND RENO'S CORPS
COMMANDED BY
MAJOR GEN. BURNSIDE
OLD SHARPSBURG ROAD
D. Beachley
J. Stevens
TOLL GATE

BATTLE OF SOUTH MOUNTAIN

SEPT. 14. 1862

SCALE OF FEET

HEADQUARTERS OF MAJ. GEN. McCLELLAN.

MAP OF THE POSITIONS AT FOX'S AND TURNER'S GAPS.

The fights of September 14th were so distinct as to time and place, and the positions of the troops were so often changed, that any single map would be misleading without analysis: (1) The early morning fight was mostly on the south side of Fox's Gap, between Cox's two Union brigades and Garland's brigade, the latter being assisted on its left by a part of Colquitt's brigade which was at Turner's Gap. By 10 o'clock Garland had been killed and his brigade routed. (2) Then Cox encountered G. B. Anderson's arriving brigade, repulsed it, and fell back to his position in the morning. (3) G. B. Anderson was then posted at Fox's Gap on both sides of the old Sharpsburg road. D. H. Hill's two other brigades came up toward noon, Ripley being joined to G. B. Anderson, and Rodes being sent to occupy a hill on the north side of Turner's Gap, near where Garnett is placed on the map. (4) About 2 o'clock, on the Union side, Cox's division was reënforced by the arriving divisions of Willcox, Sturgis, and Rodman; and Hooker's corps of three divisions was moving north of the National road by way of Mount Tabor Church (Hooker's headquarters) to flank the Confederate left. About the same time D. H. Hill's brigades at Fox's Gap were reënforced by Longstreet's brigades of G. T. Anderson, Drayton, Law, and Hood; and north of Turner's Gap three of Rodes's four regiments were sent still farther to the left. The defense was afterward strengthened by the posting of Longstreet's brigades of Garnett and Kemper, supported by Jenkins, on the hill first held by Rodes. Evans's brigade arrived later, and was of assistance to Rodes when the latter had been thrown back by Meade's flank movement. (5) The last severe engagements began at both gaps after 3 o'clock and lasted until after dark. Colquitt and Gibbon, in the center, joined desperately in the battle.— EDITORS.

successfully should let slip the fruits of victory and fall back as though defeated.

The prisoners taken were from my division, but the victors seemed to think that Longstreet's men lay hidden somewhere in the depths of those mysterious forests. Thus, it was that a thin line of men extending for miles along the crest of the mountain could afford protection for so many hours to Lee's trains and artillery and could delay the Federal advance until Longstreet's command did come up, and, joining with mine, saved the two wings of the army from being cut in two. But for the mistake about the position of our forces, McClellan could have captured Lee's trains and artillery and interposed between Jackson and Longstreet before noon on that 14th of September. The losing of the dispatch was the saving of Lee's army.

About 4 p. m. I saw what appeared to be two Federal brigades emerge from the woods south of Colquitt's position and form in an open field nearly at right angles to each other—one brigade facing toward the pike, and the other facing the general direction of the mountain. This inverted V-like formation was similar to that of the 1st Mississippi Regiment at Buena Vista. If it was made anywhere else during the Civil War, I never heard of it. The V afforded a fine target from the pike,' and I directed Captain Lane to open on it with his battery. His firing was wild, not a shot hitting the mark. The heavy batteries promptly replied, showing such excellent practice that Lane's guns were soon silenced. A small force in the edge of the woods on the west side of the old field opened fire upon the V. The Federals changed their formation, and, advancing in line of battle, brushed away their assailants and plunged into the woods, when heavy firing began which lasted possibly half an hour.

I suppose that the Federal force which I saw was the division of General Sturgis, (probably Willcox's division, with its right, refused to avoid the enfilading fire from the batteries on the mountain), and that he left behind Harland's brigade of Rodman's division to guard his flank in his advance, since Harland reports that he had no casualties. General Sturgis claims that he swept everything before him. So, do his comrades who fought on his left. On the other hand, General Hood, who came up a short time before this advance, with the brigades of Wofford and Law, claims that he checked and drove back the Federals. G. T. Anderson reports that only his skirmishers were engaged. The surviving officers under G. B. Anderson (who was killed at Sharpsburg, and left no report) say that the same thing was true of their brigade in the afternoon. Ripley's brigade was not engaged at all.

About dusk the 2nd and 13th North Carolina Regiments attacked Fairchild's brigade and the batteries protected by it on the extreme Federal left, and were repulsed disastrously. Generals Burnside and Willcox say that the fight was continued until 10 o'clock at night. Hood was mistaken, then, in thinking that he had driven back the Federal advance. The opposing lines were close together at nightfall, and the firing between the skirmishers was kept up till a late hour. Equally erroneous is the claim that any Confederates were driven except Drayton's small brigade. We held the crests of the mountain, on the National road and the old Sharpsburg road, until Lee's order for withdrawal was given. General Reno, the Federal corps commander on our right, was killed at 7 p. m., in Wise's field, where the fight began at 9 o'clock in the morning.

But on our left a commanding hill was lost before night. Batteries placed upon it next morning, acting in concert with the heavy batteries placed on our right by General Pleasonton before we were aware of his presence, would have made any position untenable on the pike or the crest of the mountain. I made that statement to General Lee about 9 p. m., when he consulted with Longstreet and myself in regard to renewing the fight the next morning. Longstreet concurred in this view, remarking that I knew the ground and the situation better than he did.

General Hooker detached Gibbon's brigade, consisting of three Wisconsin regiments and one Indiana regiment, from Hatch's division, and directed it to move directly up the pike with a section of artillery. Then the divisions of Meade and Hatch were formed on the north side of the pike, with the division of Ricketts in supporting distance in rear. A belt of woods had to be passed through, and then it was open field all the way to the summit, and the two detached peaks were in full view upon which the devoted little band of Rodes was posted—the 12th Alabama Regiment on one, and the 3rd, 5th, 6th, and 26th Alabama regiments on the other. Under the illusion that there were ten regiments and one battalion of Longstreet's command in those woods, the progress through them was slow, but, when once cleared, the advance was steady and made almost with the precision of movement of a parade day. Captain Robert E. Park, of Macon, Georgia, who commanded the forty skirmishers in the woods, thinks that he delayed the Federal advance for a long time.

★★★★★★

FOX'S GAP—THE APPROACH TO WISE'S FIELD.

This sketch and the one on the next page (from photographs made in 1885) may be regarded as parts of one picture. The old Sharpsburg or Braddock road lies between the stone-wall and the rail fence. The left distance shows the Middletown valley and the Catoctin range, from which Reno approached.

FOX'S GAP—WISE'S FIELD AS SEEN FROM THE PASTURE NORTH OF THE ROAD.

The stump in the middle of the field beyond the wall is near where Reno fell. Part of the struggle was for the wooded crest on the left of the field. The house is Wise's, at the crossing of the ridge and Old Sharpsburg roads. See map. The Confederates here were posted behind a stone-wall. The well at Wise's house was filled with the Confederate dead.

Captain Park writes:

"After passing through Boonsboro', *en route* to the scene of action, we met the dead body of the gallant General Garland, when an order from General D H. Hill, through General R. E. Rodes, to Colonel B. B. Gayle of the 12th Alabama, directed that skirmishers should be deployed in front. Colonel Gayle hurriedly ordered captains of companies to send four men each to the front to report to Lieutenant R. E. Park as sharpshooters, and I promptly reported for orders; was directed to carry my squad of forty men to the foot of South Mountain, 'and keep the enemy back as long as possible.' I hastily deployed the men, and we moved down the mountain-side.

"On our way down, we could see the enemy, in two lines of battle, in the valley below, advancing, preceded only a few steps by their dense line of skirmishers. I concealed my men behind trees, rocks, and bushes, and cautioned them to aim well before firing. We awaited with beating hearts the sure and steady approach of the 'Pennsylvania Bucktails,' who were directly in my front, and soon near enough to fire upon. I gave the command, 'Fire,' and forty guns were almost simultaneously emptied with deadly effect, and the surviving skirmishers rushed back pell-mell to their main line, disordering it greatly. The solid, well-drilled line soon rallied, and advanced steadily forward, and my small party, as soon as they were near enough, fired again, and nearly every bullet did fatal work.

"At least thirty men must have been killed or wounded at the second fire, and perhaps more at the first. Though checked for some minutes, the enemy again advanced, their officers earnestly exhorting them with 'close up' and 'forward.' I directed my men to fall back slowly, and to fire from everything which would screen them from observation. I had lost only four men wounded up to this time, but six or eight more became demoralised and, despite my commands, entreaties, and threats, left me and hastily fled to the rear.

"With the brave squad which remained, we retreated slowly, firing as rapidly as we could load, and doing fatal work with every step. The advance was very slow and cautious. It was about 3 o'clock when we had opened fire at the foot of the mountain, and now the sun was rapidly setting. Corporal Myers, of Mobile, at my request, aimed at and shot an exposed officer, receiving himself a terrible wound as he did so. I raised him tenderly, gave him water, and reluctantly was about to abandon him to his fate, when a dozen muskets were pointed at me, and I was ordered to surrender. There was a deep ravine to our left, and the 3rd Alabama skirmishers having fallen back, the Federals had got in my rear, and at the same time had closed upon me in front.

"If I had not stopped with Myers I might have escaped capture, but I was mortified and humiliated by the necessity of yielding myself a prisoner. Certain death was the only alternative. The enemy pushed forward after my capture, and came upon Colonel Gayle and the rear support. Colonel Gayle was ordered to surrender, but, drawing his pistol and firing it in their faces, he exclaimed: 'We are flanked, boys, but let's die in our tracks,' and continued to fire until he was literally riddled by bullets.

"I was accompanied to the rear by three Federal soldiers, and could but notice, as I walked down the mountain, the great execution done by my little squad as shown by the dead and wounded lying all along the route. At the foot of the mountain ambulances were being loaded. From what I saw and gathered from my captors, my little party committed fearful havoc, and the Federals imagined that several divisions of Lee's army confronted them. . . . I was carried before some prominent officer (have heard it was General Hatch), who questioned me about my regiment, brigade, division, number of troops, etc. The information I gave could not have benefited him much." D. H. H.

★★★★★★

It is not more improbable that a few active skirmishers north of the pike should prove an obstacle to progress through the forest there, than that a division on the south side should hesitate to penetrate a forest from which their foes had been completely driven. The success of the Federals on the north side was due to the fact that after getting through the belt of woods at the foot of the mountain, they saw exactly what was before them. The lack of complete success south of the pike was owing to the thick woods on that side, which were supposed to be full of hidden enemies. In the Battle of South Mountain, the imaginary foes of the Lost Dispatch were worth more to us than ten thousand men.

The advance of Hatch's division in three lines, a brigade in each, was as grand and imposing as that of Meade's division. Hatch's general and field officers were on horseback, his colours were all flying, and the alignment of his men seemed to be perfectly preserved. General Hooker, looking at the steady and precise movement from the foot of the mountain, describes it as a beautiful sight. From the top of the mountain the sight was grand and sublime, but the elements of the pretty and the picturesque did not enter into it. Doubtless the Hebrew poet whose idea of the awe-inspiring is expressed by the phrase, "terrible as an army with banners," had his view of the enemy from the top of a mountain.

There was not a single Confederate soldier to oppose the advance of General Hatch. I got some guns from the reserve artillery of Colonel Cutts to fire at the three lines; but owing to the little practice of the gunners and to the large angles of depression, the cannonade was as harmless as blank-cartridge salutes in honour of a militia general. While these ineffective missiles were flying, which the enemy did not honour by so much as a dodge, Longstreet came up in person with three small brigades, and assumed direction of affairs. He sent the brigade of Evans under Colonel Stevens to the aid of Rodes's men, sorely pressed and well-nigh exhausted. The brigade of Pickett (under Garnett) and that of Kemper were hurried forward to meet and check Hatch, advancing, hitherto, without opposition.

General Meade had moved the brigade of Seymour to the right to take Rodes's position in reverse, while the brigades of Magilton and Gallagher went straight to the front. Meade was one of our most dreaded foes; he was always in deadly earnest, and he eschewed all trifling. He had under him brigade commanders, officers, and soldiers worthy of his leadership. In his onward sweep the peak upon which the 12th Alabama was posted was passed, the gallant Colonel Gayle was killed, and his regiment was routed and dispersed. The four other regiments of Rodes made such heroic resistance that Meade, believing his division about to be flanked, sent for and obtained Duryea's brigade of Ricketts's division.

It was pitiable to see the gallant but hopeless struggle of those Alabamians against such mighty odds. Rodes claimed to have fought for three hours without support; but an over-estimate of time under such circumstances is usual and natural. He lost 61 killed, 157 wounded, and 204 missing (captured), or more than one-third of his brigade. His supports (Evans's brigade) fought gallantly and saved him from being entirely surrounded, but they got on the ground too late to effect anything else.

Evans's brigade under Stevens had been wasted by two campaigns and was small when it left Hagerstown that morning, and many had fallen out on the hot and dusty forced march. Of the four regiments in the brigade, we find in Volume XIX. of the *Official Records* only the report of one, the 17th South Carolina regiment under Colonel Mc-Master. That says that 141 men entered the fight on South Mountain, and of these 7 are reported killed, 37 wounded, and 17 missing (captured). Colonel McMaster writes to me that his was the largest regiment in the brigade; so, the brigade must have been about 550 strong. General Meade says in his report that he lost 397 men, or ten *per cent*, of his division. As he received the support of Duryea before or about the time that Rodes got the aid of Stevens, he fought Rodes with the advantage all the while of three to one.

When Ripley came up, as before described, the pressure was all at Fox's Gap. He was sent in there and his brigade was uselessly employed by him in marching and counter-marching. Had it been sent to strengthen Rodes the key of the position might not have been lost. But the vainest of all speculations and regrets are about "the might have been."

Meade encamped that night on the commanding eminence which he had won.

The strength of the two brigades sent to check General Hatch did not exceed eight hundred men, as I will show presently. They must have performed prodigies of valour, and their praises can best be spoken in the words of their enemies. General Patrick, commanding the leading Federal brigade, tells of a race between his men and a strong force of the enemy for the possession of a fence. Patrick won the race and delivered his fire from the fence, picking off the cannoneers at some of our guns. General Hatch was wounded at this fence, and the command devolved on General Doubleday.

The latter speaks of lying down behind the fence and allowing the enemy to charge up to within fifteen paces, whereupon he opened a deadly fire. Colonel Wainwright, who succeeded Doubleday in command of his brigade, was also wounded here, and Colonel Hofmann assumed command of it. Colonel Hofmann tells us that the ammunition of the brigade was just giving out when Ricketts relieved Doubleday. Several of the reports speak of the "superior force of the enemy." General Ricketts says that "he relieved Doubleday hard-pressed and nearly out of ammunition."

Before Ricketts came in person with Hartsuff's brigade, he had sent Christian's brigade to the assistance of Doubleday. The brigades of Kemper and Pickett (the latter under Garnett) must have fought valiantly, else such results could not have been achieved. General Doubleday's report contains this curious story:

> I learned from a wounded prisoner that we were engaged with four to five thousand under the immediate command of General Pickett, with heavy masses in their vicinity. He stated also that Longstreet in vain tried to rally the men, calling them his pets and using every effort to induce them to renew the attack.

Of course, the old rebel knew that Pickett was not there in person and that there were no heavy masses in the vicinity. The astonishing thing is that General Doubleday should believe that there were 4000 or 5000 men before him under the immediate command of Pickett. But Doubleday's belief of the story is a tribute to the efficiency of the 800 men who fought a division of 3500 men (the number reported by Hatch after Gibbon had been detached), and fought it so vigorously that two brigades were sent to its assistance.

Jenkins's brigade, under Walker, came up at dusk, too late to be in the fight; but it went in on the right of Garnett and took part in the irregular firing which was kept up till a late hour. Colonel Walker's report shows a loss of 3 killed and 29 wounded, which proves that he was but slightly engaged. The tired men of both sides lay down at last to rest within a hundred yards of each other. But now Gibbon was putting in earnest work on the pike. He had a choice brigade, strong in numbers and strong in the pluck of his men, all from the North-west, where habitually good fighters are reared. He had pushed forward cautiously in the afternoon with the 7th Wisconsin regiment, followed by the 6th on the north side of the pike and the 19th Indiana, supported by the 2nd Wisconsin, on the south side.

The ten imaginary regiments of the Lost Dispatch retarded his progress through the woods; and at one time, believing that the 7th Wisconsin was about to be turned on its right flank, he sent the 6th to its assistance. There were only a few skirmishers on his right, but the Lost Dispatch made him believe otherwise. About 9 p. m. the stone-wall was reached, and several gallant efforts were made in vain to carry it. When each repulse was followed by the "rebel" yells, the young men on my staff would cry out: "Hurrah for Georgia! Georgia is having a free fight." The Western men had met in the 23rd and 28th Georgia regiments men as brave as themselves and far more advanta-

59

VIEW FROM TURNER'S GAP, LOOKING SOUTH-EAST .SEE MAP.   FROM A PHOTOGRAPH TAKEN IN 1886.

The point of view is a little to the left of the Mountain House, now the home of Mrs. Dahlgren, widow of Admiral Dahlgren. Rodes was first posted on the hill, the slope of which is seen on the left; Gibbon was farther down the road in the hollow. The white patch on the mountain to the south (on the right) is Wise's field at Fox's Gap, where Reno and Garland were killed.

geously posted. Colonel Bragg, of the 6th Wisconsin, says in his report:

We sat down in the dark to wait another attack, but the enemy was no more seen.

At midnight Gorman's brigade of Sumner's corps relieved Gibbon's.

General Gibbon reports officially 318 men killed and wounded—a loss sustained almost entirely, I think, at the stone-wall. The colonel of the 7th Wisconsin reports a loss of 147 men in killed and wounded out of 375 muskets carried into action. This shows that he had brave men and that he encountered brave men. From his report, we infer that Gibbon had fifteen hundred men. On our side Colquitt had 1100 men, and lost less than 100, owing to the admirable position in which he had been placed.

And now in regard to the numbers engaged. Longstreet sent to my aid 8 brigades,—5 belonging to the division of D. R. Jones, consisting of the brigades of Drayton, Pickett, Jenkins, Gr. T. Anderson, and Kemper; and 3 belonging to an extemporised division of N. G. Evans, including the brigades of Evans, Hood, and Law. On page 886, Part I., Volume XIX. of the *Official Records*, Jones says that after Toombs joined him from Hagerstown, his 6 brigades numbered at Sharpsburg 2430 men; *i.e.*, an average of 405 men to each brigade. Now all Longstreet's officers and men know that the ranks were fuller at Sharpsburg than at South Mountain, because there were more stragglers in the forced march from Hagerstown to the battlefield of the 14th of September than there were casualties in the battle.

★★★★★★

In his official report General Hill, after stating his force on the morning of the 14th as "less than 5000 men," says: "My ranks had been diminished by some additional straggling, and the morning of the 17th (Antietam) I had but 3000 infantry." Adding to this number General Hill's losses on September 14th at Fox's and Turner's Gaps, and we have 3934 as his strength in the Battle of South Mountain, without counting these additional stragglers.

★★★★★★

The above average would give 810 as the number of men in the two brigades which confronted the division of Hatch aided by two brigades from Ricketts. But it is well known that the Virginia brigades were unusually small, because of the heavy draughts upon them for cavalry, artillery, and local service. Between pages 894 and 902, Volume XIX., *Official Records*, we have the strength at South Mountain of four of the five regiments of Pickett's brigade given officially,—the 19th Regiment, 150 men; 18th Regiment, 120 men; 56th Regiment, 80 men; 8th Regiment, 34 men. The strength of the other regiment, the 28th, is not given; but, assuming that it was 96, the average of the other four regiments, we have 480 as the number of men in Pickett's brigade at South Mountain.

But the report of the colonel of the 56th shows that he was turned off with his 80 muskets, and did not go in with his brigade; so that Garnett had in the battle but 400 of Pickett's men. From Kemper's brigade, we have but one report giving the strength of a regiment, and that comes from Colonel Corse of the 17th Virginia. He says that at Sharpsburg he had 6 officers and 49 privates in his regiment. A calculation based upon this report would show that Kemper's brigade was smaller than Pickett's.

On page 907 we have the only report from Jenkins's brigade which gives any intimation of its strength. There the 1st South Carolina regiment is said to have 106 men at Sharpsburg. It is possible the five regiments of this brigade numbered 530 in that battle. It is true that it was

BRIGADIER-GENERAL GEORGE B. ANDERSON, C. S. A.,
KILLED AT ANTIETAM.

considerably larger at Sharpsburg than at South Mountain, because the stragglers from the Hagerstown march much more than made up for the small loss (32) in the battle of the 14th. But with due allowance for that gain, the brigade must have been 450 strong at South Mountain. It is evident, then, that Kemper's brigade fell below 400 at South Mountain; otherwise, the brigade average in Jones's division would have exceeded 406.

Longstreet thinks that he had four thousand men at South Mountain. His estimate is too high, according to the records as I find them. Accepting his numbers, I would place 2200 at Fox's Gap and 1800 north of Turner's Gap. Colquitt fought mainly and Rodes entirely with Hooker's corps. Adding the 2200 men of these two brigades to Longstreet's 1800, we have 4000 as the number opposed to Hooker.

★★★★★★

According to the estimate of Mr. Thomas White, chief clerk of the adjutant-general's office at General Lee's headquarters, who had charge of the field returns during the war, the effective strength of the Confederate forces at South Mountain, or Boonsboro', was: Longstreet, 8000, D. H. Hill, 7000,—total, 15,000. According to Colonel W. H. Taylor, adjutant-general of the Army of Northern Virginia, Hill had "less than 5000"; 6 brigades of Longstreet engaged numbered 4900,—total, 9900 (with 2 of Longstreet's brigades not engaged and not included). In his official report, General D. H. Hill says "the division numbered less than 5000 men on the morning of September 14th"; of his 5 brigades, Rodes's is stated to have numbered 1200, and Garland's "scarce 1000 men." The Union returns quoted show the whole number of officers and men of all arms present for duty without deduction. If to the strength of the First and Ninth Corps on the 20th of September we add the previous losses, these numbers will show as follows: First Corps, 15,750; Ninth Corps, 13,972. Deduct one-fifth, 5944, for non-effectives,—total available Union force, 23,778. Total available Confederate force, according to Mr. White, 15,000; according to Colonel Taylor, 9900, plus the two reserve brigades of Longstreet, whose strength he does not give

★★★★★★

General McClellan puts the strength of the two attacking corps at thirty thousand. His figures are substantially corroborated by the reports of his subordinates,—division, brigade, and regimental com-

63

manders. They indicate, moreover, that there had been great straggling in the Federal Army, as well as in our own. On p. 97, General Ingalls, chief quartermaster, reports, October 1st, 1862, means of transportation for 13,707 men in the First Corps; for 12,860 men in the Ninth Corps . . . . and for 127,818 men in the entire Army of the Potomac.

******

The return of the Army of the Potomac for September 30th shows a total present for duty of 98,774 officers and men, including 5714 cavalry and headquarters guard. General Ingalls's statement, partly estimated as shown on its face (he counts cavalry 7000, it being actually 4543), is obviously in error in the figures, 30,926, set down for the Fifth Corps, which the return shows to have had 17,268 for duty, and 31,688 *present and absent.*

******

This was after the wastage of the two battles (14th and 17th of September), reported on page 204 as amounting to 15,203.

General Hooker was well pleased with the work of his corps. He says in his report:

When the advantages of the enemy's position are considered, and his preponderating numbers, the forcing of the passage of South Mountain will be classed among the most brilliant and satisfactory achievements of this army, and its principal glory will be awarded to the First Corps.

Undoubtedly that corps had gained important positions, but it is difficult to see how 4000 men could preponderate in numbers over 13,707. Hooker's division and brigade commanders, who had been well up under musketry fire, do not speak in such glowing terms of the victory. The reports of the stubborn fighters in the Federal Army on both sides of the pike are models of modest propriety. This is especially so with those who bore the heat and burden of the day,— Meade, Hatch, Cox, Willcox, Scammon, Crook, Gibbon, Ewing, Gallagher, Magilton, Phelps, White, Jackson, Callis, Bragg, and others.

In regard to the casualties of the opposing forces, the losses in killed and wounded were greater on the Federal side than on the Confederate, because the one thin line of the latter fired at the dense masses of the former, sometimes in two lines, and sometimes in three. But from their weakness the Confederates took no prisoners, while they lost over four hundred within the enveloping ranks of their enemies. The revised statement of Federal losses in Volume XIX. gives the casualties in the First Corps as 923; of the Ninth Corps as 889, total 1812, infantry and artillery; and to this number is added one cavalryman, how killed is not explained.

I lost two brigadiers and a large number of regimental commanders within three days, so that my division reports are very meagre. Of the five brigades, there is a statistical report from that of Rodes alone. By means of a very extensive correspondence I have ascertained the casualties as nearly as they can be reached at this late day:

	Killed and Wounded.	Missing.
Rodes	218	204
Colquitt	92	7
Garland	100	200
Anderson	84	29
Ripley	0	0
	494	440

Longstreet's loss must have been less than mine, as he had but four small brigades seriously engaged. Walker reports only thirty-two casualties in Jenkins's brigade; G. T. Anderson had none. Hood speaks lightly of the fight of the two brigades under him. The exact losses can, however, never be known.

In the foregoing table reference is had to prisoners taken in battle. Some of our wearied men slipped off in the woods to sleep, and were not aroused when the orders came to fall back. Colonel Parker of the 30th North Carolina regiment, a brave and efficient officer, writes to me that he could hardly keep his men awake even when the deadly missiles were flying among them. This is in confirmation of what General Hood, in charge of the rear-guard, told me when I passed him after daylight on the 15th. He said that he found it difficult to arouse and push on the tired men, who had fallen out by the wayside to get a few minutes' sleep.

If the Battle of South Mountain was fought to prevent the advance of McClellan, it was a failure on the part of the Confederates. If it was fought to save Lee's trains and artillery, and to reunite his scattered forces, it was a Confederate success. The former view was taken by the President of the United States, for he telegraphed to General McClellan on the 15th of September:

God bless you and all with you. Destroy the rebel army, if possible.

MAJOR-GENERAL R. E. RODES, C. S. A

But, from whatever standpoint it may be looked at, the Battle of South Mountain must be of interest to the military reader as showing the effect of a hallucination in enabling 9000 men to hold 30,000 at bay for so many hours, in robbing victory of its fruits, and in inspiring the victors with such caution that a simple ruse turned them back in their triumphal career.

Every battlefield of the Civil War beheld the deadly conflict of former friends with each other. South Mountain may be taken as a specimen of this unnatural and horrible state of things. The last time I ever saw Generals McClellan and Reno was in 1848, at the table of General G. W. Smith, in the city of Mexico. Generals Meade and Scammon had both been instructors while I was at West Point. Colonel Magilton, commanding a brigade in Meade's division, had been a lieutenant in my company in the Mexican war. General John Gibbon (whose brigade pressed up the pike on the 14th of September) and his brother Lardner had been "best men" at my wedding. They were from North Carolina; one brother took the Northern side, while the other took the Southern.

There is another view of the picture, however. If we had to be beaten it was better to be beaten by former friends. Every true soldier loves to have "a foeman worthy of his steel." Every true man likes to attribute high qualities to those who were once friends, though now alienated for a time. The temporary estrangement cannot obliterate the recollection of noble traits of character. Someone attempted to condole with Tom Yearwood, a famous old South Carolina bully, upon the beating given him by his own son. "Hush up," said old Tom. "I am glad that no one but my own flesh and blood had a hand in my drubbing."

The sons of the South struck her many heavy blows. Farragut, of Tennessee, rose, as a reward of merit, to the highest rank in the Federal navy. A large number of his associates were from the South. In the Federal Army, there were of Southern blood and lineage Generals Thomas, Sykes, Reno, Newton, J. J. Reynolds, Canby, Ord, Brannan, William Nelson, Crittenden, Blair, R. W. Johnson, T. J. Wood, N. B. Buford, Terrill, Graham, Davidson, Cooke, Alexander, Getty, French, Frémont, Pope, Hunter. Some of these doubtless served the South better by the side they took; most of them were fine, and some superb, officers.

Moreover, the South had three hundred thousand of her sons in the Federal Army in subordinate capacities.

★★★★★★

According to a printed statement dated at the "Adjutant-General's Office, Washington, November 9th, 1880," the slave-holding States furnished troops to the Union Army as follows: Delaware, 12,284; Maryland, 46,638; West Virginia, 32,068; District of Columbia, 16,534; Missouri, 109,111; Kentucky, 75,760; Tennessee, 31,092; Arkansas, 8289; North Carolina, 3156; Alabama, 2576; Florida, 1290; Louisiana, 5224; Mississippi, 545; Texas, 1965,—total, 346,532. This sum includes coloured troops, but their number is not stated. The territory in actual rebellion also furnished 99,337 coloured soldiers, recruited at various stations and not accredited to States. The so-called Northern, or free, States furnished to the Union Army 2,419,159 men.

★★★★★★

Her armies surrendered when a Southern-born President and a Southern-born Vice-President were at the head of the United States Government. That the wounds of defeat and humiliation have been so soon healed has been owing largely to this balm to mortified pride. The sting of shame to Frenchmen is that their magnificent capital was captured by, and their splendid armies were surrendered to, soldiers of an alien race and religion. On the other hand, the civil wars in England have left no bitter memories behind them. Compare this forgetfulness of civil strife in England with the bitterness which Ireland still feels over her subjugation; compare it with the fact that the Roman occupation of England for five hundred years made no impres-

GENERAL J. E. B. STUART

sion upon the language of the natives, so little intercourse was there between them and their conquerors; compare it with the fact that for four hundred years after the Norman conquest there was no fusion between the Norman and Saxon tongues.

In truth, all history teaches that the humiliation of defeat by a foreign foe is felt for ages, while that of defeat by the same race is temporary and soon forgotten. The late Civil War was relieved of very much of its sectional character by the presence of so many Southerners in the Union armies. Therefore, it will be in the United States as in all the unsectional civil wars of the world's history in which race and religion were not involved,—the waves of oblivion will roll over the bitter recollections of the strife. But we trust that fragrant forever will be the memory of deeds of heroism, patience, fortitude, self-denial, and constancy to principle, whether those deeds were performed by the wearers of the blue or of the gray.

Confederate Dead at the Cross-Roads by Wise's House at Fox's Gap from a Sketch Made the Day After the Battle.

Forcing Fox's Gap and Turners Gap

By Jacob D. Cox, Major-General, U. S. V.

On the 5th of September, 1862, the Kanawha Division was ordered by McClellan to report to General Burnside, commanding the Right Wing of the Army of the Potomac.

★★★★★★

The Kanawha Division transferred from West Virginia to the Potomac. The division was not engaged in the second Battle of Bull Run; but two regiments of Scammon's brigade were under fire at Bull Run Bridge, near Union Mills, August 27th.

★★★★★★

We left Upton's Hill early on the morning of the 6th, crossed the river, and marched through Washington to Leesboro, Maryland, where the First Corps (Hooker's) and the Ninth Corps, (created July 22nd, 1862, and composed of the command that Burnside brought from North Carolina), (Burnside's, under Reno), constituting the right wing, were assembling.

★★★★★★

Confusion in the numbers of the First and Twelfth Corps is found in the records and correspondence. In the Army of Virginia, Sigel's corps (Eleventh) had been designated as First, Banks's (Twelfth) had been Second, and McDowell's (First) had been Third. In the Maryland campaign Hooker was assigned to McDowell's, which was sometimes called First and sometimes Third. Mansfield was assigned to Banks's. The proper designations after the consolidation of the armies were First and Twelfth. Reno had been assigned to the First, but McClellan got authority to change it, and gave that corps to Hooker, sending Reno back to the Ninth (*Official Records*, XIX., Pt. II.)—J. D. C.

★★★★★★

Our formal assignment to the Ninth Corps was made a day or two later. On the 8th, the division was ordered to take the advance and marched to Brookville; on the 9th to Goshen; on the 11th to Ridgeville, and on the 12th, shortly after noon, to Frederick City, being the first to enter that place, and driving out the Confederate rear-guard of cavalry under General Wade Hampton. The insignificant skirmish which occurred there had a considerable influence upon the battle of the 14th, in an indirect way. The enemy's cavalry had been driven from the banks of the Monocacy River and retired into the town. The division, consisting of two brigades (Moor's and Scammon's), had crossed at the stone bridge on the National road, and Moor's, deployed on both sides of the turnpike, advanced upon the city. Colonel Moor himself, with a troop of cavalry and a single cannon, was in the road.

An impertinent criticism upon the speed of his movement, volunteered by a young staff-officer from corps headquarters, stung Moor into dashing ahead at a gallop, with his escort and staff, and the gun. Just at the outskirts of the town the road turns to the left among the houses, and cannot be seen. While we were wondering at the charge by the brigade commander and his escort, he came to the turn of the road: there was a quick, sharp rattling of carbines, and Hampton's Legion was atop of the little party. There was one discharge of the cannon, and some of the brigade staff and the escort came back in disorder.

I ordered up quickly the 11th Ohio, of Scammon's brigade, which was in column in the road, and they dashed into the town at a charge with fixed bayonets. The enemy's cavalry had not waited for them, but had retreated out of the place by the Hagerstown road. Moor had been ridden down, unhorsed, and captured. The artillerymen had unlimbered their gun, pointed it, and the gunner stood with the lanyard in his hand, when he was struck by a rushing horse; the gun was fired by the concussion, but at the same moment it was capsized into the ditch by the impact of the cavalry column.

The enemy had no time to right the gun or carry it off, nor to stop for prisoners. They forced Moor on another horse and turned tail as the charging lines of infantry came up on right and left, together with the column in the road, for there had not been a moment's pause in the advance. Those who have a fancy for learning how Munchausen could have told this story are referred to the narrative of Major Heros von Borcke, of J. E. B. Stuart's staff. Moor's capture, however, had con-

71

sequences, as we shall see. His brigade passed to the command of Colonel George Crook, of the 36th Ohio.

Frederick was a loyal city, and as Hampton's cavalry went out at one end of the street and our infantry came in at the other, while the carbine smoke and the smell of powder still lingered, the closed window-shutters of the houses flew open, the sashes went up, the windows were filled with ladies waving their handkerchiefs and the national flag, and the men came to the column with fruits and refreshments for the marching soldiers. We encamped just beyond the town. Pleasonton's cavalry, which had advanced by a different road (the one leading through Urbana), was sent forward next morning (September 13th) to reconnoiter the passes of Catoctin Mountain, and Rodman's division of our corps went as his support. Through some misunderstanding, Rodman did not advance on the Hagerstown road beyond Catoctin Mountain, but moved toward Franklin's line of march upon Crampton's Gap (southward).

About noon of the 13th, I was ordered to march with my division to Middletown, on the National road leading to Hagerstown. Mc-Clellan himself met me as my column moved out of town, and told me of the misunderstanding in Rodman's orders, adding, that if I met him on the march I should take his division also along with me. I did

MAJOR-GENERAL JESSE L. RENO,
KILLED AT FOX'S GAP.

not meet him, but his division returned to Frederick that night. The other two divisions of our corps crossed the Catoctin in the evening, and camped near the western base of the mountain.

My own camp for the night was pitched on the western side of the village of Middletown. The Catoctin or Middletown valley is beautifully included between Catoctin Mountain and South Mountain, two ranges of the Blue Ridge, running north-east and south-west. The valley is 6 or 8 miles wide, and the National road, as it goes northwestward, crosses South Mountain at a depression called Turner's Gap. The old Sharpsburg road leaves the turnpike a little west of Middletown, turns to the left, and crosses the mountain at Fox's Gap, about a mile from Turner's. The mountain crests are about 1300 feet above the Catoctin valley, and the "gaps" are from 200 to 300 feet lower than the summits near them. (These elevations are from the official map made by the U. S. Engineers—J. D. C.). These summits are like scattered and somewhat irregular hills upon the high rounded surface of the mountain-top. They are wooded, but along the south-easterly slopes, quite near the top of the mountain, are small farms with meadows and cultivated fields.

In the evening of the 13th I was ordered to support General Pleasonton in his cavalry reconnoissance to be made toward Turner's Gap in the morning. He had already been re-enforced by Benjamin's and Gibson's batteries from the corps. The notion that Pleasonton was authorised to put the infantry in position for an expected battle is wholly a mistake. No battle was expected at Turner's Gap. Lee's order, of which a copy had fallen into McClellan's hands, directed the concentration of the forces under Longstreet and D. H. Hill at Boonsboro', where they were to be joined by those under Jackson as soon as Harper's Ferry should be taken. McClellan's orders and correspondence show that he expected a battle at Boonsboro', but not at South Mountain or east of it. Pleasonton had found a rear-guard at Turner's Gap, but the support of a single brigade of infantry was assumed to be enough to enable his cavalry to clear the way.

Pleasonton asked for one brigade of infantry to report to him for the purpose stated, and I detailed the brigade under command of Colonel E. P. Scammon. At 6 o'clock in the morning of Sunday, September 14th, he marched out of camp at Middletown. His brigade consisted of the 12th, 23rd, and 30th Ohio regiments; that of Crook, which was left in camp, was made up of the 11th, 28th, and 36th Ohio, and each brigade was nearly fifteen hundred strong. Two batteries of artillery and a squadron of cavalry also belonged to the division.

I was myself on the road when Scammon marched out, and was riding forward with him to learn how Pleasonton intended to use the troops, when, just as we crossed Catoctin Creek, I was surprised to see Colonel Moor standing at the roadside. With astonishment, I rode to him and asked how he came there. He said he had been taken prisoner beyond the mountain, but had been paroled the evening before, and was now finding his way back to us on foot.

"But where are *you* going?" said he.

I answered that Scammon's brigade was going to support Pleasonton in a reconnoissance into the gap. Moor made an involuntary start, saying, "My God! be careful"; then, checking himself, said, "But I am paroled!" and turned away.

I galloped to Scammon and told him that I should follow him in close support with Crook's brigade, and as I went back along the column I spoke to each regimental commander, warning them to be prepared for anything, big or little, it might be a skirmish, it might be a battle. Hurrying back to the camp, I ordered Crook to turn out his brigade prepared to march at once. I then wrote a dispatch to General Reno, saying I suspected we should find the enemy in force on the mountain-top, and should go forward with both brigades instead of sending one. Starting a courier with this, I rode forward to find Pleasonton, who was about a mile in front of my camp, where the old Sharpsburg road leaves the turnpike.

I found that he was convinced that the enemy's position in the gap was too strong to be carried by a direct attack, and that he had determined to let his horsemen demonstrate on the main road, supporting the batteries, one of which at least (Benjamin's) was of 20-pounder Parrott guns, while Scammon should march by the Sharpsburg road and try to reach the flank of the force on the summit. Telling him of my suspicion as to the enemy, I also informed him that I had determined to support Scammon with Crook, and if it became necessary to fight with the whole division I should do so, in which case I should assume the responsibility myself as his senior officer. To this he cordially assented.

One of my batteries contained a section of 20-pounder Parrotts, and as these were too heavy to take up the rough mountain road, I ordered them to go into action beside Benjamin's battery, near the turnpike, and to remain with it till further orders. Our artillery at this time was occupying a knoll about half a mile in front of the forks of the road, and was exchanging shots with a battery of the enemy well up toward the gap. It was about half-past 7 o'clock when Crook's column filed off on the old Sharpsburg road, Scammon having perhaps half an hour's start. We had fully two miles to go before we should reach the place where our attack was made, and, as it was a pretty steep road, the men marched slowly with frequent rests.

On our way up, we were overtaken by my courier who had returned from Reno with approval of my action, and the assurance that the rest of the Ninth Corps would come forward to my support. (See map). At about half a mile from the summit, at Fox's Gap, the enemy had opened upon Scammon with case shot from the edge of the timber above the open fields, and the latter had judiciously turned off upon a country road leading still farther to the left and nearly parallel to the ridge above. Here I overtook him, his brigade being formed in line, under cover of the timber, facing open pasture fields, having a stone-wall along the upper side, with the forest again beyond this.

Crook was brought up close in his rear. The ascent and the formation of the division had occupied more than an hour, and it was now about 9 o'clock. Bayonets were fixed, and at the word the lines charged forward with loud hurrahs. The enemy opened with musketry and shrapnel; our men fell fast, but they kept up their pace, and in a few moments, they were on and over the wall, the centre of Garland's North Carolina brigade breaking before them. They hung on a little longer at right and left, and for some time it was a fierce melee, hand to hand, but the Ohio boys were the victors. We found that there was a country road behind the wall on top of the ridge, and the cover of the forest had enabled the enemy's guns to get away toward our right.

The 11th Ohio was sent from Crook's brigade beyond Scammon's left, where part of the enemy's force held a hill and summit higher than the ridge at the stone-wall. This seems to have been held by Rosser's cavalry with a battery. The 36th Ohio was, in similar manner, sent beyond Scammon's right. The whole line again sprung forward. The high knoll on the left was carried, the enemy's centre was completely broken and driven down the mountain, while on the right our men pushed the routed Carolinians beyond the Sharpsburg road, through Wise's fields, and up the slope of the crest toward the Mountain House at Turner's Gap. The regiment on the enemy's extreme right had been cut off from the others and retreated southwestwardly down the mountain toward Rohrersville. Those on their left had made such resistance as they could till they were supported by Anderson's brigade, which hurried to their assistance.

The cavalry also took refuge on a wooded hill west of the Mountain House. Although Garland's line had been broken in the first charge, the rallying and fighting had been stubborn for more than an hour. Our position was now diagonally across the mountaintop, the shape of the ridges making our formation a hollow curve with our right too much in the air, where it was exposed to a severe artillery fire, not only from the batteries near the Mountain House but from one on a high hill north of the turnpike. The batteries with Pleasonton did their best to assist us, and were admirably served. We had several hundred prisoners in our hands, and learned from them that D. H. Hill's division, consisting of five brigades, was opposed to us, and that Longstreet was said to be in near support.

Our own losses had not been trifling, and it seemed wise to contract our lines a little, so that we might have some reserve and hold the crest we had won till the rest of the Ninth Corps should arrive. Our left and centre were strongly posted, but the right was partly across Fox's Gap, at the edge of the woods beyond Wise's house, around which there had been a fierce struggle. The 30th and 36th were therefore brought back to the crest on the hither side of the gap, where we still commanded the Sharpsburg road, and making the 30th our right flank, the 36th and the 28th were put in second line. My right thus occupied the woods looking northward into Wise's fields. About noon the combat was reduced to one of artillery, and the enemy's guns had so completely the range of the sloping fields behind us that their canister shot cut long furrows in the sod, with a noise like the cutting of a melon rind.

Willcox's division reported to me at about 2 o'clock, and would have been up considerably earlier but for a mistake in the delivery of a message to him, in consequence of which he moved first toward the hill on the north of the turnpike (afterward carried by Hooker's corps), until he was recalled and given the right direction by Reno, who had arrived at Pleasonton's headquarters. As he went into position on my right, the artillery fire from the crest beyond the turnpike annoyed him, and to avoid being enfiladed by it, he formed with his right thrown back nearly at right angles to the front and facing toward the turnpike.

We were not long left idle. Longstreet's divisions had been arriving on the field faster than ours, and made a most determined effort to push us back from the ridge we held. I sent two regiments of Willcox's to extend my left, which was in danger of being turned. Their

THE WASHINGTON MONU-
MENT ON SOUTH
MOUNTAIN.

FROM PHOTOGRAPHS.

This monument, to the memory of George Washington, was first erected by the citizens of Boonsboro' and vicinity in 1827. It stands on the summit, a mile and a half north of Turner's Gap [see map, p. 568]. Originally it was twenty feet high. In its tumble-down condition, as seen on the right of the picture, it served as one of the Union signal stations during the battle of Antietam. In 1882 the monument was rebuilt, as seen on the left of the picture, by the Odd Fellows of Boonsboro'. The present height of the tower, including the observatory, is forty feet.

strongest attack fell upon the angle of Willcox's command, and for a little while there was some confusion there, due to the raking artillery fire which came from the right; but Willcox soon reformed his lines, and after a very bloody contest, pushed across the Sharpsburg road, through Wise's fields, and into the wooded slope beyond. Along the front of the Kanawha Division the line was steadily maintained and the enemy was repulsed with severe loss.

At nearly 4 o'clock, Sturgis's division arrived and relieved the left wing of Willcox's division, the latter taking ground a little more to the right and rear. Rodman was the last to arrive, and as part of Long-street's corps again threatened to pass beyond my left flank, I sent Fairchild's brigade to extend the line in that direction, the rest of that division going to the support of Sturgis and Willcox. During all this time, there was sharp fighting all along the front, the struggle being on the part of the Confederates to drive back our centre and left, where we held the highest summits of the mountain, and on our part to push forward our right so as to gain the one elevation they still held on our side of the National road, at the Mountain House. On the other side of the turnpike Hooker had by this time deployed, and his corps was fighting its way up the mountain side there.

McClellan, Burnside, and Reno had come, soon after Willcox's division, to the knoll in the valley which had been Pleasonton's position, and from that point, a central one in the midst of curving hills, had issued their orders. The Ninth Corps troops, as they came up the mountain, had reported to me for position, as I was senior on the line. Soon after the arrival of Rodman's division, the order came to advance the whole line, so as to complete the dislodgment of the enemy from the remaining summit at the Mountain House. At the centre and left the advance was not difficult, for we held the ridge and pushed our opponents down the mountain. But the right had still to climb, and the ground there was rough and rocky, a fortress in itself and stoutly held.

Good progress was made by both Sturgis and Willcox, but the fastness at the Mountain House had not been carried when darkness fell upon the field. A little before sunset, Reno came up in person, anxious to know why the right could not get forward quite to the summit. After a few moments' conversation with me he passed on to Sturgis; it seemed to me he was hardly gone before he was brought back upon a stretcher, dead. He had gone to the skirmish line to examine for himself the situation there, and had been shot down by the enemy posted among the rocks and trees. There was more or less firing in that part of the field till late in the evening, but when morning dawned, the Confederates had abandoned the last foothold above Turner's Gap.

On the north of the National road the First Corps under Hooker had been opposed by one of Hill's brigades and four of Longstreet's, and had gradually worked its way along the old Hagerstown road, crossing the heights in that direction after dark in the evening. Gibbon's brigade had advanced along the National road, crowding up quite close to Turner's Gap, and engaging the enemy under Colquitt in a lively combat. It has been my purpose, however, to limit any detailed account to what occurred under my own eye.

The peculiar character of the battle had been that it grew out of what was intended for a mere reconnoissance. The Kanawha Division had carried the crest at Fox's Gap early in the forenoon, while the rest of the army was miles away. General Hill has since argued that only part of his division could oppose us; but his brigades were all on the mountain summit within easy support of each other, and they had the day before them. It was five hours from the time of our first charge to the arrival of our first supports, and it was not till 3 o'clock in the afternoon that Hooker's corps reached the eastern base of the mountain and began its deployment north of the National road. Our effort was to attack the weak end of the Confederate line, and we succeeded in putting a stronger force there than that which opposed us.

It is for our opponent to explain how we were permitted to do it. The two brigades of the Kanawha Division numbered less than three thousand men. Hill's division was five thousand strong, even by the Confederate method of counting their effectives, which should be increased nearly one-fifth to compare properly with our reports. In addition to these, Stuart had the principal part of the Confederate cavalry on this line, and they were not idle spectators. Part of Lee's and Hampton's brigades were certainly there, and probably the whole of Lee's. With less than half the numerical strength which was opposed to it, therefore, the Kanawha Division had carried the summit, advancing to the charge for the most part over open ground in a storm of musketry and artillery fire, and had held the crests they had gained through the livelong day, in spite of all efforts to retake them.

The Ninth and the First Corps were deployed about 1 o'clock in the afternoon, and from that time till dark the proportions of the combat were enlarged to a battle which raged along two miles of mountain summits. The casualties in the Ninth Corps had been 889, of which 356 were in the Kanawha Division, which also captured some 600 of the enemy and sent them to the rear under guard. Reno on the National side and Garland on the Confederate were the officers of highest rank who were killed; but the wounded included a long list of distinguished men, among whom was Lieutenant-Colonel Rutherford B. Hayes (afterward President), who fell severely wounded in the early morning struggle on our left, where, also, Garland died, vainly trying to stay the rout of his brigade as our men covered the mountain-top.

★★★★★★

General Hooker, commander of the First Corps, in his report, thus describes the action on the right of the Union Army, for the control of Turner's Gap:

> In front of us was South Mountain, the crest of the spinal ridge of which was held by the enemy in considerable

force. Its slopes are precipitous, rugged, and wooded, and difficult of access to an infantry force even in absence of a foe in front. . . . Meade moved forward with great vigour and soon became engaged, driving everything before him.

Every step of his advance was resisted stubbornly by a numerous enemy, and, besides, he had great natural obstacles to overcome which impeded his advance, but did not check it. . . . . At this moment word was received that the enemy were attempting to turn Meade's right, when Duryea's brigade, of Ricketts's division, was dispatched to thwart it, and reached there in good time to render substantial aid in this, and also in assisting their comrades in crowning the summit with our arms. This was taken possession of in fine style between sundown and dark, and from that moment the battle was won. . . .

Meantime Hatch had pressed into the forest on the left, and, after driving in their advanced pickets, encountered a heavy fire from the enemy massed in his front. The struggle became violent and protracted, his troops displaying the finest courage and determination. . . . Hatch being outnumbered, sorely pressed, and almost out of ammunition, Christian's brigade, of Ricketts's division, was ordered forward to strengthen him, and in this rendered good service.

On this part of the held the resistance of the enemy was continued until after dark, and only subsided on his being driven from his position. It being very dark, our troops were directed to remain in position, and Hartsuff's brigade (of Ricketts's division) was brought up and formed a line across the valley, connecting with Meade's left and Hatch's right, and all were directed to sleep on their arms.

Brigadier-General John Gibbon reports:

. . . My brigade was detached from the. division and ordered to report for duty to Major-General Burnside. Late in the afternoon I was ordered to move up the Hagerstown turnpike (National road) with my brigade and one section of Gibbon's battery to attack the position of the enemy in the gorge. The 7th Wisconsin and the 19th Indiana were placed respectively on the right and left of the turnpike, to advance by the head of the company, preceded by two companies of skirmishers from the 6th and 2nd Wisconsin, and, followed by these regiments, formed in double column at half distance, the section of the battery under Lieutenant Stewart, 4th Artillery, keeping on the pike a little in rear of the first line.

The skirmishers soon became engaged and were supported by the leading regiments, while our guns moved forward on the turnpike until within range of the enemy's guns which were firing on our column from the top of the gorge, when they opened with good effect. My men steadily advanced on the enemy posted in the woods and behind stone-walls, driving him before them until he was re-enforced by three additional regiments, making five in all opposed to us. Seeing we were likely to be outflanked on our right, I directed Lieutenant-Colonel Bragg, of the 6th Wisconsin, to enter the wood on his right and deploy his regiment on the right of the 7th. This was successfully accomplished, while the 19th Indiana, supported by the 2nd Wisconsin, deployed, and, swinging around parallel to the turnpike, took the enemy in the flank. Thus, the fight continued till long after dark, Stewart using his guns with good effect over the heads of our own men. My men, with their ammunition nearly exhausted, held all the ground they had taken. . . .

The Confederate troops opposed to Meade appear to have been Rodes's brigade, of D. H. Hill's division, supported by Jenkins's, of D. R. Jones's division, while Hatch's advance appears to have been resisted by Kemper's and Garnett's brigades, of D. R. Jones's division, supported by Evans's independent brigade. Colquitt's brigade, of D. H. Hill's division, held the main turnpike against Gibbon.

★★★★★★

On Monday morning, our first duty was to bury the dead and to see that the wounded in our field-hospitals were sent back to Middletown where the general hospital had been established. During the forenoon, we received orders to march toward Sharpsburg, but the road was already occupied by other troops, and when the head of my division reached it, at the place where the fight in front of Willcox's division had been most severe, we were halted for two or three hours till the corps which had the right of way should pass. Then we turned our faces toward the Antietam.

CAVALRY SKIRMISHERS.

Notes on Crampton's Gap and Antietam

By Wm. B. Franklin, Major-General, U. S. V.

Between the 2nd and 6th of September, the Sixth Corps remained in camp near Alexandria and collected horses and transportation for ammunition and provisions, which were gradually disembarked. On the latter date, it marched to Tenallytown, beyond Georgetown, D. C, crossing the Potomac by the Long Bridge, and beginning the Maryland campaign. Its daily marches thereafter, to the date of the battle of Antietam, were regulated by orders from General McClellan, who, in turn, was in direct communication with Washington. It appears from the telegraphic correspondence which was carried on between Halleck and McClellan, that while the latter believed that General Lee's object was the invasion of Pennsylvania, the former could not divest himself of the notion that Lee was about to play the Union Army some slippery trick by turning its left, getting between it and Washington and Baltimore, and then taking each city by a *coup-de-main*.

The following are extracts from some of General Halleck's dispatches:

Sept. 9.—.... I think we must be very cautious about stripping too much the forts on the Virginia side. It may be the enemy's object to draw off the mass of our forces, and then attempt to attack from the Virginia side of the Potomac.

Sept. 11.—I think the main force of the enemy is in your front; more troops can be spared from here."(General McClellan states that he received the dispatch in this form, but as printed in the *Official Records*, Vol. XIX., Pt. II., p. 253, the sentence reads: "If the main force of the enemy is in your front, more troops can be spared from here."

Sept. 13.—I am of opinion that the enemy will send a small column toward Pennsylvania, so as to draw your forces in that direction; then suddenly move on Washington with the forces south of the Potomac, and those he may cross over.

Sept. 14.—Scouts report a large force still on Virginia side of the Potomac, near Leesburg. If so, I fear you are exposing your left flank, and that the enemy can cross in your rear.

Sept. 16.—I fear now more than ever that they (the enemy) will recross at Harper's Ferry, or below, and turn your left, thus cutting you off from Washington. . . .

On September 12th, Mr. Lincoln telegraphed General McClellan that he believed the enemy was recrossing the Potomac, and said:

Please do not let him get off without being hurt.

These dispatches demonstrate that it was McClellan's duty as a subordinate to move slowly and cautiously in his advance, although he believed that the whole of Lee's army was in his front. And during the whole Maryland campaign his army was nearer Washington than was Lee's.

On or before September 7th, General McClellan advised that Harper's Ferry should be evacuated *via* Hagerstown, so as to hold the Cumberland Valley against an advance toward Harrisburg, and on the 10th of September he asked that the garrison at Harper's Ferry should be ordered to join him. General Halleck in answer to the last request stated:

There is no way for Colonel Miles to join you at present; his only chance is to defend his works till you can open communication with him.

Yet during the night of September 11th two regiments of cavalry marched out of Harper's Ferry to Hagerstown without meeting any enemy; and the whole infantry and field-artillery force of the garrison might have escaped before the 14th had General McClellan's advice of September 7th and 10th been followed. So, the Sixth Corps moved by easy marches toward the Blue Ridge, under daily orders from the commanding general, and on the 14th of September fought the battle of Crampton's Gap, gaining the completest victory gained up to that time by any part of the Army of the Potomac.

While Burnside and Hooker were forcing Turner's Gap to open

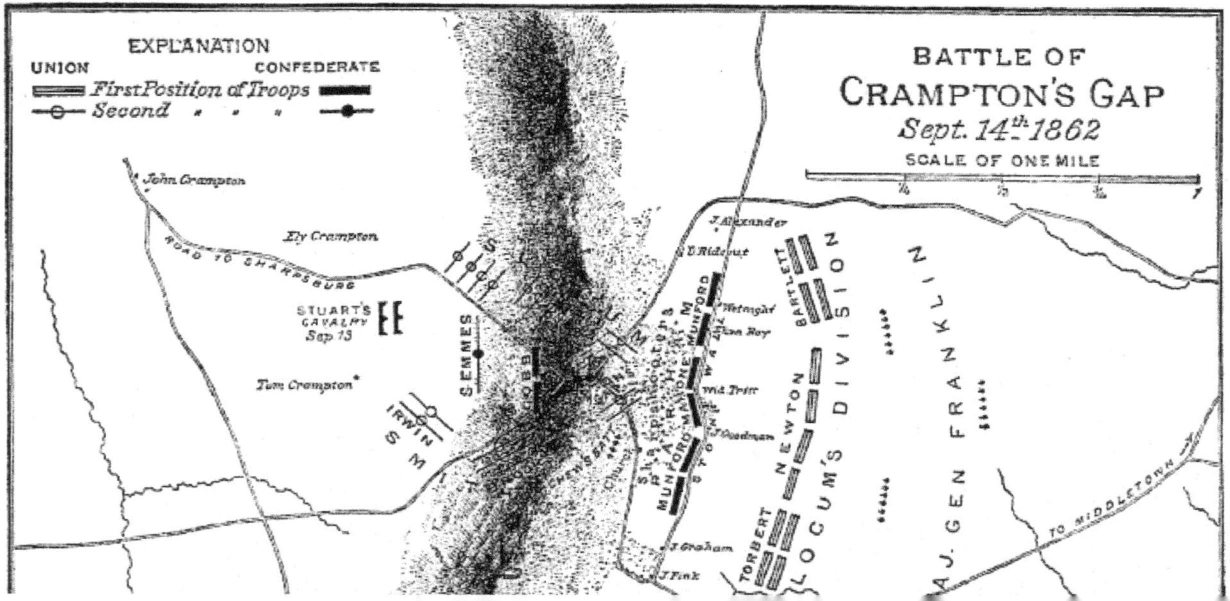

BATTLE OF
CRAMPTON'S GAP
Sept. 14th 1862
SCALE OF ONE MILE

EXPLANATION
UNION   CONFEDERATE
First Position of Troops
Second   "   "   "

A. GEN FRANKLIN

SLOCUM'S DIVISION

TORBERT   NEWTON   BARTLETT

J. Alexander
U. Ridgway
M. Cake
Wenger
Van Roy
Wm. Penn
Brougham
C. Miller

MUNFORD
MUNFORD
MAHONE
SHAW
PARHAM

COBB

SEMMES

IRWIN   S   M

STUART'S
CAVALRY
Sep. 13

ROAD TO SHARPSBURG

Ely Crampton

John Crampton

Tom Crampton

TO MIDDLETOWN

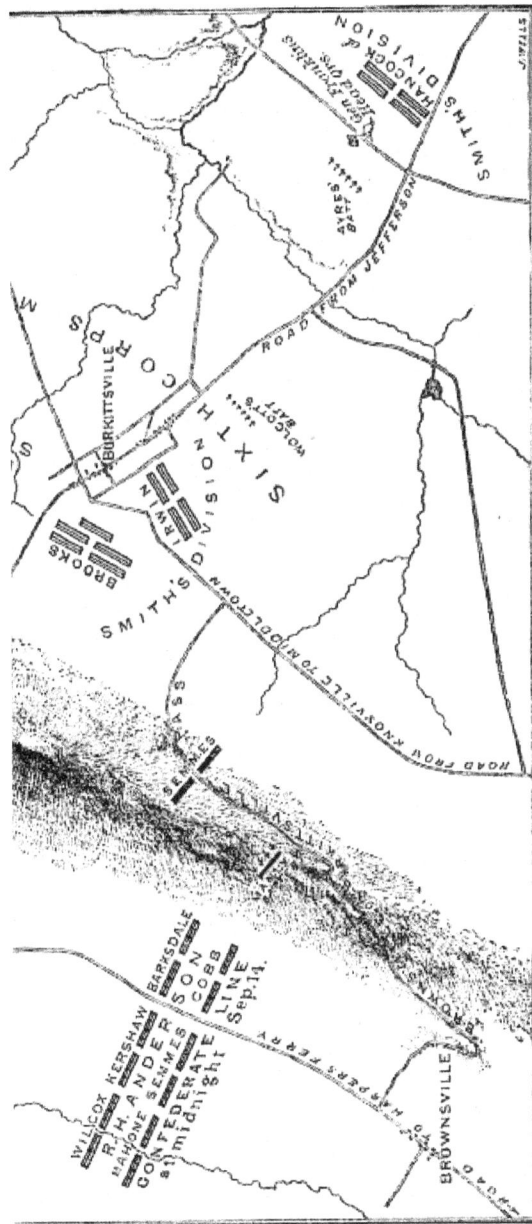

The Confederate sharp-shooters were behind their main line on higher ground, protected by trees and bowlders. After Parham's troops retired, Cobb, who had just reached the field, assumed command. — EDITORS.

the direct road to Hagerstown, I was ordered to move by Crampton's Gap, five miles farther south, and gain Rohrersville, in order to cut off McLaws and R. H. Anderson on Maryland Heights, and to relieve Harper's Ferry. About noon on the 14th of September, the head of my column, Slocum's division, came upon Munford's brigade of cavalry, comprising the 2nd and 12th Virginia regiments, with Chew's battery and a section of the Portsmouth battery of naval howitzers, supported by two regiments of Mahone's brigade of R. H. Anderson's division, under Colonel William A. Parham.

General McLaws had also posted the remainder of Mahone's brigade and the brigades of Semmes and Cobb of his own division within supporting distance, and ordered General Howell Cobb to take command and to hold the pass against us. With the remainder of Anderson's division and his own, General McLaws occupied Maryland Heights, distant five miles. I quote from my official report of the action which ensued:

> The enemy was strongly posted on both sides of the road, which made a steep ascent through a narrow defile, wooded on both sides and offering great advantages of cover and position. Their advance was posted near the base of the mountain, in the rear of a stone-wall, stretching to the right of the road at a point where the ascent was gradual and for the most part over open fields. Eight guns had been stationed on the road and at points on the sides and summit of the mountain to the left of the pass. It was evident that the position could be carried only by an infantry attack.
>
> Accordingly, I directed Major-General Slocum to advance his division through, the village of Burkittsville and commence the attack upon the right. Wolcott's 1st Maryland Battery was stationed on the left and to the rear of the village, and maintained a steady fire on the positions of the enemy until they were assailed and carried by our troops. Smith's division was placed in reserve on the east side of the village, and held in readiness to cooperate with General Slocum or support his attack as occasion might require. Captain Ayres's battery of this division was posted on a commanding ground to the left of the reserves, and kept up an uninterrupted fire on the principal battery of the enemy until the latter was driven from its position.
>
> The advance of General Slocum was made with admirable

steadiness through a well-directed fire from the batteries on the mountain, the brigade of Colonel Bartlett taking the lead, and followed at proper intervals by the brigades of General Newton and Colonel Torbert. Upon fully determining the enemy's position, the skirmishers were withdrawn and Colonel Bartlett became engaged along his entire line. He maintained his ground steadily under a severe fire for some time at a manifest disadvantage, until re-enforced by two regiments of General Newton's brigade upon his right, and the brigade of Colonel Torbert and the two remaining regiments of Newton's on his left. The line of battle thus formed, an immediate charge was ordered, and most gallantly executed.

The men swept forward with a cheer, over the stone-wall, dislodging the enemy, and pursuing him up the mountain-side to the crest of the hill and down the opposite slope. This single charge, sustained as it was over a great distance, and on a rough ascent of unusual steepness, was decisive. The enemy was driven in the utmost confusion from a position of strength and allowed no opportunity for even an attempt to rally, until the pass was cleared and in the possession of our troops.

When the division under General Slocum first became actively engaged, I directed General Brooks's brigade, of Smith's division, to advance upon the left of the road and dislodge the enemy from the woods upon Slocum's flank. The movement was promptly and steadily made under a severe artillery fire. General Brooks occupied the woods after a slight resistance, and then advanced, simultaneously with General Slocum, rapidly and in good order, to the crest of the mountain. The victory was complete, and its achievement followed so rapidly upon the first attack that the enemy's reserves, although pushed forward at the double-quick, arrived but in time to participate in the flight and add confusion to the rout. 400 prisoners, from 17 different organisations, 700 stand of arms, 1 piece of artillery, and 3 stand of colours were captured. . . .

The gun was a 12-pounder howitzer belonging to the Troup artillery attached to Cobb's brigade, and was captured by the 95th Pennsylvania, Colonel Gustavus W. Town, of Newton's brigade. General Cobb says it was "lost by an accident to the axle," but according to Colonel Town's report the artillerists fled before his advance, "merely disabling it temporarily by throwing off one wheel from the limber, which was left with the horses near at hand." Two of the colours were captured by the 4th New Jersey regiment, Colonel William B. Hatch, of Torbert's brigade, and one by the 16th New York, commanded by Lieutenant-Colonel Joel J. Seaver, of Bartlett's brigade. A fourth stand of colours, belonging to the 16th Virginia regiment, of Mahone's brigade, was taken by the 4th Vermont regiment, Lieutenant-Colonel Charles B. Stoughton, of Brooks's brigade.

No report appears to have been made by Colonel Parham, who commanded Mahone's brigade, nor by his division commander, General R. H. Anderson, who was wounded at Antietam, but the reports of Generals Cobb and Semmes and Colonel Munford sufficiently indicate the effect of our advance upon the forces under their command. Munford, who had eight guns, his two regiments of cavalry dismounted, and Mahone's brigade, was driven from his position behind a stone-wall at the foot of the pass. Cobb now came to his support, dividing his brigade to the right and left, but too late to change the result. One regiment, the 10th Georgia, of Semmes's brigade, also joined in Parham's defence, while the remaining three regiments, with nine guns of Manly's, Macon's, and Page's batteries, were posted for the defence of Burkittsville Gap, about a mile below toward our left, where the artillery is described, in the Confederate reports, as having done "good service." General Cobb says:

> As I was marching the last of the column, I received a message from you (McLaws) . . . that I must hold the gap if it cost the life of every man in my command. . . . Two of my regiments were sent to the right and two to the left to meet these movements of the enemy. In this we were successful, until the centre gave way, pressed by fresh troops of the enemy and increased numbers. Up to this time the troops had fought well and maintained their ground against greatly superior forces. The 10th Georgia regiment, of General Semmes's brigade, had been ordered to the gap from their position at the foot of the mountain and participated in the battle with great courage and energy. After the lines were broken, all my efforts to rally the troops were unsuccessful.

General Semmes, who hurried forward to offer his assistance to General Cobb, thus describes the scene he witnessed on the Confederate side of the crest:

A Battery Going into Action

Arriving at the base of, and soon after commencing the ascent of, the mountain at Crampton's Gap, I encountered fugitives from the battlefield and endeavoured to turn them back. Proceeding farther up the mountain, the troops were met pouring down the road and through the wood in great disorder, where I found General Cobb and his staff, at the imminent risk of their lives, using every effort to check and rally them. I immediately joined my efforts, and those of my staff who were with me, to General Cobb's, and cooperated with him for a considerable time in the vain effort to rally the men.

General McLaws moved Wilcox's brigade of R. H. Anderson's, and later Kershaw's and Barksdale's brigades of his own division, to the support of Cobb, but not in time to take part in the engagement. The report of General McLaws shows that he accurately appreciated the effect of our success in completely shutting up his command on Maryland Heights until the surrender of Harper's Ferry opened the door for him to cross into Virginia. Accepting the estimate of Mr. Thomas White, who was chief clerk in the adjutant-general's office at General Lee's headquarters, and had charge of the returns, the whole available force under McLaws was 8000 men, and mine, on the basis of the last returns, 12,300.

Couch's division (7219 men) of the Fourth Corps did not reach the field of the 14th until the fighting was over, and was detached from my command early the next morning. But these figures are at least one-fifth, if not one-fourth, beyond the actual effective strength. General Cobb estimates the Confederate forces actually engaged at 2200. Mine can hardly have exceeded 6500; heavy odds, indeed, but so are stone walls and a steep mountain pass. My losses were 533. The losses in Parham's (Mahone's) brigade, spoken of as heavy, are not reported; those in Cobb's and Semmes's brigades are given as 749.

At the end of the fight, after nightfall, the division of the corps which had borne the brunt of the fight (Slocum's), was, as it were, astride of the mountain. Of the other division (Smith's), the brigades of Brooks and Irwin were on the mountain, the reserve under Hancock being at the eastern base. Couch's division reported to me at 10 p. m. (In October, 1862, when Mr. Lincoln visited the army, he came through Crampton's Gap; he told me that he was astonished to see and hear of what we had done there. He thanked me for it, and said that he had not understood it before. He was in all respects very kind and complimentary. W. B. F.)

Early the next morning, Smith's division was sent into Pleasant Valley, west of the Blue Ridge, to begin the movement toward Harper's Ferry. Couch's division was sent, by order of the commanding general, to occupy Rohrersville. Slocum was to support Smith. As I was crossing the mountain about 7 a. m., on September 15th, I had a good view of the enemy's force below, which seemed to be well posted on hills stretching across the valley, which is at this place about two miles wide. When I reached General Smith, we made an examination of the position, and concluded that it would be suicidal to attack it. The whole breadth of the valley was occupied, and batteries swept the only approaches to the position. We estimated the force as quite as large as ours, and it was in a position which, properly defended, would have required a much greater force than ours to have carried.

I am unable to give the numbers, but McLaws, in his report of the operations of the day, states that he formed the line across the valley with the brigades of Kershaw and Barksdale, except one regiment and two guns of the latter, and the "remnants" of the brigades of Cobb, Semmes, Mahone, and Wilcox, which he afterward states were very small. The only force available for an attack would have been Smith's division of about 4500 men, Slocum's division being in no condition for a fight that day. Reading between the lines of General McLaws's report, he seems to have been disgusted that I did not attack him.

The evidence before the court of inquiry on the surrender of Harper's Ferry shows that the white flag was shown at 7:30 a. m., on the 15th, and the firing ceased about one hour afterward. It is evident, therefore, that a fight between General McLaws's force and mine could have had no effect upon the surrender of Harper's Ferry. Success on my part would have drawn me farther away from the army and would have brought me in dangerous nearness to Jackson's force, already set free by the surrender. McLaws's supports were three and a half miles from him, while my force was seven miles from the main army.

Later on that day the enemy withdrew from Pleasant Valley and Harper's Ferry toward Sharpsburg. Couch's division joined me, and the corps remained stationary without orders from McClellan until the evening of the 16th, when I was ordered to march the next morning to join the army and to send Couch's division to occupy Maryland Heights. Accordingly, the corps started at 5:30 a. m., and the advance reached the field of Antietam at 10 a. m., about twelve miles distant from the starting-point.

General Smith's division arrived first and was immediately brought into action in the vicinity of the Dunker Church, repelling a strong attack made by the enemy at this point. The details of the part borne by the corps in the battle are graphically given in the official reports.

While awaiting the arrival of Slocum, I went to the right, held by Sumner. I found him at the head of his troops, but much depressed. He told me that his whole corps was exhausted and could do nothing more that day. It was lying in line of battle partly in a wood from which it had driven the enemy that morning. About three hundred yards in its front, across an open field, was a wood nearer the bank of the river, strongly held by the enemy. The corps had been driven back from an attack on this wood with great loss.

When General Slocum arrived, I placed two brigades of his division on General Sumner's left and was awaiting the arrival of his third brigade, which was to be in reserve. With the two brigades, I intended to make an attack on the wood referred to, and General Sumner was informed of my intention. The two brigades were ready to move. Just as the third brigade arrived, General Sumner rode up and directed me not to make the attack, giving as a reason for his order, that if I were defeated the right would be entirely routed, mine being the only troops left on the right that had any life in them. Major Hammerstein, of McClellan's staff, was near, and I requested him to inform General McClellan of the state of affairs, and that I thought the attack ought to be made.

Shortly afterward McClellan rode up, and, after hearing the statements of Sumner and myself, decided that as the day had gone so well on the other parts of the line it would be unsafe to risk anything on the right. Of course, no advance was made by the division. Later in the day General McClellan came again to my headquarters, and there was pointed out to him a hill on the right, commanding the wood, and it was proposed that the hill should be occupied by our artillery early the next morning, and that after shelling the wood, the attack should be made by the whole corps from the position then held by it. He assented to this, and it was understood that the attack was to be made.

During the night, however, the order was countermanded. I met him about 9 o'clock on the morning of the 18th. He informed me that he countermanded the order because fifteen thousand Pennsylvania troops would soon arrive, and that upon their arrival the attack would be ordered. The troops, however, did not arrive, and the order was not renewed that day. On the 19th the corps entered the wood, expecting a fight, but the enemy had slipped off during the night.

The Opposing Forces in the Maryland Campaign

The composition, losses, and strength of each army as stated in the following pages, give the gist of all the data obtainable in the *Official Records*, k stands for killed; w for wounded; m w for mortally wounded; m for captured or missing; c for captured.

MAJOR-GENERAL E. V. SUMNER

BEFORE THE WAR

THE OPPOSING FORCES IN THE MARYLAND CAMPAIGN.

The composition, losses, and strength of each army as here stated give the gist of all the data obtainable in the Official Records. K stands for killed; w for wounded; m w for mortally wounded; m for captured or missing : c for captured.

THE UNION ARMY.

(On September 14th, the right wing of this army, consisting of the First and Ninth Corps, was commanded by Maj.-Gen. A. E. Burnside; the center, composed of the Second and Twelfth Corps, by Maj.-Gen. Edwin V. Sumner; and the left wing, comprising the Sixth Corps and Couch's division of the Fourth Corps, by Maj.-Gen. W. B. Franklin.)

ARMY OF THE POTOMAC.—Major-General George B. McClellan.

Escort, Capt. James B. McIntyre : Oneida (N. Y.) Cav., Capt. Daniel P. Mann ; A, 4th U. S. Cav., Lieut. Thomas H. McCormick; E, 4th U. S. Cav., Capt. James B. McIntyre. *Regular Engineer Battalion*, Capt. James C. Duane. *Provost Guard*, Maj. William H. Wood ; 2d U. S. Cav. (4 co's) Capt. George A. Gordon; 8th U. S. Inf. (4 co's), Capt. Royal T. Frank; G, 19th U. S. Inf., Capt. Edmund L. Smith; H, 19th U. S. Inf., Capt. Henry S. Welton. *Headquarters Guard*, Maj. Granville O. Haller: 93d N. Y., Lieut.-Col. Benjamin C. Butler. *Quartermaster's Guard:* 1st U. S. Cav. (4 co's), Capt. Marcus A. Reno.

FIRST ARMY CORPS, Maj.-Gen. Joseph Hooker (w), Brig.-Gen. George G. Meade. Staff loss: Antietam, w, 1.
  Escort: 2d N. Y. Cav. (4 co's), Capt. John E. Naylor.
  FIRST DIVISION, Brig.-Gen. Rufus King, Brig.-Gen. John P. Hatch (w), Brig.-Gen. Abner Doubleday. Staff loss: South Mountain, w, 1.
    First Brigade, Col. Walter Phelps, Jr.: 22d N. Y., Lieut.-Col. John McKie, Jr. ; 24th N. Y., Capt. John D. O'Brian (w); 30th N. Y., Col. William M. Searing; 84th N. Y. (14th Militia), Maj. William H. de Bevoise ; 2d U. S. Sharp-shooters, Col. Henry A. V. Post (w). Brigade loss: South Mountain, k, 20 ; w, 67 ; m, 8=95. Antietam, k, 30; w, 120; m, 4=154. *Second Brigade*, Brig.-Gen. Abner Doubleday, Col. William P. Wainwright (w), Lieut.-Col, J. William Hofmann : 7th Ind., Maj. Ira G. Grover; 76th N. Y., Col. William P. Wainwright, Capt. John W. Young; 95th N. Y., Maj. Edward Pye ; 56th Pa., Lieut.-Col. J. William Hofmann, Capt. Frederick Williams. Brigade loss: South Mountain, k, 3 ; w, 52 ; m, 4 =79. Antietam, w, 10. *Third Brigade*, Brig.-Gen. Marsena R. Patrick: 21st N. Y., Col. William F. Rogers; 23d N. Y., Col. Henry C. Hoffman; 35th N. Y., Col. Newton B. Lord; 80th N. Y. (20th Militia), Lieut.-Col. Theodore B. Gates. Brigade loss: South Mountain, k, 3 ; w, 19 ; m, 1 =23. Antietam, k, 30 ; w, 187; m, 17 =234. *Fourth Brigade*, Brig.-Gen. John Gibbon: 19th Ind., Col. Solomon Meredith, Lieut.-Col. Alois O. Bachman (k), Capt. William W. Dudley : 2d Wis., Col. Lucius Fairchild, Lieut.-Col. Thomas S. Allen (w) ; 6th Wis., Lieut.-Col. Edward S. Bragg (w), Maj. Rufus R. Dawes; 7th Wis., Capt. John B. Callis. Brigade loss: South Mountain, k, 37 ; w, 251 ; m, 30 =318. Antietam, k, 68 ; w, 275; m, 5 =348. *Artillery*, Capt. J. Albert Monroe: 1st N. H., Lieut. Frederick M. Edgell ; D, 1st R. I., Capt. J. Albert Monroe; L, 1st N. Y., Capt. John A. Reynolds ; B, 4th U. S., Capt. Joseph B. Campbell (w), Lieut. James Stewart. Artillery loss: Antietam, k, 12 ; w, 46; m, 8 =66.
  SECOND DIVISION, Brig.-Gen. James B. Ricketts.
    First Brigade, Brig.-Gen. Abram Duryea: 97th N. Y., Maj. Charles Northrup; 104th N. Y., Maj. Lewis C. Skinner; 105th N. Y., Col. Howard Carroll ; 107th Pa., Capt. James MacThomson. Brigade loss: South Mountain, k, 5 ; w, 16 =21. Antietam, k, 59; w, 233; m, 35 =327. *Second Brigade*, Col. William A. Christian, Col. Peter Lyle (w) : 26th N. Y., Lieut.-Col. Richard H. Richardson; 94th N. Y., Lieut.-Col. Calvin Littlefield ; 88th Pa., Lieut.-Col. George W. Gile (w); Capt. Henry R. Myers; 90th Pa., Col. Peter Lyle, Lieut.-Col. William A. Leech. Brigade loss: South Mountain, k, 2 ; w, 6 =8. Antietam, k, 28 ; w, 197; m, 29 =254. *Third Brigade*, Brig.-Gen. George L. Hartsuff (w), Col. Richard Coulter : 12th Mass., Maj. Elisha Burbank (m w), Capt. Benjamin F. Cook; 13th Mass., Maj. J. Parker Gould ; 83d N. Y. (9th Militia), Lieut.-Col. William Atterbury; 11th Pa., Col. Richard Coulter, Capt. David M. Cook. Brigade loss : South Mountain, k, 2 ; w, 4 =6. Antietam, k, 82; w, 497; m, 20 =599. *Artillery:* F, 1st Pa., Capt. Ezra W. Matthews ; C, Pa., Capt. James Thompson. Artillery loss: Antietam, k, 3 ; w, 19 ; m, 2 =24.

THIRD DIVISION (Pa. Reserves), Brig.-Gen. George G. Meade, Brig.-Gen. Truman Seymour.
    First Brigade, Brig.-Gen. Truman Seymour, Col. R. Biddle Roberts : 1st Pa., Col. R. Biddle Roberts, Capt. William C. Talley ; 2d Pa., Capt. James N. Byrnes; 5th Pa., Col. Joseph W. Fisher ; 6th Pa., Col. William Sinclair; 13th Pa. (1st Rifles), Col. Hugh W. McNeil (k), Capt. Dennis McGee. Brigade loss: South Mountain, k, 38 ; w, 133 =171. Antietam, k, 24; w, 131 =155. *Second Brigade*, Col. Albert L Magilton : 3d Pa., Lieut.-Col. John Clark; 4th Pa., Maj. John Nyce; 7th Pa., Col. Henry C. Bolinger (w), Maj. Chauncey A. Lyman ; 8th Pa., Maj. Silas M. Baily. Brigade loss: South Mountain, k, 25 ; w, 63; m, 1 =89. Antietam, k, 41; w, 181= 222. *Third Brigade*, Col. Thomas F. Gallagher (w), Lieut.-Col. Robert Anderson : 9th Pa., Lieut.-Col. Robert Anderson, Capt. Samuel B. Dick ; 10th Pa., Lieut.-Col. Adoniram J. Warner (w), Capt. Jonathan P. Smith; 11th Pa., Lieut.-Col. Samuel M. Jackson; 12th Pa., Capt. Richard Gustin. Brigade loss : South Mountain, k, 32 ; w, 100 =132. Antietam, k, 37 ; w, 136; m, 2 =175. *Artillery:* A, 1st Pa., Lieut. John G. Simpson; B, 1st Pa., Capt. James H. Cooper; C, 5th U. S., Capt. Dunbar R. Ransom. Artillery loss : Antietam, k, 3 ; w, 18 =21.

SECOND ARMY CORPS, Maj.-Gen. Edwin V. Sumner. Staff loss: Antietam, w, 2.
  Escort: D and K, 6th N. Y. Cav., Capts. Henry W. Lyon and Riley Johnson. Loss : Antietam, w, 1.
  FIRST DIVISION, Maj.-Gen. Israel B. Richardson (m w), Brig.-Gen. John C. Caldwell, Brig.-Gen. Winfield S. Hancock. Staff loss : Antietam, w, 2.
    First Brigade, Brig.-Gen. John C. Caldwell: 5th N. H., Col. Edward E. Cross ; 7th N.Y., Capt. Chas. Brestel; 61st and 64th N. Y., Col. Francis C. Barlow (w), Lieut.-Col. Nelson A. Miles; 81st Pa., Maj. H. Boyd McKeen. Brigade loss: Antietam, k, 44 ; w, 268; m, 2 =314. *Second Brigade*, Brig.-Gen. Thomas F. Meagher, Col. John Burke: 29th Mass., Lieut.-Col. Joseph H. Barnes ; 63d N. Y., Col. John Burke, Lieut.-Col. Henry Fowler (w), Maj. Richard C. Bentley (w), Capt. Joseph O'Neill ; 69th N.Y., Lieut.-Col. James Kelly (w), Maj. James Cavanagh ; 88th N. Y., Lieut.-Col. Patrick Kelly. Brigade loss : Antietam, k,113 ; w, 422; m, 5 =540. *Third Brigade*, Col. John R. Brooke: 2d Del., Capt. David L. Stricker; 52d N. Y., Col. Paul Frank; 57th N. Y., Lieut.-Col. Philip J. Parisen (k), Maj. Alford B. Chapman; 66th N. Y., Capt. Julius Wehle, Lieut.-Col. James H. Bull; 53d Pa., Lieut.-Col. Richards McMichael. Brigade loss: Antietam, k, 52 ; w, 244; m, 9 =305. *Artillery:* B, 1st N. Y., Capt. Rufus D. Pettit; A and C, 4th U. S., Lieut. Evan Thomas. Artillery loss : Antietam, k, 1 ; w, 3 =4.
  SECOND DIVISION, Maj.-Gen. John Sedgwick (w), Brig.-Gen. Oliver O. Howard. Staff loss : Antietam, w, 2.
    First Brigade, Brig.-Gen. Willis A. Gorman: 15th Mass., Lieut.-Col. John W. Kimball ; 1st Minn., Col. Alfred Sully ; 34th N. Y., Col. James A. Suiter; 82d N. Y. (2d Militia), Col. Henry W. Hudson; 1st Co. Mass. Sharp-shooters, Capt. John Saunders (k) ; 2d Co. Minn. Sharp-shooters, Capt. William F. Russell. Brigade loss: Antietam, k, 134; w, 539; m, 67 =740. *Second Brigade*,

Brig.-Gen. Oliver O. Howard, Col. Joshua T. Owen, Col. De Witt C. Baxter: 69th Pa., Col. Joshua T. Owen; 71st Pa., Col. Isaac J. Wistar (w), Lieut. Richard P. Smith, Capt. Enoch E. Lewis; 72d Pa., Col. De Witt C. Baxter; 106th Pa., Col. Turner G. Morehead. Brigade loss: Antietam, k, 93; w, 379; m, 73 = 545. *Third Brigade*, Brig.-Gen. Napoleon J. T. Dana (w), Col. Norman J. Hall: 19th Mass., Col. Edward W. Hinks (w), Lieut.-Col. Arthur F. Devereux (w); 20th Mass., Col. William R. Lee; 7th Mich., Col. Norman J. Hall, Capt. Charles J. Hunt; 42d N. Y., Lieut.-Col. George N. Bomford, Maj. James E. Mallon; 59th N. Y., Col. Wm. L. Tidball. Brigade loss: Antietam, k, 142; w, 652; m, 104 = 898. *Artillery : A*, 1st R. I., Capt. John A. Tompkins; I, 1st U. S., Lieut. George A. Woodruff. Artillery loss: Antietam, k, 4; w, 21 = 25.
THIRD DIVISION, Brig.-Gen. William H. French.
First Brigade, Brig.-Gen. Nathan Kimball: 14th Ind., Col. William Harrow; 8th Ohio, Lieut.-Col. Franklin Sawyer; 132d Pa., Col. Richard A. Oakford (k), Lieut.-Col. Vincent M. Wilcox; 7th W. Va., Col. Joseph Snider. Brigade loss: Antietam, k, 121; w, 510; m, 8 = 639. *Second Brigade*, Col. Dwight Morris: 14th Conn., Lieut.-Col. Sanford H. Perkins; 108th N. Y., Col. Oliver H. Palmer; 130th Pa., Col. Henry I. Zinn. Brigade loss: Antietam, k, 78; w, 356; m, 95 = 529. *Third Brigade*, Brig.-Gen. Max Weber (w), Col. John W. Andrews: 1st Del., Col. John W. Andrews, Lieut.-Col. Oliver Hopkinson (w); 5th Md., Maj. Leopold Blumenberg (w), Capt. E. F. M. Faehtz; 4th N. Y., Lieut.-Col. John D. MacGregor. Brigade loss: Antietam, k, 100; w, 449; m, 33 = 582.
UNATTACHED ARTILLERY: G, 1st N. Y., Capt. John D. Frank; B, 1st R. I., Capt. John G. Hazard; G, 1st R. I., Capt. C. D. Owen. Artillery loss: Antietam, k, 1; w, 9 = 10.
FOURTH ARMY CORPS.
FIRST DIVISION (attached to Sixth Army Corps), Maj.-Gen. Darius N. Couch.
First Brigade, Brig.-Gen. Charles Devens, Jr.: 7th Mass., Col. David A. Russell; 10th Mass., Col. Henry L. Eustis; 36th N. Y., Col. William H. Browne; 2d R. I., Col. Frank Wheaton. *Second Brigade*, Brig.-Gen. Albion P. Howe: 62d N. Y., Col. David J. Nevin; 93d Pa., Col. James M. McCarter; 98th Pa., Col. John F. Ballier; 102d Pa., Col. Thomas A. Rowley; 139th Pa., Col. Frank H. Collier. *Third Brigade*, Brig.-Gen. John Cochrane: 65th N. Y., Col. Alexander Shaler; 67th N. Y., Col. Julius W. Adams; 122d N. Y., Col. Silas Titus; 23d Pa., Col. Thomas H. Neill; 61st Pa., Col. George C. Spear; 82d Pa., Col. David H. Williams. Brigade loss: Antietam (Sept. 18th), w, 9. *Artillery :* 3d N. Y., Capt. William Stuart; C, 1st Pa., Capt. Jeremiah McCarthy; D, 1st Pa., Capt. Michael Hall; G, 2d U. S., Lieut. J. H. Butler.
FIFTH ARMY CORPS, Maj.-Gen. Fitz John Porter.
Escort : Detachment 1st Me. Cav., Capt. George J. Summat.
FIRST DIVISION, Maj.-Gen. George W. Morell.
First Brigade, Col. James Barnes: 2d Me., Col. Charles W. Roberts; 18th Mass., Lieut.-Col. Joseph Hayes; 22d Mass., Lieut.-Col. William S. Tilton; 1st Mich., Capt. Emory W. Belton; 13th N. Y., Col. Elisha G. Marshall; 25th N. Y., Col. Charles A. Johnson; 118th Pa., Col. Charles M. Prevost; 2d Co. Mass. Sharp-shooters, Capt. Lewis E. Wentworth. Brigade loss: Shepherdstown, k, 66; w, 125; m, 130 = 321. *Second Brigade*, Brig.-Gen. Charles Griffin: 2d D. C., Col. Charles M. Alexander; 9th Mass., Col. Patrick R. Guiney; 32d Mass., Col. Francis J. Parker; 4th Mich., Col. Jonathan W. Childs; 14th N. Y., Col. James McQuade; 62d Pa., Col. Jacob B. Sweitzer. Brigade loss: Shepherdstown, k, 1; w, 10 = 11. *Third Brigade*, Col. T. B. W. Stockton: 20th Me., Col. Adelbert Ames; 16th Mich., Lieut.-Col. Norval E. Welch; 12th N. Y., Capt. William Huson; 17th N. Y., Lieut.-Col. Nelson B. Bartram; 44th N. Y., Maj. Freeman Conner; 83d Pa., Capt. Orpheus S. Woodward; Brady's Co. Mich. Sharp-shooters, Lieut. Jonas H. Titus, Jr. Brigade loss: Shepherdstown, w, 7. *Artillery :* 3d Mass., Capt. Augustus P. Martin; C, 1st R. I., Capt. Richard Waterman; D, 5th U. S., Lieut. Charles E. Hazlett. Artillery loss: Shepherdstown, m, 1. *Sharp-shooters :* 1st U. S., Capt. John B. Isler. Loss: Shepherdstown, k, 2; w, 5 = 7.

SECOND DIVISION, Brig.-Gen. George Sykes.
First Brigade, Lieut.-Col. Robert C. Buchanan: 3d U. S., Capt. John D. Wilkins; 4th U. S., Capt. Hiram Dryer; 12th U. S. (1st Battalion), Capt. Matthew M. Blunt; 12th U. S. (2d Battalion), Capt. Thomas M. Anderson; 14th U. S. (1st Battalion), Capt. W. Harvey Brown; 14th U. S. (2d Battalion), Capt. David B. McKibbin. Brigade loss : Antietam, k, 4; w, 35 = 39. *Second Brigade*, Maj. Charles S. Lovell: 1st and 6th U. S., Capt. Levi C. Bootes; 2d and 10th U. S., Capt. John S. Poland; 11th U. S., Capt. De Lancey Floyd-Jones; 17th U. S., Maj. George L. Andrews. Brigade loss: Antietam, k, 8; w, 47; m, 1 = 56; Shepherdstown, k, 1; w, 8 = 9. *Third Brigade*, Col. Gouverneur K. Warren: 5th N. Y., Capt. Cleveland Winslow; 10th N. Y., Lieut.-Col. John W. Marshall. Brigade loss: Shepherdstown, w, 1. *Artillery :* E and G, 1st U. S., Lieut. Alanson M. Randol ; I, 5th U. S., Capt. Stephen H. Weed; K, 5th U. S., Lieut. William E. Van Reed. Artillery loss: Antietam, w, 3. Shepherdstown, k, 1; w, 2 = 3.
THIRD DIVISION (reached the field of Antietam Sept. 18th), Brig.-Gen. Andrew A. Humphreys.
First Brigade, Brig.-Gen. Erastus B. Tyler: 91st Pa., Col. Edgar M. Gregory; 126th Pa., Col. James G. Elder; 129th Pa., Col. Jacob G. Frick; 134th Pa., Col. Matthew S. Quay. *Second Brigade*, Col. Peter H. Allabach: 123d Pa., Col. John B. Clark; 131st Pa., Lieut.-Col. William B. Shaut; 133d Pa., Col. Franklin B. Speakman; 155th Pa., Col. Edward J. Allen. *Artillery :* C, 1st N. Y., Capt. Almont Barnes; L, 1st Ohio, Capt. Lucius N. Robinson.
ARTILLERY RESERVE, Lieut.-Col. William Hays:
A, B, C, and D, 1st Battalion N. Y., Lieuts. Bernhard Wever and Alfred von Kleiser, and Capts. Robert Langner and Charles Kusserow; 5th N. Y., Capt. Elijah D. Taft; K, 1st U. S., Capt. William M. Graham; G, 4th U. S., Lieut. Marcus P. Miller. Artillery loss: Antietam, k, 5; w, 5; m, 1 = 11.
SIXTH ARMY CORPS, Maj.-Gen. William B. Franklin.
Escort : B and G, 6th Pa. Cav., Capt. H. P. Muirheid.
FIRST DIVISION, Maj.-Gen. Henry W. Slocum.
First Brigade, Col. A. T. A. Torbert: 1st N. J., Lieut.-Col. Mark W. Collet; 2d N. J., Col. Samuel L. Buck: 3d N. J., Col. Henry W. Brown; 4th N. J., Col. William B. Hatch. Brigade loss: Crampton's Pass, k, 38; w, 134 = 172. Antietam, k, 2; w, 17 = 19. *Second Brigade*, Col. Joseph J. Bartlett: 5th Me., Col. Nathaniel J. Jackson; 16th N. Y., Lieut.-Col. Joel J. Seaver; 27th N. Y., Lieut.-Col. Alexander D. Adams; 96th Pa., Col. Henry L. Cake. Brigade loss: Crampton's Pass, k, 50; w, 167 = 217. Antietam, k, 1; w, 8 = 9. *Third Brigade*, Brig.-Gen. John Newton: 18th N. Y., Lieut.-Col. George R. Myers; 31st N. Y., Lieut.-Col. Francis E. Pinto; 32d N. Y., Col. Roderick Matheson (m w), Maj. George F. Lemon (m w); 95th Pa., Col. Gustavus W. Town. Brigade loss : Crampton's Pass, k, 24; w, 98; m, 2 = 124. Antietam, k, 1; w, 20 = 21. *Artillery*, Capt. Emory Upton: A, Md., Capt. John W. Wolcott; 1st Mass., Capt. Josiah Porter; 1st N. J., Capt. William Hexamer; D, 2d U. S., Lieut. Edward B. Williston. Artillery loss: Antietam, k, 1; w, 13; m, 2 = 16.
SECOND DIVISION, Maj.-Gen. William F. Smith.
First Brigade, Brig.-Gen. Winfield S. Hancock, Col. Amasa Cobb : 6th Me., Col. Hiram Burnham; 43d N. Y., Maj. John Wilson; 49th Pa., Lieut.-Col. William Brisbane; 137th Pa., Col. Henry M. Bossert; 5th Wis., Col. Amasa Cobb. Brigade loss: Antietam, w, 6. *Second Brigade*, Brig.-Gen. W. T. H. Brooks: 2d Vt., Maj. James H. Walbridge; 3d Vt., Col. Breed N. Hyde; 4th Vt., Lieut.-Col. Charles B. Stoughton; 5th Vt., Col. Lewis A. Grant; 6th Vt., Maj. Oscar L. Tuttle. Brigade loss : Crampton's Pass, k, 1; w, 18 = 19. Antietam, k, 1; w, 24 = 25. *Third Brigade*, Col. William H. Irwin : 7th Me., Maj. Thomas W. Hyde; 20th N. Y., Col. Ernest von Vegesack; 33d N. Y., Lieut.-Col. Joseph W. Corning; 49th N. Y., Lieut.-Col. William C. Alberger (w), Maj. George W. Johnson; 77th N. Y., Capt. Nathan S. Babcock. Brigade loss: Antietam, k, 64; w, 247; m, 31 = 342. *Artillery*, Capt. Romeyn B. Ayres: B, Md., Lieut. Theodore J. Vanneman; 1st N. Y., Capt. Andrew Cowan; F, 5th U. S., Lieut. Leonard Martin.

NINTH ARMY CORPS, Maj.-Gen. Ambrose E. Burnside (commanded the right wing of the army at South Mountain and exercised general command on the left at Antietam), Maj.-Gen. Jesse L. Reno (k), Brig. Gen. Jacob D. Cox. Staff loss: South Mountain, k, 1.

Escort: G, 1st Me. Cav., Capt. Zebulon B. Blethen.

FIRST DIVISION, Brig.-Gen. Orlando B. Willcox.

First Brigade, Col. Benjamin C. Christ; 28th Mass., Capt. Andrew P. Caraher; 17th Mich., Col. William H. Withington; 79th N. Y., Lieut.-Col. David Morrison; 50th Pa., Maj. Edward Overton (w), Capt. William H. Diehl. Brigade loss: South Mountain, k, 26; w, 136 = 162. Antietam, k, 43; w, 198; m, 3 = 244. *Second Brigade,* Col. Thomas Welsh: 8th Mich. (transferred to First Brigade, Sept. 16th), Lieut.-Col. Frank Graves, Maj. Ralph Ely; 46th N. Y., Lieut.-Col. Joseph Gerhardt; 45th Pa., Lieut.-Col. John I. Curtin; 100th Pa., Lieut.-Col. David A. Leckey. Brigade loss: South Mountain, k, 37; w, 151 = 188. Antietam, k, 3; w, 86; m, 4 = 93. *Artillery:* 8th Mass., Capt. Asa M. Cook; E, 2d U. S., Lieut. Samuel N. Benjamin. Artillery loss: South Mountain, k, 1; w, 4 = 5. Antietam, w, 1.

SECOND DIVISION, Brig.-Gen. Samuel D. Sturgis.

First Brigade, Brig.-Gen. James Nagle: 2d Md., Lieut.-Col. J. Eugene Duryea; 6th N. H., Col. Simon G. Griffin; 9th N. H., Col. Enoch Q. Fellows; 48th Pa., Lieut.-Col. Joshua K. Sigfried. Brigade loss: South Mountain, w, 34; m, 7 = 41. Antietam, k, 39; w, 160; m, 5 = 204. *Second Brigade,* Brig.-Gen. Edward Ferrero: 21st Mass., Col. William S. Clark; 35th Mass., Col. Edward A. Wild (w), Lieut.-Col. Sumner Carruth (w); 51st N.Y., Col. Robert B. Potter; 51st Pa., Col. John F. Hartranft. Brigade loss: South Mountain, k, 10; w, 89; m, 23 = 116. Antietam, k, 95; w, 368; m, 6 = 469. *Artillery:* D, Pa., Capt. George W. Durell; E, 4th U. S., Capt. Joseph C. Clark, Jr. Artillery loss: Antietam, k, 2; w, 4 = 6.

THIRD DIVISION, Brig.-Gen. Isaac P. Rodman (m w). Staff loss: Antietam, w, 1.

First Brigade, Col. Harrison S. Fairchild: 9th N. Y., Lieut.-Col. Edgar A. Kimball; 89th N. Y., Maj. Edward Jardine; 103d N. Y., Maj. Benjamin Ringold. Brigade loss: South Mountain, k, 2; w, 18 = 20. Antietam, k, 87; w, 321; m, 47 = 455. *Second Brigade,* Col. Edward Harland: 8th Conn., Lieut.-Col. Hiram Appelman (w), Maj. John E. Ward; 11th Conn., Col. Henry W. Kingsbury (k); 16th Conn., Col. Francis Beach; 4th R. I., Col. William H. P. Steere (w), Lieut.-Col. Joseph B. Curtis. Brigade loss: Antietam, k, 133; w, 462; m, 23 = 618. *Artillery:* A, 5th U. S., Lieut. Charles P. Muhlenberg. Loss: Antietam, w, 3.

KANAWHA DIVISION, Brig.-Gen. Jacob D. Cox, Col. Eliakim P. Scammon.

First Brigade, Col. Eliakim P. Scammon, Col. Hugh Ewing: 12th Ohio, Col. Carr B. White; 23d Ohio, Lieut.-Col. Rutherford B. Hayes (w), Maj. James M. Comly; 30th Ohio, Col. Hugh Ewing, Lieut.-Col. Theodore Jones (c), Maj. George H. Hildt; 1st Ohio Battery, Capt. James R. McMullin; Gilmore's Co., W. Va. Cav., Lieut. James Abraham; Harrison's Co., W. Va. Cav., Lieut. Dennis Delaney. Brigade loss: South Mountain, k, 63; w, 201; m, 8 = 272. Antietam, k, 28; w, 134; m, 20 = 182. *Second Brigade,* Col. Augustus Moor (c), Col. George Crook: 11th Ohio, Lieut.-Col. Augustus H. Coleman (k), Maj. Lyman J. Jackson; 28th Ohio, Lieut.-Col. Gottfried Becker; 36th Ohio, Col. George Crook, Lieut.-Col. Melvin Clarke (k), Maj. E. B. Andrews; Chicago (Ill.) Dragoons, Capt. Frederick Schambeck; Ky. Battery, Capt. Seth J. Simmonds. Brigade loss: South Mountain, k, 17; w, 64; m, 3 = 84. Antietam, k, 8; w, 58; m, 7 = 73.

UNATTACHED TROOPS: 6th N. Y. Cav. (8 co's), Col. Thomas C. Devin; 3d Co. Ohio Cav., Lieut. Jonas Seamen; L and M, 3d U. S. Art'y, Capt. John Edwards, Jr.

TWELFTH ARMY CORPS, Maj.-Gen. Joseph K. F. Mansfield (k), Brig.-Gen. Alpheus S. Williams. Staff loss: Antietam, k, 1.

Escort: L, 1st Mich. Cav., Capt. Melvin Brewer.

FIRST DIVISION, Brig.-Gen. Alpheus S. Williams, Brig.-Gen. Samuel W. Crawford (w), Brig.-Gen. George H. Gordon. Staff loss: Antietam, w, 1.

First Brigade, Brig.-Gen. Samuel W. Crawford, Col. Joseph F. Knipe: 10th Me., Col. George L. Beal (w); 28th N. Y., Capt. William H. H. Mapes; 46th Pa., Col. Joseph F. Knipe, Lieut.-Col. James L. Selfridge; 124th Pa., Col. Joseph W. Hawley (w), Maj. Isaac L. Haldeman; 125th Pa., Col. Jacob Higgins; 128th Pa., Col. Samuel Croasdale (k), Lieut.-Col. William W. Hammersly (w), Maj. Joel B. Wanner. Brigade loss: Antietam, k, 88; w, 315; m, 27 = 430. *Third Brigade,* Brig.-Gen. George H. Gordon, Col. Thomas H. Ruger (w): 27th Ind., Col. Silas Colgrove; 2d Mass., Col. George L. Andrews; 13th N. J., Col. Ezra A. Carman; 107th N. Y., Col. R. B. Van Valkenburgh; Pa. Zouaves d'Afrique; 3d Wis., Col. Thomas H. Ruger. Brigade loss: Antietam, k, 71; w, 348; m, 27 = 646.

SECOND DIVISION, Brig.-Gen. George S. Greene.

First Brigade, Lieut.-Col. Hector Tyndale (w), Maj. Orrin J. Crane: 5th Ohio, Maj. John Collins; 7th Ohio, Maj. Orrin J. Crane, Capt. Frederick A. Seymour; 66th Ohio, Lieut.-Col. Eugene Powell (w); 28th Pa., Maj. Ario Pardee, Jr. Brigade loss: Antietam, k, 61; w, 308; m, 7 = 376. *Second Brigade,* Col. Henry J. Stainrook: 3d Md., Lieut.-Col. Joseph M. Sudsburg; 102d N. Y., Lieut.-Col. James C. Lane; 111th Pa., Maj. Thomas M. Walker. Brigade loss: Antietam, k, 32; w, 128; m, 16 = 176. *Third Brigade,* Col. William B. Goodrich (k), Lieut.-Col. Jonathan Austin: 3d Del., Maj. Arthur Maginnis (w), Capt. William J. McKaig; Purnell (Md.) Legion, Lieut.-Col. Benjamin L. Simpson; 60th N. Y., Lieut.-Col. Charles R. Brundage; 78th N. Y., Lieut.-Col. Jonathan Austin, Capt. Henry R. Stagg. Brigade loss: Antietam, k, 21; w, 71; m, 7 = 99. *Artillery,* Capt. Clermont L. Best: 4th Me., Capt. O'Neil W. Robinson; 6th Me., Capt. Freeman McGilvery; M, 1st N. Y., Capt. George W. Cothran; 10th N. Y., Capt. John T. Bruen; E, Pa., Capt. Joseph M. Knap; F, Pa., Capt. R. B. Hampton; F, 4th U. S., Lieut. E. D. Muhlenberg. Artillery loss: Antietam, k, 1; w, 15; m, 1 = 17.

CAVALRY DIVISION, Brig.-Gen. Alfred Pleasonton.

First Brigade, Maj. Charles J. Whiting: 5th U. S., Capt. Joseph H. McArthur; 6th U. S., Capt. William P. Sanders. Brigade loss: Antietam, w, 1. *Second Brigade,* Col. John F. Farnsworth: 8th Ill., Maj. William H. Medill; 3d Ind., Maj. George H. Chapman; 1st Mass., Capt. Casper Crowninshield; 8th Pa., Capt. Peter Keenan. Brigade loss: Antietam, w, 6. *Third Brigade,* Col. Richard H. Rush: 4th Pa., Col. James H. Childs (k), Lieut.-Col. James K. Kerr; 6th Pa., Lieut.-Col. C. Ross Smith. Brigade loss: Antietam, k, 3; w, 10 = 13. *Fourth Brigade,* Col. Andrew T. McReynolds: 1st N. Y., Maj. Alonzo W. Adams; 12th Pa., Maj. James A. Congdon. *Fifth Brigade,* Col. Benjamin F. Davis: 8th N. Y., Col. Benjamin F. Davis; 3d Pa., Lieut.-Col. Samuel W. Owen. *Unattached,* 15th Pa. (detachment), Col. William J. Palmer. Loss: Antietam, k, 1.

The total loss of the Union Army in the three principal engagements of the campaign was as follows:

	Killed.	Wounded.	Captured or missing.	Total.
South Mountain....	325	1403	85	1813
Crampton's Pass....	113	418	2	533
Antietam............	2108	9549	753	12,410

The casualties during the entire campaign, from September 3d to 20th (exclusive of Miles's force at Harper's Ferry, for which see page 618), aggregated 2629 killed, 11,583 wounded, and 991 captured or missing = 15,203.

THE CONFEDERATE ARMY.

General Robert E. Lee.

LONGSTREET'S COMMAND, Maj.-Gen. James Longstreet. Staff loss (in the campaign): w, 2.

MCLAWS'S DIVISION, Maj.-Gen. Lafayette McLaws. Staff loss (in the campaign): k, 1.

Kershaw's Brigade, Brig.-Gen. Joseph B. Kershaw: 2d S. C., Col. John D. Kennedy (w), Maj. Franklin Gaillard; 3d S. C., Col. James D. Nance; 7th S. C., Col. D. Wyatt Aiken (w), Capt. John S. Hard; 8th S. C., Col.

John W. Henagan, Lieut.-Col. A. J. Hoole. Brigade loss (in the campaign): k, 90; w, 455; m, 6=551. *Cobb's Brigade*, Brig.-Gen. Howell Cobb, Lieut.-Col. C. C. Sanders, Lieut.-Col. William MacRae: 16th Ga., ——; ☆ 24th Ga., Lieut.-Col. C. C. Sanders, Maj. R. E. McMillan; Cobb's (Ga.) Legion, ——; 15th N. C., Lieut.-Col. William Mac- Rae. Brigade loss (in the campaign): k, 76; w, 318, m, 452=846. *Semmes's Brigade*, Brig. Gen. Paul J. Semmes: 10th Ga., Maj. Willis C. Holt (w), Capt. P. H. Loud; 53d Ga., Lieut.-Col. Thomas Sloan (w), Capt. S. W. Marsh- borne; 15th Va., Capt. E. M. Morrison (w), Capt. Edward J. Willis; 32d Va., Col. E. B. Montague. Brigade loss (in the campaign): k, 56; w, 274; m, 43=373. *Barksdale's Brigade*, Brig.-Gen. William Barksdale: 13th Miss., Lieut.-Col. Kennon McElroy (w); 17th Miss., Lieut.-Col. John C. Fiser; 18th Miss., Maj. J. C. Campbell (w), Lieut.- Col. William H. Leese; 21st Miss., Capt. John Sims, Col. Benjamin G. Humphreys. Brigade loss (in the cam- paign): k, 35; w, 272; m, 4=311. *Artillery*, Maj. S. P. Hamilton, Col. Henry C. Cabell: N. C. Battery, Capt. Basil C. Manly; Ga. Battery (Pulaski Art'y), Capt. John P. W. Read; Va. Battery (Richmond Fayette Art'y), Capt. M. C. Macon; Va. Battery (1st Co. Richmond How- itzers), Capt. E. S. McCarthy; Ga. Battery (Troup Art'y), Capt. H. H. Carlton. (Loss of the artillery included with that of the brigades to which attached.)
ANDERSON'S DIVISION, Maj.-Gen. Richard H. Anderson (w), Brig.-Gen. Roger A. Pryor. Staff loss (in the campaign): w, 1.
Wilcox's Brigade, Col. Alfred Cumming: 8th Ala. ——; 9th Ala., ——; 10th Ala., ——; 11th Ala., ——; Bri- gade loss (in the campaign): k, 34; w, 181; m, 29 = 244. *Mahone's Brigade*, Col. W. A. Parham: 6th Va., ——; 12th Va., ——; 16th Va., ——; 41st Va., ——; 61st Va., ——. Brigade loss (in the campaign): k, 8; w, 92; m, 127=227. *Featherston's Brigade*, Col. Carnot Posey: 12th Miss., ——; 16th Miss., Capt. A. M. Feltus; 19th Miss., ——; 2d Miss. Battalion, ——. Brigade loss (in the campaign): k, 45; w, 233; m, 36=319. *Armistead's Bri- gade*, Brig.-Gen. Lewis A. Armistead, Col. J. G. Hodges: 9th Va., ——; 14th Va., Col. J. G. Hodges; 38th Va., ——; 53d Va., ——; 57th Va., ——. Brigade loss (in the campaign): k, 5; w, 29; m, 1=35. *Pryor's Bri- gade*, Brig.-Gen. Roger A. Pryor: 14th Ala., ——; 2d Fla., ——; 8th Fla., ——; 3d Va., ——. Brigade loss (in the campaign): k, 48; w, 285; m, 49=382. *Wright's Brigade*, Brig.-Gen. Ambrose R. Wright: 44th Ala., ——; 3d Ga., ——; 22d Ga., ——; 48th Ga., ——. Brigade loss (in the campaign): k, 32; w, 192; m, 34=258. *Artil- lery*, Maj. J. S. Saunders: La. Battery (Donaldsville Art'y), Capt. Victor Maurin; Va. Battery (Huger's); Va. Battery, Lieut. C. R. Phelps; Va. Battery (Thompson's or Grimes's). (Loss of artillery not separately reported.)
JONES'S DIVISION, Brig.-Gen. David R. Jones.
Toombs's Brigade, Brig.-Gen. R. Toombs (in temporary command of a division), Col. Henry L. Benning: 2d Ga., Lieut.-Col. William R. Holmes (k), Maj. Skidmore Harris (w); 15th Ga., Col. William T. Millican (k); 17th Ga., Capt. J. A. McGregor; 20th Ga., Col. John B. Cumming. Brigade loss (in the campaign): k, 16; w, 122; m, 22=160. *Drayton's Brigade*, Brig.-Gen. Thomas F. Drayton: 50th Ga., Lieut.-Col. F. Kearse; 51st Ga., ——; 15th S. C., Col. W. D. De Saussure. Brigade loss (in the campaign): k, 82; w, 280; m, 179=541. *Pickett's Brigade*, Brig.-Gen. Richard B. Garnett: 8th Va., Col. Eppa Hunton; 18th Va., Maj. George C. Cabell; 19th Va., Col. J. B. Strange (m w), Capt. John L. Cochran, Lieut. William N. Wood; 28th Va., Capt. W. L. Wingfield; 56th Va., Col. William D. Stuart, Capt. John B. McPhail. Brigade loss (in the campaign): k, 30; w, 199; m, 32=261. *Kemper's Brigade*, Brig.-Gen. James L. Kemper: 1st Va., ——; 7th Va., ——; 11th Va., Maj. Adam Clement; 17th Va., Col. Montgomery D. Corse (w), Maj. Arthur Herbert; 24th Va., ——. Brigade loss (in the campaign): k, 15; w, 102; m, 27 =144. *Jenkins's Brigade*, Col. Joseph Walker: 1st S. C., Lieut.-Col. D. Livingston (w); 2d S. C. (rifles) ——; 5th S. C., Capt. T. C. Beckham; 6th S. C., Lieut.-Col. J. M. Steedman, Capt. E. B. Cantey (w); 4th S. C. Battal-

ion, ——; Palmetto (S. C.) Sharp-shooters, ——. Bri- gade loss (in the campaign): k, 27; w, 196; m, 12=235. *Anderson's Brigade*, Col. George T. Anderson: 1st Ga. (Regulars), Col. William J. Magill; 7th Ga., ——; 8th Ga. ——; 9th Ga., ——; 11th Ga., Maj. F. H. Little; Va. Battery (Wise Art'y), Capt. J. S. Brown (w). Bri- gade loss (in the campaign): k, 8; w, 80; m, 6=94.
WALKER'S DIVISION, Brig.-Gen. John G. Walker.
Walker's Brigade, Col. Van H. Manning (w), Col. E. D. Hall: 3d Ark., Capt John W. Reedy; 27th N. C., Col. John R. Cooke; 46th N. C., Col. E. D. Hall, Lieut.-Col. William A. Jenkins; 48th N. C., Col. R. C. Hill; 30th Va., ——; Va. Battery, Capt. Thomas B. French. Brigade loss (in the campaign); k, 140; w, 684; m, 93=917. *Ran- som's Brigade*, Brig.-Gen. Robert Ransom, Jr.: 24th N. C., Lieut.-Col. John L. Harris; 25th N. C., Col. H. M. Rutledge; 35th N. C., Col. M. W. Ransom; 49th N. C., Lieut.-Col. Lee M. McAfee; Va. Battery, Capt. James R. Branch. Brigade loss (in the campaign): k, 41; w, 141; m, 4=186.
HOOD'S DIVISION, Brig.-Gen. John B. Hood.
Hood's Brigade, Col. W. T. Wofford: 18th Ga., Lieut.- Col. S. Z. Ruff; Hampton (S. C.) Legion, Lieut.-Col. M. W. Gary; 1st Tex., Lieut.-Col. P. A. Work; 4th Tex., Lieut.-Col. B. F. Carter; 5th Tex., Capt. Ike N. M. Tur- ner. Brigade loss (in the campaign): k, 69; w, 417; m, 62=548. *Law's Brigade*, Col. E. McIver Law: 4th Ala., Lieut.-Col. O. K. McLemore (m w), Capt. L. H. Scruggs (w); 2d Miss., Col. J. M. Stone (w), 11th Miss., Col. P. F. Liddell (m w), Lieut.-Col. S. F. Butler (w); 6th N. C., Maj. Robert F. Webb (w). Brigade loss (in the campaign): k, 53; w, 390; m, 25=468. *Artillery*, Maj. B. W. Frobel: S. C. Battery (German Art'y), Capt. W. K. Bachman; S. C. Battery (Palmetto Art'y), Capt. H. R. Garden; N. C. Battery (Rowan Art'y), Capt. James Reilly. Artillery loss (in the campaign): k, 4; w, 19=23.
EVANS'S BRIGADE, Brig.-Gen. Nathan G. Evans (in tem- porary command of a division), Col. P. F. Stevens: 17th S. C., Col. F. W. McMaster; 18th S. C., Col. W. H. Wall- ace; 22d S. C., Lieut.-Col. Thomas C. Watkins (k), Maj. M. Hilton; 23d S. C., Capt. S. A. Durham (w), Lieut. E. R. White; Holcombe's (S. C.) Legion, ——; S. C. Battery (Macbeth Art'y), Capt. R. Boyce. Brigade loss (in the campaign): k, 40; w, 185; m, 65=290.
ARTILLERY. *Washington (La.) Artillery*, Col. J. B. Walton: 1st Co., Capt. C. W. Squires; 2d Co., Capt. J. B. Richardson; 3d Co., Capt. M. B. Miller; 4th Co., Capt B. F. Eshleman. Loss (in campaign): k, 4; w, 28; m, 2, = 34. *Lee's Battalion*, Col. S. D. Lee: Va. Battery (Ashland Art'y), Capt. Pichegru Woolfolk, Jr.; Va. Battery (Bed- ford Art'y), Capt. T. C. Jordan; S. C. Battery (Brooks's Art'y), Lieut. William Elliott; Va. Battery, Capt. J. L. Eubank; La. Battery (Madison Light Art'y), Capt. Geo. V. Moody; Va. Battery, Capt. W. W. Parker. Loss (in the campaign): k, 11; w, 75=86.
JACKSON'S COMMAND, Maj.-Gen. T. J. Jackson.
EWELL'S DIVISION, Brig.-Gen. A. R. Lawton (w), Brig.- Gen. Jubal A. Early. Staff loss: Antietam w, 2.
Lawton's Brigade, Col. M. Douglass (k), Maj. J. H. Lowe, Col. John H. Lamar: 13th Ga., ——; 26th Ga., ——; 31st Ga., Lieut.-Col. J. T. Crowder; 38th Ga., ——; 60th Ga., ——; 61st Ga., Col. John H. Lamar. Brigade loss: Antietam, k, 106; w, 440; m, 21=567. Shepherds- town, w, 7. *Early's Brigade*, Brig.-Gen. Jubal A. Early, Col. William Smith (w): 13th Va., Capt. F. V. Winston; 25th Va., ——; 31st Va., ——; 44th Va., ——; 49th Va., Col. William Smith; 52d Va., Col. M. G. Harman; 58th Va., ——. Brigade loss: Antietam, k, 18; w, 167; m, 9 =194. *Trimble's Brigade*, Col James A. Walker (w): 15th Ala., Capt. I. B. Feagin; 12th Ga., Capt. James G. Rodgers (k); 21st Ga., Maj. Thomas C. Glover (w); 21st N. C. (1st N. C. Battalion attached), Capt. F. P. Miller (k); Va. Battery, Capt. John R. Johnson. Brigade loss: Antietam, k, 27; w, 202; m, 8=237. Shepherdstown, w, 1. *Hays's Brigade*, Col. H. B. Strong, Brig.-Gen. Harry T. Hays; 5th La., ——; 6th La., Col. H. B. Strong (k); 7th La., ——; 8th La., ——; 14th La., ——; La. Battery, Capt. Louis E. D'Aquin. Brigade loss: Antietam, k, 45;

☆ The dash indicates that the name of the commanding officer has not been found in the "Official Records."

w, 289; m, 2 = 336. *Artillery*, Maj. A. R. Courtney: 1st Md. Battery, Capt. William F. Dement; Md. Battery (Chesapeake Art'y), Capt. William D. Brown; Va. Battery (Courtney Art'y), Capt. J. W. Latimer; Va. Battery (Staunton Art'y), Lieut. A. W. Garber. Artillery not engaged at Antietam.

LIGHT DIVISION, Maj.-Gen. Ambrose P. Hill.
Branch's Brigade, Brig.-Gen. L. O'B. Branch (k), Col. James H. Lane: 7th N. C., ——; 18th N. C., Lieut.-Col. T. J. Purdie; 28th N. C., Col. James H. Lane; 33d N. C., ——; 37th N. C., ——. Brigade loss: Harper's Ferry, w, 4. Antietam, k, 21; w, 79; m, 4 = 104. Shepherdstown, k, 3; w, 71 = 74. *Gregg's Brigade*, Brig.-Gen. Maxcy Gregg (w): 1st S. C. (Prov. Army), Col. D. H. Hamilton; 1st S. C. (Rifles), Lieut.-Col. James M. Perrin (w); 12th S. C., Col. Dixon Barnes (k), Maj. W. H. McCorkle; 13th S. C., Col. O. E. Edwards; 14th S. C., Lieut.-Col. W. D. Simpson. Brigade loss: Antietam, k, 28; w, 135; m, 2 = 165. Shepherdstown, k, 10; w, 53 = 63. *Field's Brigade*, Col. J. M. Brockenbrough: 40th Va., ——; 47th Va., ——; 55th Va., ——; 22d Va.Battalion, ——. Brigade loss not separately reported. *Archer's Brigade*, Brig.-Gen. James J. Archer, Col. Peter Turney: 5th Ala. Battalion, Capt. Charles M. Hooper; 19th Ga., Maj. James H. Neal, Capt. F. M. Johnston; 1st Tenn. (Prov. Army), Col. Peter Turney; 7th Tenn., Maj. S. G. Shepard, Lieut. G. A. Howard; 14th Tenn., Lieut.-Col. J. W. Lockert, Col. William McComb (w). Brigade loss: Harper's Ferry, k, 1; w, 22 = 23. Antietam, k, 15; w, 90 = 105. Shepherdstown, k, 6; w, 49 = 55. *Pender's Brigade*, Brig.-Gen. William D. Pender: 16th N. C., Lieut.-Col. W. A. Stowe; 28d N. C., Maj. C.C.Cole; 34th N.C., ——; 38th N.C., ——. Brigade loss: Harper's Ferry, k, 2; w, 20 = 22. Antietam, k, 2; w, 28 = 30. Shepherdstown, k, 8; w, 55 = 63. *Thomas's Brigade*, Col. Edward L. Thomas: 14th Ga., Col. R. W. Folsom; 35th Ga., ——; 45th Ga., Maj. W. L. Grice; 49th Ga., Lieut.-Col. S. M. Manning. Brigade not at Antietam; losses elsewhere not separately reported. *Artillery*, Lieut.-Col. R. L. Walker: Va. Battery, Capt. William G. Crenshaw; Va. Battery (Fredericksburg Art'y), Capt. Carter M. Braxton, Lieut. E. A. Marye; Va. Battery (Letcher Art'y), Capt. Greenlee Davidson; Va. Battery (Purcell Art'y), Capt. W. J. Pegram (w); S. C. Battery (Pee Dee Art'y), Capt. D. G. McIntosh. Artillery loss not separately reported. Division loss (in the campaign) : k, 99; w, 605; m, 6 = 710. JACKSON'S DIVISION, Brig.-Gen. John R. Jones (w), Brig.-Gen. William B. Starke (k), Col. A. J. Grigsby. Staff loss: Antietam, k, 1; m, 1 = 2.
Winder's Brigade, Col. A. J. Grigsby, Lieut.-Col. R. D. Gardner, Maj. H. J. Williams: 2d Va. (detached at Martinsburg), Capt. R. T. Colston; 4th Va., Lieut.-Col. R. D. Gardner; 5th Va., Maj. H. J. Williams; 27th Va., Capt. Frank C. Wilson; 33d Va., Capt. Jacob B. Golladay, Lieut. David H. Walton. Brigade loss: Antietam, k, 11; w, 77 = 88. *Taliaferro's Brigade*, Col. E. T. H. Warren, Col. James W. Jackson, Col. James L. Sheffield: 47th Ala., Col. James W. Jackson; 48th Ala., Col. James L.Sheffield; 10th Va., ——; 23d Va., ——; 37th Va., ——. Brigade loss: Antietam, k, 41; w, 132 = 173. *Jones's Brigade*, Col. Bradley T. Johnson, Capt. John E. Penn (w), Capt. A. C. Page (w), Capt. R. W. Withers: 21st Va., Capt. A. C. Page; 42d Va., Capt. R. W. Withers; 48th Va., Capt. John H. Candler; 1st Va. Battalion, Lieut. C. A. Davidson. Brigade loss not separately reported. *Starke's Brigade*, Brig.-Gen. William E. Starke, Col. Leroy A. Stafford (w), Col. Edmund Pendleton: 1st La., Lieut.-Col. M. Nolan (w); 2d La.,Col. J. M. Williams (w); 9th La., Col. Leroy A. Stafford; 10th La., Capt. H. D. Monier; 15th La., Col. Edmund Pendleton; 1st La. Battalion (Zouaves), Lieut.-Col. G. Coppens. Brigade loss (partial): Antietam, k, 81; w, 189; m, 17 = 287. *Artillery*, Maj. L. M. Shumaker: Md. Battery (Baltimore Battery), Capt. J. B. Brockenbrough; Va. Battery (Alleghany Art'y), Capt. Joseph Carpenter; Va. Battery (Danville Art'y), Capt. George W. Wooding; Va. Battery (Hampden Art'y), Capt. William H. Caskie; Va. Battery, (Lee Battery), Capt. Charles I. Raine; Va. Battery (Rockbridge Art'y), Capt. W. T. Poague. Artillery loss not separately reported.

HILL'S DIVISION, Maj.-Gen. Daniel H. Hill.
Ripley's Brigade, Brig.-Gen. Roswell S. Ripley (w), Col. George Doles: 4th Ga., Col. George Doles; 44th Ga., Capt. John C. Key; 1st N. C., Lieut.-Col. Hamilton A. Brown; 3d N. C., Col. William L. De Rosset (w). Brigade loss: South Mountain and Antietam, k, 110; w, 506; m, 124 = 740. *Rodes's Brigade*, Brig.-Gen. R. E. Rodes (w): 3d Ala., Col. C. A. Battle; 5th Ala., Maj. E. L. Hobson; 6th Ala., Col. J. B. Gordon (w), Lieut.-Col. J. N. Lightfoot (w); 12th Ala., Col. B. B. Gayle (k); 26th Ala., Col. E. A. O'Neal (w). Brigade loss: South Mountain, k, 61; w, 157; m, 204 = 422. Antietam, k, 50; w, 132; m, 21 = 203. *Garland's Brigade*, Brig.-Gen. Samuel Garland, Jr., (k), Col. D. K. McRae: 5th N. C., Col. D. K. McRae, Capt. Thomas M. Garrett; 12th N. C., Capt. S. Snow; 13th N. C., Lieut.-Col. Thomas Ruffin, Jr. (w), Capt. J. H. Hyman; 20th N. C., Col. Alfred Iverson; 23d N. C., Col. Daniel H. Christie. Brigade loss: South Mountain and Antietam, k, 46; w, 210; m, 187 = 443. *Anderson's Brigade*, Brig.-Gen. George B. Anderson (m w), Col. R. T. Bennett (w): 2d N. C., Col. C. C. Tew (k), Capt. G. M. Roberts; 4th N. C., Col. Bryan Grimes, Capt. W. T. Marsh (k), Capt. D. P. Latham (k); 14th N. C., Col. R. T. Bennett, Lieut.-Col. William A. Johnston (w); 30th N. C., Col. F. M. Parker (w), Maj. William W. Sillers. Brigade loss: South Mountain and Antietam, k, 64; w, 229; m, 202 = 505. *Colquitt's Brigade*, Col. A. H. Colquitt: 13th Ala., Col. B. D. Fry (w), Lieut.-Col. W. H. Betts (w); 6th Ga., Lieut.-Col. J. M. Newton (k); 23d Ga., Col.W.P. Barclay (k); 27th Ga., Col. Levi B. Smith (k); 28th Ga., Maj. Tully Graybill, Capt. N. J. Garrison (w). Brigade loss: South Mountain and Antietam, k, 129; w, 518; m, 184 = 831. *Artillery*, Maj. S. F. Pierson: Ala. Battery, Capt. R. A. Hardaway; Ala. Battery (Jeff Davis Art'y), Capt. J. W. Bondurant; Va. Battery, Capt. William B. Jones; Va. Battery (King William Art'y), Capt. Thomas H. Carter. Brigade loss: South Mountain and Antietam, k, 4; w, 30; m, 3 = 37.

RESERVE ARTILLERY, Brig.-Gen. William N. Pendleton.
Brown's Battalion (1st Va. Art'y), Col. J. Thompson Brown: Powhatan Art'y., Capt. Willis J. Dance; 2d Co. Richmond Howitzers, Capt. D. Watson; 3d Co. Richmond Howitzers, Capt. Benjamin H. Smith, Jr.; Salem Art'y, Capt. A. Hupp; Williamsburg Art'y, Capt. John A. Coke. *Cutts's Battalion*, Lieut.-Col. A. S. Cutts: Ga. Battery, Capt. James Ap Blackshear; Ga. Battery (Irwin Art'y), Capt. John Lane; N. C. Battery, Capt. W. P. Lloyd; Ga. Battery, Capt. G. M. Patterson; Ga. Battery, Capt. H. M. Ross. *Jones's Battalion*, Maj. H. P. Jones: Va. Battery (Morris Art'y), Capt. R. C. M. Page; Va. Battery (Orange Art'y), Capt. Jefferson Peyton; Va. Battery (Turner's); Va. Battery, Capt. A. Wimbish. *Nelson's Battalion*, Maj. William Nelson: Va. Battery (Amherst Art'y), Capt. T. J. Kirkpatrick; Va. Battery (Fluvanna Art'y), Capt. John J. Ancell; Va. Battery, Capt. Charles T. Huckstep; Va. Battery, Capt. Marmaduke Johnson; Ga. Battery (Milledge Art'y), Capt. John Milledge. *Miscellaneous:* Va. Battery, Capt. W. E. Cutshaw; Va. Battery (Dixie Art'y), Capt. W. H. Chapman; Va. Battery (Magruder Art'y), Capt. T. J. Page, Jr.; Va. Battery, Capt. W. H. Rice.

CAVALRY, Maj.-Gen. James E. B. Stuart.
Hampton's Brigade, Brig.-Gen. Wade Hampton: 1st N. C., Col. L. S. Baker; 2d S. C., Col. M. C. Butler: 10th Va., ——; Cobb's (Ga.) Legion, Lieut.-Col. P. M. B. Young (w), Maj. William G. Delony; Jeff. Davis (Miss.) Legion, Lieut.-Col. W. T. Martin. *Lee's Brigade*, Brig.-Gen. Fitzhugh Lee: 1st Va., Lieut.-Col. L. T. Brien; 3d Va., Lieut.-Col. John T. Thornton (m w); 4th Va., Col. W. C. Wickham; 5th Va., Col. Thomas L. Rosser; 9th Va., ——. *Robertson's Brigade*, Col. Thomas T. Munford: 2d Va., Lieut.-Col. Richard H. Burks; 7th Va., Capt. S. B. Myers; 12th Va., Col. A. W. Harman. *Horse Artillery:* Va. Battery, Capt. R. P. Chew; S. C. Battery, Capt. J. F. Hart; Va. Battery, Capt. John Pelham. Cavalry and Horse Artillery loss (in the campaign): k, 10; w, 45; m, 6 = 61.

According to the report of Lee's medical director (Dr. Guild), there was a loss of 1567 killed and 8724 wounded

101

in the battles of South Mountain, Crampton's Pass, Harper's Ferry, Sharpsburg (or Antietam), and Shepherdstown. Dr. Guild does not give the number of missing and prisoners, and he also omits the casualties in Jones's brigade of Jackson's division, Rodes's brigade of D. H. Hill's division, and the whole of A. P. Hill's division. The corps and division commanders report 1890 killed, 9770 wounded, and 2304 captured or missing during the campaign, making a total of 13,964. Estimating four-fifths of these for the battle of Antietam, we have the following comparative result in that engagement:

	Killed.	*Wounded.*	*Captured or Missing.*	*Total.*
Union Army	2108	9549	753	12,410
Confederate Army	1512	7816	1844	11,172

There is not the slightest reason for doubting that many of the "missing" of Lee's army were killed, and that if the number could be ascertained, it would materially increase that class of casualties. General McClellan (Vol. XIX., Pt. I., p. 67, "Official Records"), says that "about 2700 of the enemy's dead were . . . counted and buried upon the battle-field of Antietam"; also, that "a portion of their dead had been previously buried by the enemy."

RELATIVE STRENGTH OF THE ARMIES.

According to McClellan's report the number of combatants in his command was 87,164; but the brunt of the battle was borne by not above 60,000 men.

Comparing the *available* strength of the two armies, undoubtedly McClellan's doubled that of Lee's. In his official report General Lee says, "This great battle was fought by less than 40,000 men on our side."

The Finding of Lee's Lost Order

By Silas Colgrove, Brevet Brigadier-General, U. S. V.

In reply to your request for the particulars of the finding of General Lee's lost dispatch, "Special Orders No. 191," and the manner in which it reached General McClellan, I beg leave to submit the following account:

The Twelfth Army Corps arrived at Frederick, Maryland, about noon on the 13th of September, 1862. The 27th Indiana Volunteers, of which I was colonel at that date, belonged to the Third Brigade, First Division, of that corps.

We stacked arms on the same ground that had been occupied by General D. H. Hill's division the evening before.

Within a very few minutes after halting, the order was brought to me by First Sergeant John M. Bloss and Private B. W. Mitchell, of Company F, 27th Indiana Volunteers, who stated that it was found by Private Mitchell near where they had stacked arms. When I received the order, it was wrapped around three cigars, and Private Mitchell stated that it was in that condition when found by him.

General A. S. Williams was in command of our division. I immediately took the order to his headquarters, and delivered it to Colonel S. E. Pittman, General Williams's adjutant-general. The order was signed by Colonel Chilton, General Lee's adjutant-general, and the signature was at once recognised by Colonel Pittman, who had served with Colonel Chilton at Detroit, Michigan, before the war, and was acquainted with his handwriting. It was at once taken to General McClellan's headquarters by Colonel Pittman. It was a general order giving directions for the movement of General Lee's entire army, designating the route and objective point of each corps. Within an hour after finding the dispatch, General McClellan's whole army was on the move, and the enemy were overtaken next day, the 14th, at South

Mountain, and the battle of that name was fought.

During the night of the 14th General Lee's army fell back toward the Potomac River, General McClellan following the next day. On the 16th they were overtaken again, and the Battle of Antietam was fought mainly on the 17th. General D. H. Hill says in his article in the May *Century*, that the Battle of South Mountain was fought in order to give General Lee time to move his trains, which were then parked in the neighbourhood of Boonsboro'. It is evident from General Lee's movements from the time he left Frederick City, that he intended to recross the Potomac without hazarding a battle in Maryland, and had it not been for the finding of this lost order, the Battle of South Mountain, and probably that of Antietam, would not have been fought.

For confirmation of the above statements in regard to the finding of the dispatch, you are respectfully referred to Colonel Samuel E. Pittman, of Detroit, Michigan, and Captain John M. Bloss, of Muncie, Indiana.

Washington, D. C, June 2nd, 1886.

★★★★★★

Note.—Mr. W. A. Mitchell, the son of Private Mitchell, who, as General Silas Colgrove describes above, was the finder of Lee's order, writes to say that his father was severely wounded at Antietam. After eight mouths in hospital he completed his term of enlistment, three years, and three years after his discharge died at his home in Bartholomew, Indiana. As his family were then destitute, some efforts are said to have been made to procure a pension for the widow, but General Colgrove (in a letter to the editor of the *Century*, dated Washington. November 15th, 1886) states that "neither the soldier nor the widow has ever filed a claim for pension, and any seeming failure of recognition is not due to neglect on the part of the Pension Office."

The following letter from General McClellan to the son is of interest:

> Trenton, New Jersey,
> November 18th, 1879.
> W. A. Mitchell, Esq., La Cynge, Kansas.—Dear sir: Your Letter of the 9th inst. has reached me. I cannot, at this interval of time, recall the name of the finder of the papers to which you refer—it is doubtful whether I ever knew the name. All that I can say is that on or about

the 13th of September, 1862—just before the battles of South Mountain and Antietam,—there was handed to me by a member of my staff a copy (original) of one of General Lee's orders of march, directed to General D. H. Hill, which order developed General Lee's intended operations for the next few days, and was of very great service to me in enabling me to direct the movements of my own troops accordingly. This order was stated to have been found on one of the abandoned campgrounds of the Confederate troops by a private soldier, and, as I think, of an Indiana regiment. Whoever found the order in question and transmitted it to the headquarters showed intelligence and deserved marked reward, for he rendered an infinite service. The widow of that soldier should have her pension without a day's delay. Regretting that it is not in my power to give the name of the finder of the order,

I am very truly yours,

Geo. B. Mcclellan.

★★★★★★

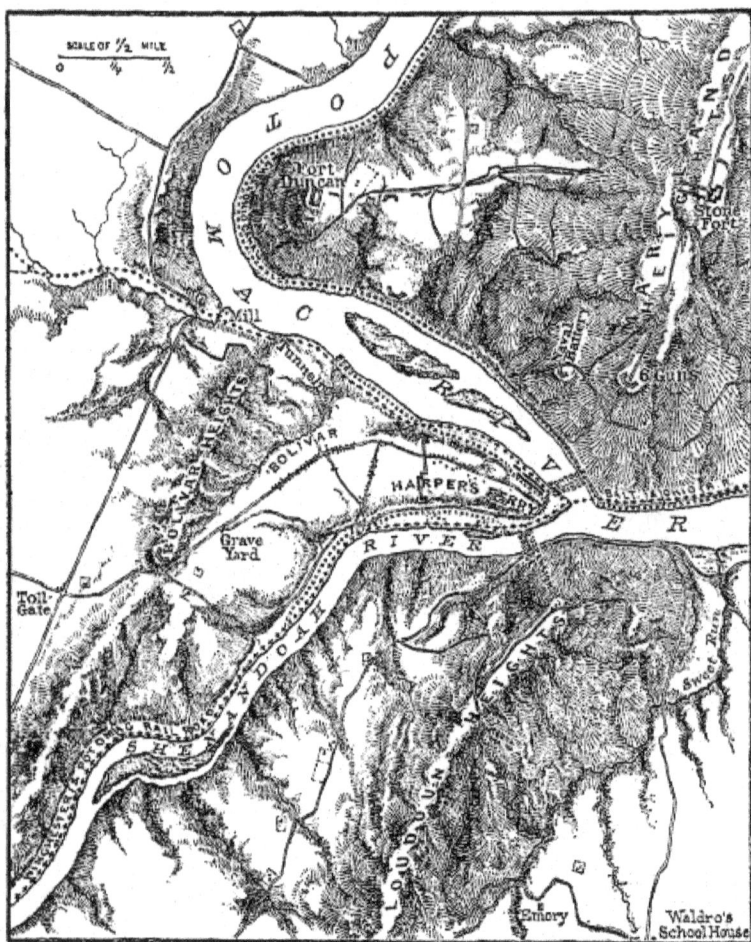

MAP OF THE DEFENSES AND APPROACHES OF HARPER'S FERRY.

Jackson's Capture of Harper's Ferry

By John G. Walker, Major-General, C. S. A.

When General Lee began his campaign against Pope I was in command of a division (of three brigades) which, was not a part of either of the two corps of the Army of Northern Virginia. I was left on the James for the defence of Richmond, but after the evacuation of Harrison's Landing by McClellan's army (August 14th to 20th), the Confederate capital being no longer threatened, I was ordered by the Secretary of War to leave one of my brigades at Richmond and proceed with the other two to join General Lee in the field. Leaving Daniel's brigade on the James, I marched northward with my old brigade, the strongest and the one which had seen most service, at that time commanded by Colonel Van H. Manning, and with the brigade of General Robert Ransom.

It was our hope that we should overtake General Lee in time to take part in the fight with Pope; but when we reached the field of Bull Run we found it strewn with the still unburied dead of Pope's army, and learned that Lee was pushing for the fords of the Upper Potomac. Following him rapidly, on the night of the 6th of September my division reached the vicinity of Leesburg, and the next morning crossed the Potomac at Cheek's Ford, at the mouth of the Monocacy, and about three miles above White's Ford, where Stonewall Jackson had crossed.

At Cheek's Ford, I overtook G. B. Anderson's brigade of D. H. Hill's division and crossed into Maryland with it. The next day we reached the neighbourhood of Frederick. I went at once to General Lee, who was alone. After listening to my report, he said that as I had a division which would often, perhaps, be ordered on detached service, an intelligent performance of my duty might require a knowledge of the ulterior purposes and objects of the campaign.

Tracing with his finger on a large map, he said:

"Here is the line of our communications, from Rapidan Station to Manassas, thence to Frederick. It is too near the Potomac, and is liable to be cut any day by the enemy's cavalry. I have therefore given orders to move the line back into the Valley of Virginia, by way of Staunton, Harrisonburg, and Winchester, entering Maryland at Shepherdstown. (See map.)

"I wish you to return to the mouth of the Monocacy and effectually destroy the aqueduct of the Chesapeake and Ohio canal. By the time that is accomplished you will receive orders to cooperate in the capture of Harper's Ferry, and you will not return here, but, after the capture of Harper's Ferry, will rejoin us at Hagerstown, where the army will be concentrated. My information is that there are between 10,000 and 12,000 men at Harper's Ferry, and 3000 at Martinsburg. The latter may escape toward Cumberland, but I think the chances are that they will take refuge at Harper's Ferry and be captured.

"Besides the men and material of war which we shall capture at Harper's Ferry, the position is necessary to us, not to garrison and hold, but because in the hands of the enemy it would be a break in our new line of communications with Richmond.

"A few days' rest at Hagerstown will be of great service to our men. Hundreds of them are barefooted, and nearly all of them are ragged. I hope to get shoes and clothing for the most needy. But the best of it will be that the short delay will enable us to get up our stragglers not stragglers from a shirking disposition, but simply from inability to keep up with their commands.

★★★★★★

During the Maryland campaign, the Federals as well as the Confederates were greatly weakened by straggling. On October 7th twenty days after the Battle of Antietam, General Halleck, in a letter to General McClellan, said:

> Straggling is the great curse of the army, and must be checked by severe measures. . . . I think, myself, that shooting them while in the act of straggling from their commands, is the only effective remedy that can be applied. If you apply the remedy you will be impatient at the want of activity of your army, and we must push it on. . . . There is a decided want of legs in our troops. . . . The real difficulty in they are not sufficiently exercised in marching; they lie still in camp too long. After a hard

march one day is time enough to rest. Lying still beyond that time does not rest the men. If we compare the average distances marched per month by our troops for the last year, with that of the rebels, or with European armies in the field, we will see why our troops march no better. They are not sufficiently exercised to make them good and efficient soldiers.

★★★★★★

"I believe there are not less than from eight to ten thousand of them between here and Rapidan Station. Besides these we shall be able to get a large number of recruits who have been accumulating at Richmond for some weeks. I have now requested that they be sent forward to join us. They ought to reach us at Hagerstown. We shall then have a very good army, and, (he smilingly added), one that I think will be able to give a good account of itself.

"In ten days from now, if the military situation is then what I confidently expect it to be after the capture of Harper's Ferry, I shall concentrate the army at Hagerstown, effectually destroy the Baltimore and Ohio road, and march to this point, (placing his finger at Harrisburg, Pennsylvania). That is the objective point of the campaign. You remember, no doubt, the long bridge of the Pennsylvania railroad over the Susquehanna, a few miles west of Harrisburg.

"Well, I wish effectually to destroy that bridge, which will disable the Pennsylvania railroad for a long time. With the Baltimore and Ohio in our possession, and the Pennsylvania railroad broken up, there will remain to the enemy but one route of communication with the West, and that very circuitous, by way of the Lakes. After that I can turn my attention to Philadelphia, Baltimore, or Washington, as may seem best for our interests."

I was very much astonished at this announcement, and I suppose he observed it, for he turned to me and said:

"You doubtless regard it hazardous to leave McClellan practically on my line of communication, and to march into the heart of the enemy's country?"

I admitted that such a thought had occurred to me.

"Are you acquainted with General McClellan?" he inquired.

I replied that we had served together in the Mexican war, under General Scott, but that I had seen but little of him since that time.

"He is an able general but a very cautious one. His enemies among his own people think him too much so. His army is in a very demoralised and chaotic condition, and will not be prepared for offensive operations or he will not think it so for three or four weeks. Before that time, I hope to be on the Susquehanna."

Our conversation was interrupted at this point by the arrival of Stonewall Jackson, and after a few minutes Lee and Jackson turned to the subject of the capture of Harper's Ferry. I remember Jackson seemed in high spirits, and even indulged in a little mild pleasantry about his long neglect of his friends in "the Valley," General Lee replying that Jackson had "some friends" in that region who would not, he feared, be delighted to see him. The arrival of a party of ladies from Frederick and vicinity, to pay their respects to Lee and Jackson, put an end to the conversation, and soon after I took my departure. Retracing our steps toward the Potomac, at 10 p. m. of the 9th my division arrived at the aqueduct which conveys the waters of the Chesapeake and Ohio canal across the Monocacy.

The attempted work of destruction began, but so admirably was the aqueduct constructed and cemented that it was found to be virtually a solid mass of granite. Not a seam or crevice could be discovered in which to insert the point of a crowbar, and the only resource was in blasting. But the drills furnished to my engineer were too dull and the granite too hard, and after several hours of zealous but ineffectual effort the attempt had to be abandoned. Dynamite had not then been invented, so we were foiled in our purpose, and about 3 o'clock a. m. of the 10th went into bivouac about two miles and a half west of the Monocacy.

Late in the afternoon a courier from General Lee delivered me a copy of his famous "Special Orders No. 191," directing me to co-operate with Jackson and McLaws in the capture of Harper's Ferry. That order contained the most precise and detailed information respecting the position, at its date, of every portion of the Confederate Army, where it would be during the next five or six days at least, and inferentially revealed the ulterior designs of the Confederate commander. Possessed of the information it contained, the Federal general would be enabled to throw the weight of his whole force on that small portion of the Confederate army then with Lee, before Jackson, McLaws, and Walker could effect the capture of Harper's Ferry and go to its assistance.

General McClellan did get possession, on the 13th of September, of a copy of this order, addressed to General D. H. Hill. In what manner, this happened is not positively known. General Bradley T. Johnson says that there is a tradition in Frederick that General Hill was seen to drop a paper in the streets of that town, which was supposed to be the order in question. The Comte de Paris says it was found in a house in Frederick which had been occupied by General Hill. But General Hill informed me, two years after the war, that he never received the order, and never knew of its existence until he read it in McClellan's report. (See General D. H. Hill's statement; General Colgrove's, and the text of the order).

To whatever circumstance General McClellan owed its possession, it certainly enabled him to thwart General Lee's designs for the invasion of Pennsylvania, or a movement upon Washington. But that he obtained all the advantages he might have done will hardly be contended for by General McClellan's warmest admirer. By the exercise of greater energy, he might easily have crushed Lee on the afternoon of the 15th or early on the 16th, before the arrival of Jackson from Harper's Ferry. On receiving my copy of the order, I was so impressed with the disastrous consequence which might result from its loss that I pinned it securely in an inside pocket.

In speaking with General Longstreet on this subject afterward, he remarked that the same thought had occurred to him, and that, as an absolutely sure precaution, he memorised the order and then "chewed it up." Informed of the presence of a superior Federal force at Cheek's Ford, where I was ordered to pass the Potomac, and learning that the crossing at the Point of Rocks was practicable, I moved my division to that place and succeeded in landing everything safe on the Virginia shore by daylight of the 11th. About the same time a heavy rain set in, and as the men were much exhausted by their night march, I put them into bivouac.

I would here remark that the Army of Northern Virginia had long since discarded their tents, capacious trunks, carpet-bags, bowie-knives, mill-saw swords, and six-shooters, and had reduced their "kits" to the simplest elements and smallest dimensions. Resuming our march on the morning of the 12th, we reached Hillsboro' and halted for the night. During the night, I was sent for from the village inn by a woman who claimed my attendance on the ground that she was just from Washington, and had very important information to give me. Answering the call, I found seated in the hotel parlour a young woman of perhaps twenty-five, of rather prepossessing appearance, who claimed to have left Washington the morning before, with important information from "our friends" in the Federal capital which

LOUDOUN HEIGHTS. VIEW FROM WALKER'S POSITION ON LOUDOUN
HEIGHTS OF THE UNION CAMP AND POSITION ON MARYLAND HEIGHTS.
FROM A WAR-TIME SKETCH.

she could communicate only to General Lee himself, and wished to know from me where he could be found. I saw at once that I had to do with a Federal spy; but as I did not wish to be encumbered with a woman prisoner, I professed ignorance of General Lee's whereabouts and advised her to remain quietly at the hotel, as I should, no doubt, have some information for her the next morning.

Before resuming our march the next day, I sent her under guard to Leesburg, directing the provost marshal at that place to hold her for three or four days and then release her. Resuming the march at daylight on the 13th, we reached the foot of Loudoun Heights about 10 o'clock. Here I was joined by a detachment of signal men and Captain White's company of Maryland cavalry. I detached two regiments,—the 27th North Carolina and 30th Virginia,—under Colonel J. R. Cooke, directing him to ascend Loudoun Mountain and take possession of the heights, but, in case he found no enemy, not to reveal his presence to the garrison of Harper's Ferry. I sent with him the men of the Signal Corps, with orders to open communication if possible with Jackson, whose force ought to be in the neighbourhood, coming from the west. I then disposed of the remainder of the division around the point of the mountain, where it abuts on the Potomac.

About 2 p. m. Colonel Cooke reported that he had taken unopposed possession of Loudoun Heights, but that he had seen nothing of Jackson, yet from the movements of the Federals he thought he was close at hand. By 8 o'clock the next morning five long-range Parrott rifles were on the top of the mountain in a masked position, but ready to open fire. About half-past 10 o'clock my signal party succeeded in informing Jackson of my position and my readiness to attack.

At a reunion of the Association of the Army of Northern Virginia held at Richmond on October 23rd, 1884, in an address delivered by General Bradley T. Johnson, occurs this passage:

McLaws, having constructed a road up Maryland Heights and placed his artillery in position during the 14th, while fighting was going on at Crampton's Gap and Turner's Gap, signalled to Jackson that he was ready; whereupon Jackson signalled the order both to McLaws and Walker 'Fire at such positions of the enemy as will be most effective.'

I am, of course, ignorant of what Jackson may have signalled McLaws, but it is certain that I received no such order. On the contrary, as soon as he was informed that McLaws was in possession of

113

Maryland Heights, Jackson signalled me substantially the following dispatch:

> Harper's Ferry is now completely invested. I shall summon its commander to surrender. Should he refuse I shall give him twenty-four hours to remove the non-combatants, and then carry the place by assault. *Do not fire unless forced to.* (See statements by General Bradley T. Johnson and Colonel H. Kyd Douglas).

Jackson at this time had, of course, no reason to suspect that McClellan was advancing in force, and doubtless supposed, as we all did, that we should have abundant leisure to rejoin General Lee at Hagerstown. But about noon I signalled to Jackson that an action seemed to be in progress at Crampton's Gap, that the enemy had made his appearance in Pleasant Valley in rear of McLaws, and that I had no doubt McClellan was advancing in force.

To this message Jackson replied that it was, he thought, no more than a cavalry affair between Stuart and Pleasonton. It was now about half-past 12 and every minute the sound of artillery in the direction of South Mountain was growing louder, which left no doubt on my mind of the advance of the whole Federal Army. If this were the case, it was certain that General Lee would be in fearful peril should the capture of Harper's Ferry be much longer delayed. I thereupon asked permission to open fire, but receiving no reply, I determined to be "forced."

For this purpose, I placed the two North Carolina regiments under Colonel (afterward Major-General, and now U. S. Senator) M. W. Ransom, which had relieved those under Cooke, in line of battle in full view of the Federal batteries on Bolivar Heights. As I expected, they at once opened a heavy, but harmless, fire upon my regiments, which afforded me the wished-for pretext. Withdrawing the infantry to the safe side of the mountain, I directed my batteries to reply.

It is possible that some of my military readers may question the propriety of my course, and allege that it amounted virtually to disobedience of orders. This I freely admit, but plead the dire urgency of the case. Had Jackson compromised himself by agreeing to allow the Federal commander twenty-four hours, as he proposed, General Lee would undoubtedly have been driven into the Potomac before any portion of the Confederate force around Harper's Ferry could have re-enforced him. The trouble was that Jackson could not be made to believe that McClellan's whole army was in movement.

I never knew whether or not Jackson actually made a formal demand for the surrender of the Federal garrison, but I had his own word for it that he intended to do so. Besides, such a course was in harmony with the humanity of his generous nature, and with his constant practice of doing as little harm as possible to non-combatants.

About an hour after my batteries opened fire those of A. P. Hill and Lawton followed suit, and about 3 o'clock those of McLaws. But the range from Maryland Heights being too great, the fire of McLaws's guns was ineffective, the shells bursting in mid-air without reaching the enemy. From my position on Loudoun Heights my guns had a plunging fire on the Federal batteries a thousand feet below and did great execution. By 5 o'clock our combined fire had silenced all the opposing batteries except one or two guns east of Bolivar Heights, which kept up a plucky but feeble response until night put a stop to the combat.

During the night of the 14th-15th, Major (afterward Brigadier-General) R. Lindsay Walker, chief of artillery of A. P. Hill's division, succeeded in crossing the Shenandoah with several batteries, and placing them in such a position on the slope of Loudoun Mountain, far below me, as to command the enemy's works. McLaws got his batteries into position nearer the enemy, and at daylight of the 15th the batteries of our five divisions were pouring their fire on the doomed garrison. The fire of my batteries, however, was at random, as the enemy's position was entirely concealed by a dense fog clinging to the sides of the mountain far below. But my artillerists trained their guns by the previous day's experience and delivered their fire through the fog.

The Federal batteries replied promptly, and for more than an hour maintained a spirited fire; but after that time, it grew more and more feeble until about 8 o'clock, when it ceased altogether, and the garrison surrendered. Owing to the fog I was ignorant of what had taken place, but surmising it, I soon ordered my batteries to cease firing. Those of Lawton, however, continued some minutes later. This happened unfortunately, as Colonel Dixon S. Miles, the Federal commander, was at this time mortally wounded by a fragment of shell while waving a white flag in token of surrender.

It was pleasing to us, perched upon the top of the mountain, to know that more than twelve thousand "boys in blue" below us were stacking arms. Such a situation has its pathetic side too, for after the first feeling of exultation has passed there comes one of sympathy for the humiliation of the brave men, who are no longer enemies, but unfortunate fellow-soldiers.

Some hours later, accompanied by two of my staff, I rode into Harper's Ferry, and we were interested in seeing our tattered Confederates fraternising in the most cordial manner with their well-dressed prisoners. I was introduced by General A. P. Hill to Federal Brigadier-General White. He explained to me that although of superior rank to Colonel Miles he had declined to assume command of the garrison, since he was at Harper's Ferry by accident—"an unfortunate accident too," he added.

I am of the opinion that it would have been practicable for Colonel Miles to have escaped with the infantry of his garrison during the night of the 14th-15th, as did a body of thirteen hundred cavalry under Colonel "Grimes" Davis. (Colonel Benjamin F. Davis of the 8th New York Cavalry, familiarly known at West Point and among his old army associates as "Grimes" Davis. He was killed at Beverly Ford, June 9th, 1863). This enterprising young officer crossed his cavalry to the Maryland side of the Potomac over the pontoon bridge, and followed the road on the berme side of the Chesapeake and Ohio canal, leading north to Sharpsburg. Mention of this very meritorious action is made in neither Federal nor Confederate accounts of the capture of Harper's Ferry that have fallen under my notice. (Mentioned by General McClellan).

There is a strong probability that the infantry of the garrison could have done the same. It should be stated that Davis not only escaped capture, but that he passed through Sharpsburg at daylight of the 15th, (according to a paper read by Captain William M. Luff, 12th Illinois Cavalry, before the Illinois Commandery of the Loyal Legion, the hour was 10 p. m. of the 14th), and in crossing the Hagerstown and Williamsport road he destroyed the greater part of Longstreet's reserve ordnance trains.

★★★★★★

Narrowly missing an encounter with the Reserve Artillery under General William N. Pendleton, which crossed Davis's track about eight miles north of Sharpsburg, about sunrise on the 15th. General Pendleton says Davis was "perhaps less than an hour ahead of us," and speaks of the large wagon train then passing, which he took immediate measures to protect.

★★★★★★

This escape of Davis from Harper's Ferry and Forrest's escape from

Fort Donelson under very similar circumstances show what a bold subordinate may achieve after his superior has lost heart. No sooner had the surrender of Harper's Ferry been assured than my division took up its line of march to join General Lee. At 2 a. m. of the 16th my advance overtook the rear of Jackson's force, and about 8 o'clock in the morning (of the day of the battle), after seeing our commands safe across the river at the ford below Shepherdstown, Jackson and myself went forward together toward Sharpsburg. As we rode along I mentioned my ruse in opening fire on Harper's Ferry. Knowing the strictness of Jackson's ideas in regard to military obedience, I felt a little doubtful as to what he would say. When I had finished my confession, he was silent for some minutes, and then remarked:

It was just as well as it was; but I could not believe that the fire you reported indicated the advance of McClellan in force. It seemed more likely to be merely a cavalry affair.

Then after an interval of silence, as if to himself, he continued: "I thought I knew McClellan" (they were classmates at West Point), "but this movement of his puzzles me."

ARMY WATER-CART.

The Capitulation of Harper's Ferry

By Julius White. Brigadier-General, U. S. V.

On the 8th of September, 1862, being then in command of the Union forces at Martinsburg, Virginia, about 2500 of all arms, I reported to General Wool at Baltimore, commanding the Department, that the enemy was approaching from the north in a force estimated at 15,000 to 20,000, and asked for instructions. General Wool replied:

If 20,000 men should attack you, you will of course fall back. Harper's Ferry would be the best position I could recommend.

After reconnoissance, and some skirmishing with the enemy's advance (Sept. 11th), demonstrating that his force was too large to be opposed with success, especially as there were no defences at Martinsburg, the post, in accordance with General Wool's views, was evacuated, and on the 12th Harper's Ferry was reached. Upon my reporting to Colonel Miles, the officer in command, he showed me the following dispatch:

Washington, D. C, Sept. 7th, 1862. Colonel Miles, Harper's Ferry: Our army (McClellan's) is in motion; it is important that Harper's Ferry he held to the latest moment. The Government has the utmost confidence in you, and is ready to give you full credit for the defence it expects you to make. H. W. Halleck, General-in-Chief.

In view of the foregoing dispatch, and of the fact that I had been ordered from Harper's Ferry to the command at Martinsburg a few days before by General Wool, it was manifest that the authorities intended to retain Colonel Miles in command very properly so, as he was an officer of forty years' experience. The defences of Harper's Ferry, if worthy of the name, comprised a small work on the crest of

Maryland Heights called Stone Fort; another well down the western slope, where a battery of heavy naval guns was established; and a line of intrenchments terminating at a work near the Potomac called Fort Duncan, but this line was not occupied except at the upper end. (See map.)

On Bolivar Heights, a line of rifle-pits extended from near the Potomac southward to the Charlestown road, where a small work for the protection of artillery was situated. In the rear of this line eastward, and in the upper part of the town, was an earth-work known as Camp Hill. Loudoun Heights (east of the Shenandoah) were not occupied by our troops. The troops constituting the garrison were originally disposed by Colonel Miles as follows: on Maryland Heights, about 2000; on Bolivar Heights, from the Potomac to the Charlestown road, thence at a right angle to the Shenandoah, a distance in all of at least a mile and a half, 7000 men; in the work at Camp Hill, about 800; while the remainder, about 1000, guarded the bridges and other points on the rivers.

The distance from Maryland Heights to the nearest point on Bolivar Heights by way of the pontoon bridge was two and a quarter miles; to the intersection of the Charlestown road, three miles. Thus, the principal points to be defended were not within supporting distance of each other in case of assault, nor was either of them properly fortified.

On the 13th the divisions of Generals McLaws and R. H. Anderson, by order of General Lee, reached Maryland Heights, and attacked the force stationed there, under Colonel Ford, who after some fighting abandoned the position—as he stated, by order of Colonel Miles; the latter, however, denied having given such an order. Be this as it may, it is certain that the enemy could easily have taken it with the force at his command whenever he chose.

On the same day General Walker, with a force of the enemy estimated at eight thousand, had taken possession of Loudoun Heights, and General Jackson with a much larger force had reached a position in front of Bolivar Heights—thus completing the investment of Harper's Ferry.

It has generally been considered that Colonel Miles should have tried to hold Maryland Heights (on the north side of the Potomac), even if it became necessary to mass his whole force there. The reasons given by him to the writer for not doing so were: (1) That his orders required him to hold Harper's Ferry, and this would be a violation of such orders; (2) that water would be inaccessible. Moreover, it was manifest that if the town of Harper's Ferry and the defensive line on Bolivar Heights were evacuated, the entire forces of the enemy on the Virginia side of the Potomac would recross to the north side, enveloping our small force and at the same time concentrating Lee's entire army in front of McClellan; while we should have given up the river-crossing, which, as the contending armies were then placed, constituted the only strategic value of Harper's Ferry.

Whether this view was correct or not, it is a fact that the maintenance of the line on Bolivar Heights till the morning of September 15th prevented the presence of the divisions of Generals A. P. Hill, McLaws, and Anderson with Lee, until the 17th, the day of Antietam, being four full days after General McClellan had received a copy of General Lee's orders directing the movement against Harper's Ferry, and disclosing the fact that fully one third of his army was south of the Potomac, and much more than that, including the force under General McLaws, engaged in the movement against Harper's Ferry. Distinguished officers of the Confederate Army (Generals Longstreet and Walker and Colonel Douglas) describe the situation of that part of Lee's army north of the Potomac during the 14th, 15th, and 16th of September as one of "imminent peril," "very serious," etc., etc., virtually admitting that it might then have been defeated.

Thus, it will be seen that there were two sides to the question whether Maryland Heights was the key to Harper's Ferry under the then existing circumstances, and that the detention of the Confederate forces around that place was prolonged, instead of abbreviated, by the continued occupation of Bolivar Heights by Colonel Miles.

In the afternoon of the 14th General Jackson moved forward with a view to occupy the ridge which is a prolongation of Bolivar Heights south of the Charlestown road and descends toward the Shenandoah River.

To oppose this movement troops were advanced, but after a spirited engagement it was manifest that we could not prevent his establishment in the position sought, and at night our force was withdrawn within the lines of defence.

During the evening of the 13th a consultation took place between the writer, then temporarily in command of the cavalry, Colonel B. F. Davis of the 8th New York, and Lieutenant-Colonel Hasbrouck Davis of the 12th Illinois, at which it was agreed that the mounted force could be of little use in the defence—that the horses and equipments would be of great value to the enemy if captured, and that an attempt to reach McClellan ought therefore to be made.

This proposition, made by Colonel B. F. Davis, was warmly seconded by Colonel Davis of the 12th Illinois. The question whether the whole force might not also escape was considered, but was negatived on the ground that infantry and artillery could not march fast enough to succeed. Besides, Colonel Miles considered that he had no right under his orders to evacuate the post.

After some hesitation and some sharp words between Colonels Miles and B. F. Davis, the former issued the order directing the cavalry to move out on the evening of the 14th, under the general command of the senior officer, Colonel Arno Voss, of the 12th Illinois. Under the inspiration and immediate direction of the two Davises, who rode together at the head of the column, the escaping force accomplished the brilliant achievement of reaching the Union lines without the loss of a man, capturing on the way a Confederate ammunition train of 97 wagons and its escort of 600 men.

Graphic accounts of this daring and successful exploit have been published by Major Thomas Bell of the 8th New York, Major W. M. Luff of the 12th Illinois, and Sergeant Pettengill of the 1st Rhode Island Cavalry—all of whom were participants, and I regret that the limits of this article do not permit the recital here. (*The Rhode Island Gunners: Four Accounts by Union Army Artillerymen from the 1st Rhode Island Light Artillery During the American Civil War*, by G. C. Sumner, J. A. Monroe & E. K. Parker is also published by Leonaur).

There were other incidents in the history of the events under consideration highly creditable to the troops constituting the garrison of Harper's Ferry. General Kershaw's report to General McLaws of the capture of Maryland Heights, on the 13th, states that he met with a "most obstinate resistance" from our force stationed there, "a fierce fire being kept up at a distance of one hundred yards," and it was not till he had sent General Barksdale's brigade to attack the works in rear that the heights were evacuated.

The fighting with Jackson's advance in front of Bolivar Heights, on the afternoon of the 14th and on the morning of the 15th, by the troops posted in that quarter, was deliberate, systematic, and plucky. The artillery was admirably handled, and if there had been anything like an equality of position, its effect would have been more decided. It would be invidious to specify the action of certain brigades, regiments, or batteries, but common justice to these troops requires that the foregoing statement of their service be made.

Soon after daylight on the morning of the 15th fire was opened by the enemy's artillery, comprising nearly or quite fifty pieces. Those established at the southern extremity of Bolivar Heights completely enfiladed that part of our line extending from the Charlestown road northward to the Potomac; those placed on the south-western slope of Loudoun Heights, and on the west side of the Shenandoah nearby, delivered their fire at an acute angle to our line, being half enfilade; those at or near the crest of Loudoun Heights took us in reverse; and still others in the valley beyond Bolivar Heights fired directly at our front.

The fire was chiefly converged upon the batteries we had established at and near the intersection of Bolivar Heights and the Charlestown road, that being the point upon which it was manifest that General Jackson would deliver the expected assault.

The writer, being in command of the forces in this quarter, ordered the massing of the artillery there and the movements of the regiments holding Camp Hill to the front. These orders, as I afterward learned, were countermanded by Colonel Miles, who deemed it necessary to retain a force near the river-crossing; at all events, the order was not executed.

The artillery fire continued until half-past 8 in the morning, when it was apparent the assault might be expected immediately. At this time Colonel Miles visited the work at the Charlestown road and said to the writer that the situation seemed hopeless, and that the place might as well be surrendered without further sacrifice of life. It was replied that such a step should only be taken upon the judgment of a council of war; whereupon Colonel Miles called the commanders of brigades together, who, after consultation, and with great reluctance on the part of some, voted unanimously for capitulation if honourable terms could be obtained, for the following reasons:

First. The officer commanding had lost all confidence in his ability further to defend the place, and was the first to advise surrender.

Second. There was no reason to hope that the attenuated line on Bolivar Heights could be maintained, even for half an hour, against the greatly superior force massed for the assault, supported if necessary by an attack on our rear by Generals Walker and McLaws.

Third. Great as was the disparity in numbers, the disparity in position was greater. Harper's Ferry and Bolivar Heights were dominated by Maryland and Loudoun Heights, and the other positions held by the enemy's artillery. The crest of Maryland Heights is at an elevation of 1060 feet; the southern point, nearest Harper's Ferry, 649 feet; Loudoun Heights, 954 feet. The south-western slope of the latter and the grounds nearly, west of the Shenandoah, where batteries of the enemy were placed, were 300 to 600 feet high.

The elevation of Bolivar Heights is about 300 feet, while Camp Hill and the town of Harper's Ferry are still lower. Thus, all our movements of men or guns during the engagements of the 14th and 15th, as well as the effect of their own plunging fire, were plainly visible from the enemy's signal-station on Loudoun Heights. No effective reply could be made to the fire from these elevated positions, no suitable defences existed from which to resist the assault, and there was no opportunity on the morning of the 15th to change our position, even if there had been a better one to occupy.

Fourth. To await the assault, then impending, with no hope of even a temporary successful resistance, did not seem to justify the sacrifice of life consequent upon such a course—the situation being regarded as one of the unfortunate chances of war, unavoidable under existing circumstances.

I was appointed by Colonel Miles commissioner to arrange the terms of capitulation, and at the urgent request of other officers I accepted the unwelcome duty, in the hope of obtaining honourable conditions. Immediately after the council broke up Colonel Miles was mortally wounded; he died the next day.

As commissioner, I was received very courteously by the Confederate officers, and the terms of capitulation agreed upon with General A. P. Hill provided that all private property of individuals and the side-arms of officers should be retained by them. Refugees, of whom there were a considerable number, were not to be treated as prisoners, except such, if any, as were deserters from the Confederate army. There were none of this class. All the Union troops were immediately paroled, not to serve again until regularly exchanged. A number of the prominent officers of the Confederate Army spoke of our situation as hopeless from the hour when the investment was completed.

Harper's Ferry is not defensible by a force inferior to that attacking it, unless the surrounding heights be well fortified, and each of them held by a force sufficient to maintain itself unsupported by the others. It was this which doubtless prompted the advice given by General McClellan to General Halleck, before the investment, that the garrison be withdrawn.

The Battle of South Mountain was fought by General McClellan, on the 14th of September, against a force of the enemy not more than two-thirds as large as that encountered by him at Antietam.

After the mountain passes had been carried, if a prompt advance down Pleasant Valley had been made by his largely preponderating force, there seems good reason to believe that Harper's Ferry would have been relieved, the river-crossing at that place secured, the reunion of Lee's army, separated as it was by the Potomac, rendered difficult, if not impossible, and the capture or dispersion of a large part of it probable.

The orders issued by General McClellan to General Franklin, commanding the Sixth Corps, on the night of the 13th, announced his purpose to do these very things, and directed that Crampton's Gap—the pass nearest Harper's Ferry—be carried at whatever cost. The enemy in front of General Franklin was then to be "cut off, destroyed, or captured, and Harper's Ferry relieved." The dispatch concludes with the remark:

> My general idea is to cut the enemy in two, and beat him in detail.

The column to be thus interposed between the enemy and Harper's Ferry consisted of General Franklin's corps only—subsequently re-enforced by General Couch's division of the Fourth Corps. The imminent peril of Harper's Ferry had been known to General McClellan from the inception of the campaign. He had advised the withdrawal of the garrison, and had predicted its loss if left there, before he left Washington.

No direct measures were taken by him, however, for the relief of the post, until after his receipt on the 13th of General Lee's order detaching a large part of his army for its capture, which force had then completed its investment. Early on the morning of the 14th General McClellan had been informed by Colonel Miles, through Major Russell of the 1st Maryland Cavalry, who, with great courage and tact, had made his way during the night through the enemy's lines, that Harper's Ferry could not be held more than forty-eight hours—from the time the courier left—*viz.*, till the 15th.

Thus, the time within which to relieve that post had been reduced to the minimum, so that success depended upon the prompt and vigorous advance of a force large enough to readily overcome such of the enemy as stood in the way. Unfortunately, General Franklin's command was not sufficient to accomplish this vitally important purpose.

After receiving the orders, he was not able to get his command into action until midday of the 14th, and met with such determined resistance that it was not until near nightfall, and after a loss of more than five hundred in killed and wounded, that he had forced the pass and found himself on the west side of the mountain in Pleasant Valley, confronted by an increased force of the enemy, with plenty of artillery advantageously posted.

The attack on Turner's Gap by the main body of the army, although successful, did not result, as General McClellan had expected, in relieving General Franklin of the enemy in his front; and the latter, as shown in his dispatches of the morning of the 15th, declined to attack unless re-enforced.

But the time within which it was possible to relieve Harper's Ferry had then passed, even if the place had been held during the whole of that day. During the afternoon of the 14th our guns at Harper's Ferry, engaged with Jackson's forces, were cheeringly responded to by those of General Franklin at Crampton's Gap; but after 4 o'clock of that day, and on the morning of the 15th, there was no sound of conflict in that direction, and the hope of relief from McClellan, which the proximity of the firing had inspired, was abandoned. Harper's Ferry was doomed, and as affecting this result, it did not matter whether the garrison occupied the town or either of the adjacent heights, nor whether the surrender took place before or after our assault, *because it was surrounded by the whole of Lee's army.*

I must not be understood as presuming to criticise the conduct of this campaign by General McClellan. The object of this article, as before stated, is only to relate the historical facts bearing upon the subject in hand; therefore, no commentary is made upon the questions whether his advice that the garrison of Harper's Ferry be withdrawn should have been adopted, whether he might have marched his army toward Harper's Ferry faster, or whether he might and should have detached a larger force for the purposes indicated in his orders to General Franklin. Manifestly it was his design to relieve that post, but the measures taken did not succeed.

It has been often asserted that Harper's Ferry might have held out a day or two longer, but of those who have claimed that it could have been longer held, no one has yet, so far as the writer is informed, stated *how* a garrison mostly of recruits under fire for the first time could have successfully defended an area of three square miles, assailed from all sides by veterans three times their number, posted, with artillery, in positions commanding the whole field. The writer, with due deference, expresses the opinion that the force under Jackson could have carried the place by assault within an hour after his arrival before it, or at any time thereafter prior to the surrender, in spite of any resistance which under the circumstances could have been made.

★★★★★★

The report of the Military Commission censured Colonels Miles and Ford and Major Baird. It affirmed that there was nothing in the conduct of Colonels D'Utassy and Trimble to call for censure; and that General Julius White merited the approbation of the Commission, adding, "He appears from the evidence to have acted with decided capability and courage."

★★★★★★

Stonewall Jackson's Intentions at Harper's Ferry

1. By Bradley T. Johnson, Brigadier-General, C. S. A.

Major-General J. G. Walker, in his interesting paper in *The Century* (June, 1886), states that after he had occupied Loudoun Heights on September 11th, he received a dispatch from General Jackson, by signal, substantially as follows:

> Harper's Ferry is now completely invested. I shall summon its commander to surrender. Should he refuse, I will give him twenty-four hours to remove the non-combatants, and then carry the place by assault. Do not fire unless forced to.

Referring to the statement made by me in an address before the Association of the Army of Northern Virginia, October 23rd, 1884, that on the 14th of September General Jackson signalled the order to both McLaws and Walker:

> Fire at such positions of the enemy as will be most effective.

General Walker says:

> I am, of course, ignorant of what Jackson may have signalled McLaws, but it is certain I received no such order.

General Walker then goes on to show that Jackson determined to give the commanding officer of Harper's Ferry twenty-four hours before he carried the place; that he, General Walker, was satisfied that the delay of twenty-four hours would be fatal to General Lee,—as it would have been; that, therefore, against orders not to fire until he was forced to, he determined to be forced; and that he secured this end by the display of two North Carolina regiments, under Colonel M. W. Ransom, in line of battle on Loudoun Heights, in full view of the

Federal batteries on Bolivar Heights.

As he expected, he says:

> They at once opened a heavy but harmless fire upon my regiments, which afforded me the wished-for pretext. Withdrawing the infantry to the safe side of the mountain, I directed my batteries to reply.

Thus, it would appear that General Walker forced the attack on Harper's Ferry, and prevented the delay of twenty-four hours which General Jackson proposed to give; and that to this prompt attack was due the capture of Harper's Ferry, and the salvation of that part of the Army of Northern Virginia which, with Lee, Longstreet, and D. H. Hill, was waiting at Sharpsburg the reduction of the force at the former place, and the re-enforcement of Lee by Jackson, McLaws, and Walker after Harper's Ferry had fallen. Twenty-four hours' delay would have postponed the fall of Harper's Ferry, and the battle of the 17th would have been fought by Longstreet and D. H. Hill alone, who would have been destroyed by McClellan before Jackson could have come up.

I prepared the address before the Association of the Army of Northern Virginia after careful study of the records and reports of both sides, and all accessible accounts of the battle of Sharpsburg, and believe every statement made by me can be substantiated by the record, or by the statements of eye-witnesses. Unless General Walker has a copy of the dispatch referred to by him, I respectfully submit that his recollection is in error: that no intention was ever entertained by Jackson of giving twenty-four hours' delay; and that General Jackson himself gave the order to Walker and McLaws to open fire, exactly as stated by me.

The reasons for believing that General Walker is mistaken in thinking that he ever received the order referred to by him, or one in any way intimating an intention of giving twenty-four hours' delay, seem to me to conclusive. Colonel H. Kyd Douglas was *aide-de-camp* to Jackson, and occupied, particularly in that campaign, peculiarly confidential relations to him. His home was near Sharpsburg and Shepherdstown, the scene of operations, and he probably knew as much of General Jackson's intentions as any man living. He tells me he never heard of any such projected delay. The "lost order" No. 191—from General Lee to Jackson, Walker, and McLaws—specially directs Walker and McLaws to be in position on Loudoun and Maryland Heights respectively by Friday morning, September 12th, and Jackson to take possession of the Baltimore and Ohio railroad by Friday morning and "intercept such of the enemy as may attempt to escape from Harper's Ferry." Jackson's advance division reached the vicinity of Harper's Ferry during Saturday forenoon, the 13th; Walker and McLaws reached the designated points Saturday night, but were not in position for offensive action until September 14th.

Now when the army was moving to the positions assigned by "Special Orders No. 191," it was a matter of common knowledge that McClellan's advance was in contact with our rear. Hampton had a sharp affair in the streets of Frederick late on the 12th. Fitz Lee, hanging on to the advance, located McClellan and reported his presence to Stuart, who held the mountain pass over Catoctin at Hagan's. During the 13th Stuart delayed the advance of the Federal infantry through Middletown Valley by sturdily defending the practicable points on the National road. On the 14th, when, according to General Walker, Jackson, then a day late, proposed to give the commander of Harper's Ferry twenty-four hours' delay, and General Walker, in order to prevent that delay, drew the fire of the Federal guns on him on Loudoun Heights, Franklin's corps attacked Crampton's Gap about noon, and after a sharp defence drove Munford through the mountain pass.

Now Crampton's Gap is in full sight of Loudoun Heights, not four miles off as the crow flies, and is in rear of McLaws's position on Maryland Heights. Jackson then knew that McClellan was thundering in his rear. Walker and McLaws could see the battle and hear the guns at Crampton's and Walker could also see the fight at South Mountain.

It would have been contrary to every known characteristic of the chief of the "Foot Cavalry" for him to have given his adversary twenty-four hours' breathing-time, under any circumstances, anywhere, and utterly impossible for him to have done so under these circumstances at this time. General Jackson did send General Walker an order by signal:

> I do not desire any of the batteries to open until all are ready on both sides of the river, except you should find it necessary, of which you must judge for yourself. I will let you know when to open all the batteries.

In the War Records office may be seen the report of Captain J. L. Bartlett, signal officer of Jackson's corps. It contains the order to Walker and McLaws quoted by me in my address:

Fire at such positions of the enemy as will be most effective.

This order General Walker does not recollect to have received. It certainly was sent by Captain Bartlett to Walker's signal officer, and just as certainly received by the latter. It is hardly possible that so important an order, at such a time, should not have been forwarded by the signal officer to General Walker. The following order was also sent from Captain Bartlett's signal-station to General Walker's officer on Loudoun Heights:

Special Orders Headquarters Valley District,
No. — September 14, 1862.
1. Today Major-General McLaws will attack so as to sweep with his artillery the ground occupied by the enemy, take his batteries in reverse, and otherwise operate against him as circumstances may justify.

2. Brigadier-General Walker will take in reverse the battery on the turnpike, and also sweep with his artillery the ground occupied by the enemy, and silence the battery on the island in the Shenandoah, should he find a battery there.

3. Major-General A. P. Hill will move along the left bank of the Shenandoah, and thus turn the enemy's left flank and enter Harper's Ferry.

4. Brigadier-General Lawton will move along the turnpike for the purpose of supporting General Hill and otherwise operating against the enemy on the left of General Hill.

5. Brigadier-General Jones will, with one of his brigades and a battery of artillery, make a demonstration against the enemy's right: the remaining part of his division will constitute the reserve and move along the turnpike.

By order of Major-General Jackson:

William L. Jackson,
Acting Assistant Adjutant-General.

Captain Bartlett, after reporting all messages and orders sent through his station, among which were the foregoing, says:

If any other dispatches or orders were sent at Harper's Ferry, it was done at other posts than mine.

Now, there was no signal officer except Captain Bartlett attached to Jackson's headquarters, communicating with Loudoun Heights, and his report thus shows all the orders sent by Jackson to Walker. The one quoted by General Walker is not among them; the one quoted by me is. Therefore, inasmuch as it appears that the investing force under Jackson was twenty-four hours behind the time fixed by General Lee for completing the investment of Harper's Ferry, and that Generals Jackson and McLaws knew that McClellan had been in Frederick on the 12th, only twenty miles off; and that McClellan was actually attacking at Crampton's, three or four miles from Harper's Ferry; and that Lee, Longstreet, and D. H. Hill were then north of the Potomac, and in imminent danger of being cut off from the rest of the army at Harper's Ferry: and that General Jackson did, in fact, send the order, cited by me, to Walker and McLaws to fire at such positions of the enemy as would be most effective, and did, in fact, as soon as his troops were in position, completing the investment, issue an order of battle for the assault on Harper's Ferry: taking all these facts into consideration, we must believe that General Walker is mistaken as to the order he thinks he received, and that General Jackson never issued such order, nor entertained the idea of delaying the attack.

2. By Henry Kyd Douglas, Colonel, C. S. A.

In his article in *The Century* for June, 1885, on "Harper's Ferry and Sharpsburg," General John G. Walker said, in substance, that General Jackson, after Harper's Ferry was invested, informed him that he intended to summon the Federal commander to surrender, and, should he refuse, then to give him twenty-four hours to remove the non-combatants before making an assault; but that he, General Walker, being better advised as to the movements of General McClellan, became impatient of the delay, and by a piece of mild strategy forced the assault, and thereby hastened the surrender of Harper's Ferry, saved Jackson from being " compromised," and Lee from being driven into the Potomac.

With the help of such notes as I have, confirming my recollection, and the official reports corroborating them, I will briefly examine General Walker's statement.

I think I may safely assume that General Jackson, being in immediate communication, by signal, with General McLaws (who was in contact with the enemy), and with General Lee both by signal through McLaws and by a constant line of couriers, knew at least as much about the movements of General McClellan and the situation of the rest of our army as General Walker, on Loudoun Heights, could possibly know.

Jackson reached Harper's Ferry on Saturday, September 13th, and immediately shut up his side of the pen. McLaws and Walker were not yet in position, their delay being doubtless unavoidable. Let us see whether Jackson was in danger of compromising himself by want of activity. The next day at 7:20 a. m., in anticipation that McLaws and Walker would soon be ready, he sent to McLaws a characteristic letter of instructions. As will appear, a copy of this letter was doubtless sent to Walker, and will help to explain one of the errors into which he has fallen. That letter looks to quick work. But although Jackson was ready, there were obstacles in the way of immediate action.

General Jackson says that, separated by the Potomac and Shenandoah from McLaws and Walker, he resorted to signals, "and that before the necessary orders were thus transmitted the day was far advanced." General A. P. Hill says, in effect, that it was afternoon before the signals from Maryland and Loudoun Heights notified Jackson that "all was ready," and then Jackson ordered him against the enemy. General McLaws says the morning of the 11th was occupied cutting a road for artillery, and that by 2 p. m. he had four pieces in position on Maryland Heights. General Walker says that at half-past 10 he succeeded in notifying Jackson that he was ready, and Captain Bartlett, the signal officer of Jackson, reports to the same effect. Jackson then ordered Walker to "wait" for McLaws.

Everyone at headquarters knew how impatient General Jackson was at the unavoidable loss of time. He had written the McLaws letter very early in the morning, and in further preparation for prompt and decisive action he dictated to Colonel Jackson his "special order" for the attack, and as soon as it was practicable issued it. It speaks for itself. He also issued his joint order to McLaws and Walker—

Fire at such positions of the enemy as will be most effective.

Walker opened fire about 1 p. m.—whether shortly before or shortly after this joint order does not appear, and is of little importance. McLaws began about 2 p. m. He says Walker and Jackson were both at it before him. Hill moved promptly, and did enough of work that afternoon and night, as he says, "to seal the fate of Harper's Ferry," with the assistance of McLaws and Walker. At 3 o'clock the next morning I was sent by General Jackson to direct the movement of Jones's division at first dawn, and at daylight everybody was in action, and Harper's Ferry speedily surrendered. In energy, Jackson at

Harper's Ferry simply paralleled himself; he could do no more. "Let the work be done thoroughly," he had said to McLaws; and it was.

Was General Jackson pushed to this activity by General Walker, and would he otherwise have given Colonel Miles twenty-four hours to remove non-combatants before assault, and thus have imperilled General Lee beyond hope? I will treat this question soberly, as becomes the gravity of General Walker's statement and his regard for General Jackson's reputation. But, as the matter now presents itself, I will submit the reasons for thinking General Walker is mistaken in regard to the dispatch he says he received from General Jackson respecting the twenty-four hours' delay. It is known now that Jackson never did summon the enemy to surrender, and in his report, he makes no mention of such a purpose. I find in my notes this item in regard to the 11th:

> It was late in the afternoon when McLaws was ready for action—too late to effect anything on that day. Preparations were made for an assault early the next morning. I am not aware that General Jackson made any demand for the surrender of the garrison.

There is nothing in the reports of Hill, McLaws, Jones, or Walker, touching the matter of a contemplated demand for surrender, or any delay by reason thereof. Captain Bartlett's report as signal officer—the only one known to have sent signal dispatches between Jackson and Walker—contains no such order as the one quoted by General Walker. If such a message had been sent to Walker, it would, of course, have been sent also to Hill and McLaws, and they make no mention of it. It could not have gone to McLaws except through Bartlett, and he surely would have made a note of it.

General Walker says it was after Jackson was informed that McLaws was in possession of Maryland Heights that the dispatch was sent to him. This was not earlier than 2 p. m., and before that time Walker had opened fire, and Jackson had issued the joint order, "Fire," etc. and had followed it up with his specific "special order," prepared beforehand. In fact, General Jackson knew the urgency of the situation better than General Walker, and it is simply incredible that he contemplated a delay of twenty-four hours for any purpose. General Walker must be mistaken. It does not follow, however, that he has no ground for his mistake. I have said that the substance of Jackson's early letter to McLaws must have been sent to Walker. That letter looks to an attack by Walker on an island battery in the Shenandoah, and during the morning a dispatch to Jackson from Loudoun Heights says:

Walker can't get position to bear on island.

. . . .showing that Walker had in some way been instructed with regard to it. (It would seem that Jackson's "special order" must have been prepared in the morning and before the receipt of the dispatch from Walker, for in it he gives instructions to Walker touching that island battery.) In the McLaws letter, Jackson speaks of a flag of truce to get out non-combatants should the enemy not surrender; but the spirit of that letter is against any delay. I remember the question of a demand for surrender was vaguely talked of at headquarters by the staff. It is likely they got the idea from the McLaws letter, for I never heard the general (Jackson) say anything on the subject, and every indication was against any delay in making the assault. I merely throw out the suggestion to account for the error of memory into which I think General Walker has fallen.

Whatever purpose General Jackson at first had to demand a surrender or to consider non-combatants, his ruling anxiety was for the speedy fall of Harper's Ferry. It maybe that a little reflection satisfied him, after writing the McLaws letter, that the citizens of the town would be in little danger from the firing of McLaws and Walker at the enemy on Bolivar Heights, and that he dismissed that consideration from his mind. If this humane purpose ever took definite shape in his intentions, there was never any occasion to execute it, and it would now be of little consequence had not General Walker attempted to give it such strange form and significance.

THE OPPOSING FORCES AT HARPER'S FERRY, VA.
September 12–15, 1862.

The composition, losses, and strength of each army as here stated give the gist of all the data obtainable in the Official Records. K stands for killed; w for wounded; m w for mortally wounded; m for captured or missing; c for captured.

THE UNION FORCES.
Col. Dixon S. Miles (m w), Brig.-Gen. Julius White.

Brigade Commanders: Colonels F. G. D'Utassy, William H. Trimble, Thomas H. Ford, and William G. Ward. *Troops:* 12th Ill. Cav., Col. Arno Voss; M, 2d Ill. Art'y, Capt. John C. Phillips; 65th Ill., Col. Daniel Cameron; 15th Ind. Battery, Capt. John C. H. von Sehlen; Ind. Battery, Capt. Silas F. Rigby; 1st Md. Cav. (detachment), Capt. Charles H. Russell; Battalion Md. Cav., Maj. Henry A. Cole; 1st Md., P. H. Brigade, Col. William P. Maulsby; 3d Md., P. H. Brigade, Lieut.-Col. Stephen W. Downey; 8th N. Y. Cav., Col. Benjamin F. Davis; A, 5th N. Y. H. Art'y, Capt. John H. Graham; F, 5th N. Y. H. Art'y, Capt. Eugene McGrath; 12th N. Y. (militia), Col. William G. Ward; 39th N. Y., Maj. Hugo Hildebrandt; 111th N. Y., Col. Jesse Segoine; 115th N. Y., Col. Simeon Sammon; 125th N. Y., Col. George L. Willard; 126th N. Y., Col. Eliakim Sherrill (w), Maj. William H. Baird; Ohio Battery, Capt. Benjamin F. Potts; 32d Ohio, Maj. Sylvester M. Hewitt; 60th Ohio, Lieut.-Col. Noah H. Hixon; 87th Ohio, Col. Henry B. Banning; 7th Squadron R. I. Cav., Maj. Augustus W. Corliss; 9th Vermont, Col. George J. Stannard.

The total Union loss in the actions on Maryland Heights and at Harper's Ferry and Bolivar Heights was 44 killed, 173 wounded, and 12,520 captured = 12,737. (Most of the wounded were probably counted among the captured.)

The Confederate force employed at Harper's Ferry consisted of the commands of Generals Jackson, McLaws (including R. H. Anderson's division), and Walker.

For compostion of these forces in detail see earlier lists.

The Historical Basis of Whittier's "Barbara Frietchie"

(Condensed from a contribution to the *Philadelphia Times*
for July 21st, 1886)
By George O. Seilheimer

That Barbara Frietchie lived is not denied. That she died at the advanced age of 96 years and is buried in the burial-ground of the German Reformed Church in Frederick is also true.

There is only one account of Stonewall Jackson's entry into Frederick, and that was written by a Union army surgeon who was in charge of the hospital there at the time. The doctor wrote on the 21st of September:

> Jackson, I did not get a look at to recognise him, though I must have seen him, as I witnessed the passage of all the troops through the town.

Not a word about Barbara Frietchie and this incident. Br. Oliver Wendell Holmes, too, was in Frederick soon afterward, on his way to find his son, reported mortally wounded at Antietam. Such a story, had it been true, could scarcely have failed to reach his ears, and he would undoubtedly have told it in his delightful chapter of war reminiscences, *My Hunt for the Captain*, had he heard it.

Barbara Frietchie had a flag, and it is now in the possession of Mrs. Handschue and her daughter, Mrs. Abbott, of Frederick. Mrs. Handschue was the niece and adopted daughter of Mrs. Frietchie, and the flag came to her as part of her inheritance, a cup out of which General Washington drank tea when he spent a night in Frederick in 1791 being among the Frietchie heirlooms. This flag which Mrs. Handschue and her daughter so religiously preserve is torn, but the banner was not rent with seam and gash from a rifle-blast; it is torn—only this and nothing more. That Mrs. Frietchie did not wave the flag at Jackson's men Mrs. Handschue positively affirms. The flag-waving act was done, however, by Mrs. Mary S. Quantrell, another Frederick woman: but Jackson took no notice of it, and as Mrs. Quantrell was not fortunate enough to find a poet to celebrate her deed she never became famous.

Colonel Henry Kyd Douglas, who was with General Jackson every minute of his stay in Frederick, declares in an article in *The Century* for June, 1886, that Jackson never saw Barbara Frietchie, and that Barbara never saw Jackson. This story is borne out by Mrs. Frietchie's relatives.

As already said, Barbara Frietchie had a flag and she waved it, not on the 6th to Jackson's men, but on the 12th to Burnside's. Here is the story as told by Mrs. Abbott, Mrs. Handschue's daughter:

Jackson and his men had been in Frederick and had left a short time before. We were glad that the rebels had gone and that our troops came. My mother and I lived almost opposite aunt's place. She and my mother's cousin, Harriet Yoner, lived together. Mother said I should go and see aunt and tell her not to be frightened. You know that aunt was then almost ninety-six years old. When I reached aunt's place she knew as much as I did about matters, and cousin Harriet was with her. They were on the front porch, and aunt was leaning on the cane she always carried. When the troops marched along aunt waved her hand, and cheer after cheer went up from the men as they saw her. Some even ran into the yard. 'God bless you, old lady,' 'Let me take you by the hand,' 'May you live long, you dear old soul,' cried one after the other, as they rushed into the yard.

Aunt being rather feeble, and in order to save her as much as we could, cousin Harriet Yoner said, 'Aunt ought to have a flag to wave.' The flag was hidden in the family Bible, and cousin Harriet got it and gave it to aunt. Then she waved the flag to the men and they cheered her as they went by. She was very patriotic and the troops all knew of her. The day before General Reno was killed he came to see aunt and had a talk with her.

The manner in which the Frietchie legend originated was very simple. A Frederick lady visited Washington some time after the invasion of 1862 and spoke of the open sympathy and valour of Barbara Frietchie. The story was told again and again, and it was never lost in

UNION HOSPITAL IN A BARN NEAR ANTIETAM CREEK. AFTER A SKETCH MADE AT THE TIME.

the telling. Mr. Whittier received his first knowledge of it from Mrs. E. D. E. N. Southworth, the novelist, who is a resident of Washington. When Mrs. Southworth wrote to Mr. Whittier concerning Barbara, she enclosed a newspaper slip reciting the circumstances of Barbara Frietchie's action when Lee entered Frederick.

When Mr. Whittier wrote the poem, he followed as closely as possible the account sent him at the time.

★★★★★★

Writing to the editor of *The Century* on the 10th of June, 1886, Mr. Whittier said: "The poem *Barbara Frietchie* was written in good faith. The story was no invention of mine. It came to me from sources which I regarded as entirely reliable; it had been published in newspapers, and had gained public credence in Washington and Maryland before my poem was written. I had no reason to doubt its accuracy then, and I am still constrained to believe that it had foundation in fact. If I thought otherwise, I should not hesitate to express it. I have no pride of authorship to interfere with my allegiance to truth." Mr. Whittier, writing March 7th, 1888, informs us further that he "also received letters from several other responsible persons wholly or partially confirming the story, among whom was the late Dorothea L. Dix."

★★★★★★

He has a cane made from the timber of Barbara's house,—a present from Dr. Stiener, a member of the Senate of Maryland. The flag with which Barbara Frietchie gave a hearty welcome to Burnside's troops has but thirty-four stars, is small, of silk, and attached to a staff probably a yard in length.

Barbara Frietchie was born at Lancaster, Pennsylvania. Her maiden name was Hauer. She was born December 3rd, 1766, her parents being Nicholas and Catharine Hauer. She went to Frederick in early life, where she married John C. Frietchie, a glover, in 1806. She died December 18th, 1862, Mr. Frietchie having died in 1849. In 1868 the waters of Carroll Creek rose to such a height that they nearly wrecked the old home of the heroine of Whittier's poem.

Stonewall Jackson in Maryland
By Henry Kyd Douglas, Colonel, C. S. A.

On the 3rd of September, 1862, the Federal army under General Pope having been confounded. General Lee turned his columns toward the Potomac, with Stonewall Jackson in front. On the 5th of September Jackson crossed the Potomac at White's Ford, a few miles beyond Leesburg. The passage of the river by the troops marching in fours, well closed up, the laughing, shouting, and singing, as a brass band in front played "Maryland, my Maryland," was a memorable experience.

★★★★★★

We had been faring very badly since we left Manassas Junction, having had only one meal that included bread and coffee. Our diet had been green corn, with beef without salt, roasted on the end of ramrods. We heard with delight of the 'plenty' to be had in Maryland; judge of our disappointment when, about 2 o'clock at night, we were marched into a dank clover-field and the order came down the line, 'Men, go into that cornfield and get your rations—and be ready to march at 5 in the morning. Don't burn any of these fence-rails.' Of course, we obeyed orders as to the corn, but, the rails suffered."—Extract from a letter written by Lieut. Robert Healy, of Jackson's corps.

★★★★★★

The Marylanders in the corps imparted much of their enthusiasm to the other troops, but we were not long in finding out that if General Lee had hopes that the decimated regiments of his army would be filled by the sons of Maryland he was doomed to a speedy and unqualified disappointment. However, before we had been in Maryland many hours, one enthusiastic citizen presented Jackson with a gigantic gray mare. She was a little heavy and awkward for a war-horse, but as

ROASTING GREEN CORN AT THE CAMP-FIRE

the general's "Little Sorrel" had a few days before been temporarily stolen, the present was a timely one, and he was not disposed to "look a gift horse in the mouth."

Yet the present proved almost a Trojan horse to him, for the next morning when he mounted his new steed and touched her with his spur the loyal and undisciplined beast reared straight into the air, and, standing erect for a moment, threw herself backward, horse and rider rolling upon the ground.

The general was stunned and severely bruised, and lay upon the ground for some time before he could be removed. He was then placed in an ambulance, where he rode during the day's march, having turned his command over to his brother-in-law, General D. H. Hill, the officer next in rank.

Early that day the army went into camp near Frederick, and Generals Lee, Longstreet, Jackson, and for a time "Jeb" Stuart, had their headquarters near one another in Best's grove. Hither in crowds came the good people of Frederick, especially the ladies, as to a fair. General Jackson, still suffering from his hurt, kept to his tent, busying himself with maps and official papers, and declined to see visitors. Once, however, when he had been called to General Lee's tent, two young girls waylaid him, paralyzed him with smiles and embraces and questions, and then jumped into their carriage and drove off rapidly, leaving him there, cap in hand, bowing, blushing, and speechless. But once safe in his tent he was seen no more that day.

★★★★★★

Lieutenant Robert Healy, of the 55th Virginia, in Stonewall
Jackson's command, tells the following incident of the march
into Maryland:

> The day before the corps waded the Potomac at White's
> Ford, they marched through Leesburg, where an old
> lady with upraised hands, and with tears in her eyes ex-
> claimed: 'The Lord bless your dirty ragged souls!' Lieu-
> tenant Healy adds: 'Don't think we were any dirtier than
> the rest, but it was our luck to get the blessing.'

★★★★★★

The next evening, Sunday, he went into Frederick for the first
time to attend church, and there being no service in the Presbyterian
Church he went to the German Reformed. As usual he fell asleep, but
this time more soundly than was his wont. His head sunk upon his
breast, his cap dropped from his hands to the floor, the prayers of the
congregation did not disturb him, and only the choir and the deep-
toned organ awakened him. Afterward I learned that the minister was
credited with much loyalty and courage because he had prayed for the
President of the United States in the very presence of Stonewall Jackson. Well, the general didn't hear the prayer, and if he had he would
doubtless have felt like replying as General Ewell did, when asked at
Carlisle, Pennsylvania, if he would permit the usual prayer for President Lincoln—"Certainly; I'm sure he needs it."

General Lee believed that Harper's Ferry would be evacuated as
soon as he interposed between it and Washington. But he did not
know that Halleck, and not McClellan, held command of it. When
he found that it was not evacuated he knew someone had blundered,
and took steps to capture the garrison and stores. On Tuesday, the
9th, he issued an order, directing General Jackson to move the next
morning, cross the Potomac near Sharpsburg, and envelop Harper's
Ferry on the Virginia side. In the same order, he directed General
McLaws to march on Harper's Ferry byway of Middletown and seize
Maryland Heights, and General Walker to cross the Potomac below
Harper's Ferry and take Loudoun Heights, all to be in position on the
12th, except Jackson, who was first to capture, if possible, the troops
at Martinsburg.

Early on the 10th Jackson was off. In Frederick, he asked for a map
of Chambersburg and its vicinity, and made many irrelevant inquiries
about roads and localities in the direction of Pennsylvania. To his staff,

who knew what little value these inquiries had, his questions only illustrated his well-known motto, "*Mystery, mystery is the secret of success.*" I was then assistant inspector-general on his staff, and also acting *aide-de-camp*. It was my turn this day to be intrusted with the knowledge of his purpose. Having finished this public inquiry, he took me aside, and after asking me about the different fords of the Potomac between Williamsport and Harper's Ferry, told me that he was ordered to capture the garrison at Harper's Ferry, and would cross either at Williamsport or Shepherdstown, as the enemy might or might not withdraw from Martinsburg. I did not then know of General Lee's order.

The troops being on the march, the general and staff rode rapidly out of town and took the head of the column. Just a few words here in regard to Mr. Whittier's touching poem, *Barbara Frietchie*. An old woman, by that now immortal name, did live in Frederick in those days, but she never saw General Jackson, and General Jackson never saw "Barbara Frietchie." I was with him every minute of the time he was in that city,—he was there only twice,—and nothing like the scene so graphically described by the poet ever happened. Mr. Whittier must have been misinformed as to the incident.

On the march that day, the captain of the cavalry advance, just ahead, had instructions to let no civilian go to the front, and we entered each village we passed before the inhabitants knew of our coming. In Middletown two very pretty girls, with ribbons of red, white, and blue floating from their hair, and small Union flags in their hands, rushed out of a house as we passed, came to the kerbstone, and with much laughter waved their flags defiantly in the face of the general. He bowed and raised his hat, and, turning with his quiet smile to his staff, said; "We evidently have no friends in this town." And this is about the way he would have treated Barbara Frietchie!

Having crossed South Mountain, at Turner's Gap, the command encamped for the night within a mile of Boonsboro'. Here General Jackson must determine whether he would go on to Williamsport or turn toward Shepherdstown. I at once rode into the village with a cavalryman to make some inquiries, but we ran into a squadron of Federal cavalry, who without ceremony proceeded to make war upon us. We retraced our steps, and although we did not stand upon the order of our going, a squad of them escorted us out of town with great rapidity. When I tried a couple of Parthian shots at them with my revolver, they returned them with interest, and shot a hole in my new hat, which, with the beautiful plume that a lady in Frederick had

JACKSON'S MEN WADING THE POTOMAC AT WHITE'S FORD

placed there, rolled in the dust.

This was of little moment, but at the end of the town, reaching the top of the hill, we discovered, just over it. General Jackson, walking slowly toward us, leading his horse. There was but one thing to do. Fortunately, the chase had become less vigorous, and, with a cry of command to unseen troops, we turned and charged the enemy. They, suspecting trouble, turned and fled, while the general quickly galloped to the rear. I recovered my hat and plume, and as I returned to camp I picked up the gloves which the general had dropped in mounting, and took them to him. Although he had sent a regiment of infantry to the front as soon as he went back, the only allusion he made to the incident was to express the opinion that I had a very fast horse.

The next morning, having learned that the Federal troops still occupied Martinsburg, General Jackson took the direct road to Williamsport. He there forded the Potomac, the troops now singing, and the bands playing, "Carry me back to ole Virginny!" We marched on Martinsburg. General A. P. Hill took the direct turnpike, while Jackson, with the rest of his command, followed a side road, so as to approach Martinsburg from the west, and encamped four miles from the town. His object was to drive General White, who occupied Martinsburg, toward Harper's Ferry, and thus "corral" all the Federal troops in that military pen.

As the Comte de Paris puts it:

> He organised a kind of grand hunting match through the lower valley of Virginia, driving all the Federal detachments before him and forcing them to crowd into the blind alley of Harper's Ferry.

Fatigued by the day's march, Jackson was persuaded by his host of the night to drink a whisky toddy—the only glass of spirits I ever saw him take. While mixing it leisurely, he remarked that he believed he liked the taste of whisky and brandy more than any soldier in the army; that they were more palatable to him than the most fragrant coffee, and for that reason, with others, he rarely tasted them.

The next morning the Confederates entered Martinsburg. Here the general was welcomed with great enthusiasm, and a great crowd hastened to the hotel to greet him. At first, he shut himself up in a room to write dispatches, but the demonstration became so persistent that he ordered the door to be opened. The crowd, chiefly ladies, rushed in and embarrassed the general with every possible outburst of affection, to which he could only reply, "Thank you, you're very kind." He gave them his autograph in books and on scraps of paper, cut a button from his coat for a little girl, and then submitted patiently to an attack by the others, who soon stripped the coat of nearly all the remaining buttons. But when they looked beseechingly at his hair, which was thin, he drew the line there, and managed to close the interview. These blandishments did not delay his movements, however, for in the afternoon he was off again.

On the 13th he invested Bolivar Heights and Harper's Ferry. On this day, General McClellan came into possession, by carelessness or accident, of General Lee's order of the 9th, and he was thus notified of the division of the Confederate Army and the intention to capture Harper's Ferry. From this moment, General Lee's army was in peril, imminent in proportion to the promptness with which the Federal commander might use the knowledge he thus obtained. The plans of the latter were quickly and skilfully made. Had they been executed more rapidly, or had Jackson been slower and less sure, the result must have been a disastrous one to us. But military critics disposed to

A GLIMPSE OF STONEWALL JACKSON.

censure General McClellan for not being equal to his opportunities should credit him with the embarrassment of his position. He had not been in command of this army two weeks.

It was a large army, but a heterogeneous one, with many old troops dispirited by recent defeat, and many new troops that had never been under fire. With such an army, a general as cautious as McClellan does not take great risks, nor put the safety of his army rashly "to the touch, to win or lose it all." General McClellan was inclined by nature to magnify the forces of the enemy, and had he known General Lee's weakness he would have ventured more. Yet when we remember what Pope had done and suffered just before, and what happened to Burnside and Hooker not long after, their friends can hardly sit in judgment upon McClellan.

On the afternoon of the 13th Colonel Miles, in command at Harper's Ferry, made the fatal mistake of withdrawing his troops from Maryland Heights, and giving them up to McLaws. Napier has said:

> He who wars walks in a mist through which the keenest eyes cannot always discern the right path.

But it does seem that Colonel Miles might have known that to abandon these heights under the circumstances was simply suicidal.

★★★★★★

General Julius White says in his report (*Official Records*, Vol. XIX., Pt. I., p. 523):

> It will be noticed that Colonel Ford claims to have been ordered by Colonel Miles to evacuate the heights. Colonel Miles, however, denied to me ever having given such an order, but said he gave orders that if it became necessary to abandon the heights the guns were to be spiked and dismounted.

See also General White's statements.

★★★★★★

Jackson met with so much delay in opening communication with McLaws and Walker, and ascertaining whether they were in position, that much of the 14th was consumed. But late in the afternoon A. P. Hill gained a foothold, with little resistance, well up on the enemy's left, and established some artillery at the base of Loudoun Heights and across the Shenandoah, so as to take the Federal line on Bolivar Heights in rear. (General Hill had been placed under arrest by General Jackson, before crossing the Potomac into Maryland, for disobedience of orders, and the command of his division devolved upon General Branch, who was killed a few days later at Antietam.

Believing a battle imminent, General Hill requested General Jackson to reinstate him in command of his division until the approaching engagement was over. No one could appreciate such an appeal more keenly than General Jackson, and he at once restored General Hill to his command. The work the Light Division did at Harper's Ferry and Sharpsburg proved the wisdom of Hill's request and of Jackson's compliance with it.)

During the 14th, while Jackson was fixing his clamps on Harper's Ferry, McClellan was pushing against Lee's divided forces at Turner's Gap. Hooker and Reno, under Burnside and under the eye of General McClellan, were fighting the battle of South Mountain against D. H. Hill and Longstreet. Here Reno and Garland were killed on opposite sides, and night ended the contest before it was decided. At the same time Franklin was forcing his way through Crampton's Gap, driving out Howell Cobb commanding his own brigade and one regiment of Semmes's brigade, both of McLaws's division, Parham's brigade of R. H. Anderson's division, and two regiments of Stuart's cavalry under Colonel Munford. The military complications were losing their simplicity.

Being advised of these movements, Jackson saw that his work must be done speedily. On Monday morning, at 3 o'clock, he sent me to the left to move Jones forward at first dawn, and to open on Bolivar Heights with all his artillery. This feint was executed promptly and produced confusion on the enemy's right. Troops were moved to strengthen it. Then the guns from Maryland and Loudoun Heights opened fire, and very soon, off on our right, the battle-flags of A. P. Hill rose on Bolivar Heights, and Harper's Ferry was doomed. Returning, I found General Jackson at the church in the wood on the Bolivar and Halltown turnpike, and just as I joined him a white flag was raised on Bolivar and all the firing ceased.

Under instructions from General Jackson, I rode up the pike and into the enemy's lines to ascertain the purpose of the white flag. Near the top of the hill I met General White and staff and told him my mission. He replied that Colonel Miles had been mortally wounded, that he was in command and desired to have an interview with General Jackson. Just then General Hill came up from the direction of his line, and at his request I conducted them to General Jackson, whom I found sitting on his horse where I had left him.

LIEUTENANT-GENERAL AMBROSE P. HILL, C. S. A.

He was not, as the Comte de Paris says, leaning against a tree asleep, but exceedingly wide-awake.

The contrast in appearances there presented was striking. General White, riding a handsome black horse, was carefully dressed and had on untarnished gloves, boots, and sword. His staff were equally comely in costume. On the other hand, General Jackson was the dingiest, worst-dressed, and worst-mounted general that a warrior who cared for good looks and style would wish to surrender to. The surrender was unconditional, and then General Jackson turned the matter over to General A. P. Hill, who allowed General White the same liberal terms that Grant afterward gave Lee at Appomattox.

★★★★★★

Of the expectations of Jackson's men, Lieutenant Robert Healy says, in a letter written in 1886:

> On the evening of the 14th we took position within six hundred yards of a Federal fort on Bolivar Heights. We lay that night in a deep ravine, perpendicular to the Shenandoah. The next morning by dawn I crept up the hill to see how the land lay. A few strides brought me to the edge of an abatis which extended solidly for two hundred yards, a narrow bare field being between the abatis and the foot of the fort, which was garnished with thirty guns. They were searching the abatis lazily with

grape-shot, which flew uncomfortably near at times. I thought I had never seen a more dangerous trap in my life. The order had been given that we were to charge at sunrise. I went back, and Austin Brockenbrough asked, 'How is it?' '

Well,' said I, 'we'll say our prayers and go in like men.'

'Not as bad as that?'

'Every bit; see for yourself.'

He went up and came back looking very grave. Meanwhile from the east, north-west, and north-east our cannon opened and were answered by the Federal guns from Bolivar. Heights. We were down in a ravine; we could see nothing; we could only hear. Presently, along our line came the words, 'Prepare to charge!' We moved steadily up the hill; the sun had just risen; someone said: 'Colonel, what is that on the fort?'

'Halt,' cried the colonel, 'they have surrendered.' A glad shout burst from ten thousand men. We got into the place as soon as we could, but the way was so difficult it took us a half hour.

★★★★★★

The fruits of the surrender were 12,520 prisoners (*Official Records*), 13,000 arms, 73 pieces of artillery, and several hundred wagons.

General Jackson, after sending a brief dispatch to General Lee announcing the capitulation, rode up to Bolivar and down into Harper's Ferry. The curiosity in the Union Army to see him was so great that the soldiers lined the sides of the road. Many of them uncovered as he passed, and he invariably returned the salute. One man had an echo of response all about him when he said aloud:

Boys, he's not much for looks, but if we'd had him we wouldn't have been caught in this trap!

General Jackson lost little time in contemplating his victory. When night came, he started for Shepherdstown with J. R. Jones and Lawton, leaving directions to McLaws and Walker to follow the next morning. He left A. P. Hill behind to finish up with Harper's Ferry. His first order had been to take position at Shepherdstown to cover Lee's crossing into Virginia, but, whether at his own suggestion or not, the order was changed, and after daylight on the 16th he crossed the Potomac there and joined Longstreet at Sharpsburg. General McClellan had, by that time, nearly all his army in position on the east bank of the Antietam, and General Lee was occupying the irregular range of high ground to the west of it, with the Potomac in his rear. Except some sparring between Hooker and Hood on our left, the 16th was allowed to pass without battle, fortunately for us. In the new dispositions of that evening, Jackson was placed on the left of Lee's army. (See map further on)

The first onset, early on the morning of the 17th, told what the day would be. The impatient Hooker, with the divisions of Meade, Doubleday, and Ricketts, struck the first blow, and Jackson's old division caught it and struck back again. Between such foes the battle soon waxed hot. Step by step and marking each step with dead, the thin Confederate line was pushed back to the wood around the Dunker Church. Here Lawton, Starke (commanding in place of Jones, already wounded), and D. H. Hill with part of his division, engaged Meade. And now in turn the Federals halted and fell back, and left their dead by Dunker Church. Next Mansfield entered the fight, and beat with resistless might on Jackson's people. The battle here grew angry and bloody. Starke was killed, Lawton wounded, and nearly all their general and field officers had fallen; the sullen Confederate line again fell back, killing Mansfield and wounding Hooker, Crawford, and Hartsuff.

And now D. H. Hill led in the rest, of his division; Hood also took part, to the right and left, front and rear of Dunker Church. The Federal line was again driven back, while artillery added its din to the incessant rattle of musketry. Then Sumner, with the fresh division of Sedgwick, re-formed the Federal line and renewed the offensive. Hood was driven back, and Hill partly; the Dunker Church wood was passed, the field south of it entered, and the Confederate left turned. Just then McLaws, hurrying from Harper's Ferry, came upon the field, and hurled his men against the victorious Sedgwick. He drove Sedgwick back into the Dunker wood and beyond it, into the open ground.

Farther to our right, the pendulum of battle had been swinging to and fro, with D. H. Hill and R. H. Anderson hammering away at French and Richardson, until the sunken road became historic as "bloody lane." Richardson was mortally wounded and Hancock assumed command of his division.

For a while there was a lull in the storm. It was early in the day, but hours are fearfully long in battle. About noon Franklin, with Slocum

BRIGADIER-GENERAL WILLIAM E. STARKE—FROM A TINTYPE.

In the cannonade which began with dawn of the 17th, General J. R. Jones, commanding the left division of Jackson, was stunned and injured by a shell which exploded directly over his head. General Starke was directed to take command of the division, which he led against Hooker, and a half-hour later he fell pierced by three minie-balls. Of that terrible struggle Stonewall Jackson says in his report: "The carnage on both sides was terrific. At this early hour General Starke was killed. Colonel Douglass, commanding Lawton's brigade, was also killed. General Lawton, commanding division, and Colonel Walker, commanding brigade, were severely wounded. More than half of the brigades of Lawton and Hays were either killed or wounded, and more than a third of Trimble's, and all the regimental commanders in those brigades, except two, were killed or wounded."

and W. F. Smith, marched upon the field to join the unequal contest. Smith tried his luck and was repulsed. Sumner then ordered a halt. Jackson's fight was over, and a strange silence reigned around Dunker Church.

General Lee had not visited the left that day. As usual he trusted to Jackson to fight his own battle and work out salvation in his own way. How well he did it, against the ablest and fiercest of McClellan's lieutenants, history has told.

During all this time Longstreet, stripped of his troops,—sent to the help of Jackson,—held the right almost alone, with his eye on the centre. He was now called into active work on his own front, for there were no unfought troops in Lee's army at Sharpsburg; every soldier on that field tasted battle.

General Burnside, with his corps of fourteen thousand men, had been lying all day beyond the bridge which now bears his name. Ordered to cross at 8 o'clock he managed to get over at 1, and by 3 was ready to advance. (See General Cox's statements). He moved against the hill which D. R. Jones held with his little division of 2500 men. Longstreet was watching this advance. Jackson was at General Lee's headquarters on a knoll in rear of Sharpsburg. A. P. Hill was coming, but had not arrived, and it was apparent that Burnside must be stayed, if at all, with artillery. One of the sections, transferred to the right from Jackson at the request of General Lee, was of the Rockbridge Artillery, and as it galloped by, the youngest son of the general-in-chief, Robert E. Lee, Jr., a private at the guns, black with the grime and powder of a long day's fight, stopped a moment to salute his father and then rushed after his gun. Where else in this war was the son of a commanding general a private in the ranks?

Going to put this section in place, I saw Burmside's heavy line move up the hill, and the earth seemed to tremble beneath their tread. It was a splendid and fearful sight, but for them to beat back Jones's feeble line was scarcely war. The artillery tore, but did not stay them. They pressed forward until Sharpsburg was uncovered and Lee's line of retreat was at their mercy. But then, just then, A. P. Hill, picturesque in his red battle-shirt, with 3 of his brigades, 2500 men, who had marched that day 17 miles from Harper's Ferry and had waded the Potomac, appeared upon the scene. Tired and footsore, the men forgot their woes in that supreme moment, and with no breathing time braced themselves to meet the coming shock. They met it and stayed it. The blue line staggered and hesitated, and, hesitating, was lost.

At the critical moment A. P. Hill was always at his strongest. Quickly advancing his battle-flags, his line moved forward, Jones's troops rallied on him, and in the din of musketry and artillery on either flank the Federals broke over the field. Hill did not wait for his other brigades, but held the vantage gained until Burnside was driven back to the Antietam and under the shelter of heavy guns. The day was done. Again A. P. Hill, as at Manassas, Harper's Ferry, and elsewhere, had struck with the right hand of Mars. No wonder that both Lee and Jackson, when, in the delirium of their last moments on earth, they stood again to battle, saw the form of A. P. Hill leading his columns on; but it is a wonder and a shame that the grave of this valiant Virginian in Hollywood cemetery has not a stone to mark it and keep it from oblivion.

The battle at Sharpsburg was the result of unforeseen circumstances and not of deliberate purpose. It was one of the bloodiest of the war, and a defeat for both armies. The prestige of the day was with Lee, but when on the night of the 18th he recrossed into Virginia, although, as the Comte de Paris says, he "*left not a single trophy of his nocturnal retreat in the hands of the enemy*," he left the prestige of the result with McClellan. And yet when it is known that General McClellan had 87,000 troops at hand, and. General Lee fought the battle with less than 35,000, (see notes earlier for strength of forces on each side), an army depleted by battles, weakened by privations, broken down by marching, and "ruined by straggling," it was unquestionably on the Confederate side the best-fought battle of the war.

North of the Dunker Church—A Union Charge Through the Cornfield.

The Battle of Antietam

By Jacob D. Cox, Major-General, U. S. V.

It was not till some time past noon of the 15th of September that, the way being clear for the Ninth Corps at South Mountain, we marched through Fox's gap to the Boonsboro' and Sharpsburg turnpike, and along this road till we came up in rear of Sumner's command. Hooker's corps, which was part of the right wing (Burnside's), had been in the advance, and had moved off from the turnpike to the right near Keedysville. I was with the Kanawha Division, assuming that my temporary command of the corps ended with the battle on the mountain.

When we approached the line of hills bordering the Antietam, we received orders to turn off the road to the left, and halted our battalions closed in mass. It was now about 3 o'clock in the afternoon. McClellan, as it seemed, had just reached the field, and was surrounded by a group of his principal officers, most of whom I had never seen before. I rode up with General Burnside, dismounted, and was very cordially greeted by General McClellan. He and Burnside were evidently on terms of most intimate friendship and familiarity. He introduced me to the officers I had not known before, referring pleasantly to my service with him in Ohio and West Virginia, putting me upon an easy footing with them in a very agreeable and genial way.

We walked up the slope of the ridge before us, and looking westward from its crest the whole field of the coming battle was before us. Immediately in front the Antietam wound through the hollow, the hills rising gently on both sides. In the background on our left was the village of Sharpsburg, with fields enclosed by stone fences in front of it. At its right was a bit of wood (since known as the West Wood), with the little Dunker Church standing out white and sharp against it. Farther to the right and left the scene was closed in by wooded

157

UNION SIGNAL STATION ON ELK MOUNTAIN,
FIVE OR SIX MILES SOUTH-EAST OF SHARPSBURG.

ridges with open farm lands between, the whole making as pleasing and prosperous a landscape as can easily be imagined. We made a large group as we stood upon the hill, and it was not long before we attracted the enemy's attention. A puff of white smoke from a knoll on the right of the Sharpsburg road was followed by the screaming of a shell over our heads. McClellan directed that all but one or two should retire behind the ridge, while he continued the reconnoissance, walking slowly to the right.

I noted with satisfaction the cool and business-like air with which he made his examination under fire. The Confederate artillery was answered by a battery, and a lively cannonade ensued on both sides, though without any noticeable effect. The enemy's position was revealed, and he was evidently in force on both sides of the turnpike in front of Sharpsburg, covered by the undulations of the rolling ground which hid his infantry from our sight.

The examination of the enemy's position and the discussion of it continued till near the close of the day. Orders were then given for the Ninth Corps to move to the left, keeping off the road, which was occupied by other troops. We moved through fields and farm lands, an hour's march in the dusk of the evening, going into bivouac about a mile south of the Sharpsburg bridge, and in rear of the hills bordering the Antietam.

On Tuesday, September 16th, we confidently expected a battle, and I kept with my division. In the afternoon I saw General Burnside, and learned from him that McClellan had determined to let Hooker make a movement on our extreme right to turn Lee's position. Burnside's manner in speaking of this implied that he thought it was done at Hooker's solicitation and through his desire, openly evinced, to be independent in command.

I urged Burnside to assume the immediate command of the corps and allow me to lead only my own division. He objected that as he had been announced as commander of the right wing of the army composed of two corps (his own and Hooker's), he was unwilling to waive his precedence or to assume that Hooker was detached for anything more than a temporary purpose. I pointed out that Reno's staff had been granted leave of absence to take the body of their chief to Washington, and that my division staff was too small for corps duty; but he met this by saying that he would use his staff for this purpose and help me in every way he could, till the crisis of the campaign should be over.

The 16th passed without serious fighting, though there was desultory cannonading and picket firing. It was hard to restrain our men from showing themselves on the crest of the long ridge in front of us, and whenever they did so they drew the fire from some of the enemy's batteries, to which ours would respond. In the afternoon McClellan reconnoitered the line of the Antietam near us, Burnside being with him. As the result of this we were ordered to change our positions at nightfall, staff-officers being sent to guide each division to its new camp. Rodman's division went half a mile to the left, where a country road led to a ford in a great bend in the Antietam curving deeply into the enemy's side of the stream.

★★★★★★

The information obtained from the neighbourhood was that no fords of the Antietam were passable at that time, except one about halfway between the two upper bridges and another less than half a mile below Burnside's Bridge. We, however, found during the engagement another ford a short distance above

159

Burnside's Bridge, The inquiry and reconnoissance for the fords was made by engineer officers of the general staff, and our orders were based on their reports.—J. D. C.

★★★★★★

J Sturgis's division was placed on the sides of the road leading to the stone bridge, since known as Burnside's Bridge (below the Sharpsburg bridge). Willcox's was put in reserve in rear of Sturgis. My own division was divided, Scammon's brigade going with Rodman, and Crook's going with Sturgis. Crook was ordered to take the advance in crossing the bridge, in case we should be ordered to attack. This selection was made by Burnside himself, as a compliment to the division for the vigour of its assault at South Mountain. While we were moving, we heard Hooker's guns far off on the right and front, and the cannonade continued an hour or more after it became dark.

The morning of Wednesday, the 17th, broke fresh and fair. The men were astir at dawn, getting breakfast and preparing for a day of battle. The artillery opened on both sides as soon as it was fairly light, and the positions which had been assigned us in the dusk of the evening were found to be exposed in some places to the direct fire of the Confederate guns, Rodman's division suffering more than the others. Fairchild's brigade alone reported thirty-six casualties before they could find cover. It was not till 7 o'clock that orders came to advance toward the creek as far as could be done without exposing the men to unnecessary loss. Rodman was directed to acquaint himself with the situation of the ford in front of him, and Sturgis to seek the best means of approach to the stone bridge. All were then to remain in readiness to obey further orders.

When these arrangements had been made, I rode to the position Burnside had selected for himself, which was upon a high knoll northeast of the Burnside Bridge, near a hay-stack which was a prominent landmark. Nearby was Benjamin's battery of 20-pounder Parrotts, and a little farther still to the right, on the same ridge, General Sturgis had sent in Durell's battery. These were exchanging shots with the enemy's guns opposite, and had the advantage in range and weight of metal.

Whatever the reason, McClellan had adopted a plan of battle which practically reduced Sumner and Burnside to the command of one corps each, while Hooker had been sent far off on the right front, followed later by Mansfield, but without organising the right wing as a unit so that one commander could give his whole attention to handling it with vigour. In his preliminary report, made before he was

160

DOUBLEDAY'S DIVISION OF HOOKER'S CORPS CROSSING THE UPPER FORDS OF THE ANTIETAM.

relieved from command, McClellan says:

> The design was to make the main attack upon the enemy's
> left—at least to create a diversion in favour of the main at-
> tack, with the hope of something more, by assailing the enemy's
> right——and, as soon as one or both of the flank movements
> were fully successful, to attack their centre with any reserve I
> might then have in hand.

McClellan's report covering his whole career in the war, dated
August 4th, 1863 (and published February, 1864, after warm contro-
versies had arisen and he had become a political character), modifies
the above statement in some important particulars. It says:

> My plan for the impending general engagement was to attack
> the enemy's left with the corps of Hooker and Mansfield, sup-
> ported by Sumner's, and if necessary by Franklin's, and as soon
> as matters looked favourably there to move the corps of Burn-
> side against the enemy's extreme right upon the ridge running
> to the south and rear of Sharpsburg, and having carried their
> position, to press along the crest toward our right, and when-
> ever either of these flank movements should be successful, to
> advance our centre with all the forces then disposable.

The opinion I got from Burnside as to the part the Ninth Corps
was to take was fairly consistent with the design first quoted, *viz.*,
that when the attack by Sumner, Hooker, and Franklin should be
progressing favourably, we were "to create a diversion in favour of the
main attack, with the hope of something more." It would also appear
probable that Hooker's movement was at first intended to be made
by his corps alone, taken up by Sumner's two corps as soon as he was
ready to attack, and shared in by Franklin if he reached the field in
time, thus making a simultaneous oblique attack from our right by
the whole army except Porter's corps, which was in reserve, and the
Ninth Corps, which was to create the "diversion" on our left and prevent the enemy from stripping his right to re-enforce his left.

It is hardly disputable that this would have been a better plan than
the one actually carried out. Certainly the assumption that the Ninth
Corps could cross the Antietam alone at the only place on the field
where the Confederates had their line immediately upon the stream
which must be crossed under fire by two narrow heads of column, and
could then turn to the right along the high ground occupied by the

The Sharpsburg Bridge over the Antietam.

hostile army before that army had been broken or seriously shaken elsewhere, is one which would hardly be made till time had dimmed the remembrance of the actual positions of Lee's divisions upon the field.

The evidence that the plan did not originally include the wide separation of two corps to the right, to make the extended turning movement, is found in Hooker's incomplete report, and in the wide interval in time between the marching of his corps and that of Mansfield. Hooker was ordered to cross the Antietam at about 2 o'clock in the afternoon of the 16th by the bridge in front of Keedysville and the ford below it. He says that after his troops were over and in march, he rode back to McClellan, who told him that he might call for re-enforcements and that when they came they should be under his command.

Somewhat later McClellan rode forward with his staff to observe the progress making, and Hooker again urged the necessity of re-enforcements. Yet Sumner did not receive orders to send Mansfield to support Hooker till evening, and the Twelfth Corps marched only half an hour before midnight, reaching its bivouac, about a mile and a half in rear of that of Hooker, at 2 a. m. of the 17th. Sumner was also ordered to be in readiness to march with the Second Corps an hour before day, but his orders to move did not reach him till nearly half-past 7 in the morning.

GERMAN REFORMED CHURCH, KEEDYSVILLE, USED AS UNION HOSPITAL.

By this time. Hooker had fought his battle, had been repulsed, and later in the morning was carried wounded from the field. Mansfield had fallen before his corps was deployed, and General Alpheus S. Williams who succeeded him was fighting a losing battle at all points but one—where Greene's division held the East Wood.

After crossing the Antietam, Hooker had shaped his course to the westward, aiming to reach the ridge upon which the Hagerstown turnpike runs, and which is the dominant feature of the landscape. This ridge is some two miles distant from the Antietam, and for the first mile of the way no resistance was met. However, Hooker's progress had been observed by the enemy, and Hood's two brigades were taken from the centre and passed to the left of D. H. Hill. Here they occupied an open wood (since known as the East Wood), north-east of the Dunker Church. Hooker was now trying to approach the Confederate positions, Meade's division of the Pennsylvania Reserves being in the advance.

A sharp skirmishing combat ensued and artillery was also brought into action on both sides, the engagement continuing till after dark. On our side Seymour's brigade had been chiefly engaged, and had felt the enemy so vigorously that Hood supposed he had repulsed a serious effort to take the wood. Hooker was, however, aiming to pass quite beyond the flank, and kept his other divisions north of the hollow beyond the wood, and upon the ridge which reaches the turnpike near the largest re-entrant bend of the Potomac, which is here only half a mile distant.

Here he bivouacked upon the northern slopes of the ridge, Doubleday's division resting with its right upon the turnpike, Ricketts's division upon the left of Doubleday, and Meade covering the front of both with the skirmishers of Seymour's brigade. Between Meade's skirmishers and the ridge were the farmhouse and barn of J. Poffenberger on the east of the road, where Hooker made his own quarters for the night. Half a mile farther in front was the farm of D. R. Miller, the dwelling on the east, and the barn surrounded by stacks on the west of the road.

★★★★★★

Hooker's unfinished report says he slept in the barn of D. R. Miller, but he places it on the east of the road, and the spot is fully identified as Poffenberger's by General Gibbon, who commanded the right brigade, and by Major Rufus R. Dawes

EXPLANATION

UNION CONFEDERATE

RESERVE CAVALRY

CONFED LINE EVENING SEP.16

SEP.17

SCALE OF ONE MILE

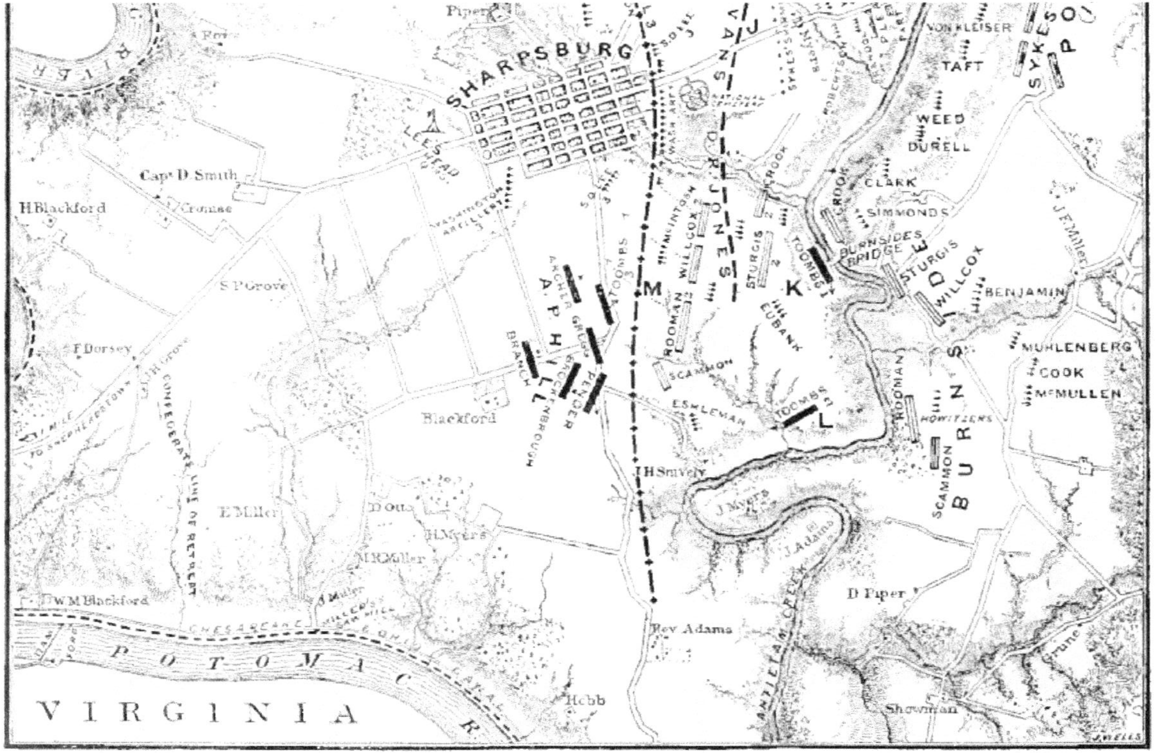
SHARPSBURG
VIRGINIA
POTOMAC R.
RIVER
ANTIETAM CREEK
CHESAPEAKE & OHIO CANAL
CONFEDERATE LINE OF RETREAT
TO SHEPHERDSTOWN
BURNSIDES BRIDGE
NATIONAL CEMETERY
LEE'S HEAD QRS.
WASHINGTON ARTILLERY
A. P. HILL
ARCHER
GREGG
PENDER
BRANCH
BROCKENBROUGH
TOOMBS
D. R. JONES
EUBANK
ESHLEMAN
BURNS
RODMAN
SCAMMON
HOWITZERS
STURGIS
WILLCOX
CROOK
BENJAMIN
MUHLENBERG
COOK
McMULLEN
CLARK
SIMMONDS
WEED
DURELL
TAFT
VON KLEISER
SYKES
McINTOSH
Capt. D. Smith
H. Blackford
Crouse
S. P. Grove
F. Dorsey
Blackford
E. Miller
H. Myers
M. R. Miller
Dr. W. M. Blackford
I. H. Snively
J. Myers
J. Adams
D. Piper
Rev. Adams
Hebb
Showman
J. F. Miller
Piper
J. WELLS

THE FIELD OF ANTIETAM.

On the afternoon of September 16th, Hooker's corps crossed at the two fords and the bridge north of McClellan's headquarters.

A.—From near sunset till dark Hooker engaged Hood's division (of Longstreet's corps) about the "East Wood," marked A on the map. Hood was relieved by two brigades of Jackson's corps, which was in and behind the Dunker Church wood (or West Wood), C.

B.—At dawn on the 17th, Hooker and Jackson began a terrible contest which raged in and about the famous corn-field, B, and in the woods, A and C. Jackson's reserves regained the corn-field. Hartsuff's brigade, of Hooker's corps, and Mansfield's corps charged through the corn-field into the Dunker Church wood, General Mansfield being mortally wounded in front of the East Wood.

C.—Summer's corps formed line of battle in the center, Sedgwick's division facing the East Wood, through which it charged over the corn-field again, and through Dunker Church wood to the edge of the fields beyond. McLaws's division (of Longstreet's corps), just arrived from Harper's Ferry, assisted in driving out Sedgwick, who was forced to retreat northward by the Hagerstown pike.

Jackson, with the aid of Hood, and a part of D. H. Hill's division, again cleared the Dunker Church wood. J. G. Walker's division, taken from the extreme right of the Confederate line, charged in support of Jackson and Hood.

D.—About the time that Sedgwick charged, French and Richardson, of Sumner's corps, dislodged D. H. Hill's line from Roulette's house.

E.—Hill re-formed in the sunken road, since known as the "Bloody Lane," where his position was carried by French and Richardson, the latter being mortally wounded in the corn-field, E.

F.—Irwin and Brooks, of Franklin's corps, moved to the support of French and Richardson. At the point F, Irwin's brigade was repelled.

G.—D. H. Hill, reënforced by R. H. Anderson's division of Longstreet's corps, fought for the ground about Piper's house.

H.—Stuart attempted a flank movement north of the Dunker Church wood, but was driven back by the thirty guns under Doubleday.

J.—Pleasonton, with a part of his cavalry and several batteries, crossed the Boonsboro' bridge as a flank support to Richardson, and to Burnside on the south. Several battalions of regulars from Porter's corps came to his assistance and made their way well up to the hill which is now the National Cemetery.

K.—Toombs (of Longstreet) had defended the lower bridge until Burnside moved Rodman and Scammon to the fords below.

L.—Then Toombs hurried south to protect the Confederate flank. Sturgis and Crook charged across the Burnside bridge and gained the heights. Toombs was driven away from the fords.

M.—After 3 o'clock, Burnside's lines, being re-formed, completed the defeat of D. R. Jones's division (of Longstreet), and on the right gained the outskirts of Sharpsburg. Toombs, and the arriving brigades of A. P. Hill, of Jackson's corps, saved the village and regained a part of the lost ground.

(afterward Brevet Brigadier-General), both of whom subsequently visited the field and determined the positions.—J. D. C.

★★★★★★

Mansfield's corps, marching as it did late in the night, kept farther to the right than Hooker's, but moved on a nearly parallel course and bivouacked upon the farm of another J. Poffenberger near the road which, branching from the Hagerstown turnpike at the Dunker Church, intersects the one running from Keedysville through Smoketown to the same turnpike about a mile north of Hooker's position.

On the Confederate side, Hood's division had been so severely handled that it was replaced by Jackson's (commanded by J. R. Jones), which, with Ewell's, had been led to the field from Harper's Ferry by Jackson, reaching Sharpsburg in the afternoon of the 16th. These divisions were formed on the left of D. H. Hill and almost at right angles to his line, crossing the turnpike and facing northward. Hood's division, on being relieved, was placed in reserve near the Dunker Church, and spent part of the night in cooking rations, of which its supply had been short for a day or two. The combatants on both sides slept upon their arms, well knowing that the dawn would bring bloody work.

When day broke on Wednesday morning, the 17th, Hooker, looking south from the Poffenberger farm along the turnpike, saw a gently rolling landscape, of which the commanding point was the Dunker Church, whose white brick walls appeared on the west side of the road backed by the foliage of the West Wood, which came toward him, filling a slight hollow which ran parallel to the turnpike, with a single row of fields between. Beyond the Miller house and barns, the ground dipped into a little depression. Beyond this was seen a large cornfield between the East Wood and the turnpike, rising again to the higher level.

There was, however, another small dip beyond, which could not be seen from Hooker's position; and on the second ridge, near the church, and extending across the turnpike eastward into the East Wood, could be seen the Confederate line of gray, partly sheltered by piles of rails taken from the fences. They seemed to Hooker to be at the farther side of the cornfield and at the top of the first rise of ground beyond Miller's. It was plain that the high ground about the little white church was the key of the enemy's position, and if that could be carried Hooker's task would be well done.

The Confederates opened the engagement by a rapid fire from a

THE PRY HOUSE, GENERAL MCCLELLAN'S HEADQUARTERS
AT THE BATTLE OF ANTIETAM

battery near the East Wood as soon as it was light, and Hooker answered the challenge by an immediate order for his line to advance.
Doubleday's division was in two lines. Gibbon's and Phelps's brigades
in front, supported by Patrick and Hofmann. Gibbon had the right
and guided upon the turnpike. Patrick held a small wood in his rear,
which is upon both sides of the road a little north of Miller's house.
Some of Meade's men were supposed to be in the northernmost extension of the West Wood, and thus to cover Gibbon's right flank as
he advanced. Part of Battery B, 4th United States Artillery (Gibbon's
own battery), was run forward to Miller's barn and stack-yard on the
right of the road, and fired over the heads of the advancing regiments.
Other batteries were similarly placed more to the left.

The line moved swiftly forward through Miller's orchard and
kitchen garden, breaking through a stout picket fence on the near side,
down into the moist ground of the hollow, and up through the corn,
which was higher than their heads, and shut out everything from view.
At the southern side of the field they came to a low fence, beyond
which was an open field, at the farther side of which was the enemy's

line. But Gibbon's right, covered by the corn, had outmarched the left, which had been exposed to a terrible fire, and the direction taken had been a little oblique, so that the right wing of the 6th Wisconsin, the flanking regiment, had crossed the turnpike and was suddenly assailed by a sharp fire from the West Wood on its flank.

They swung back into the road, lying down along the high, stout post-and-rail fence, keeping up their fire by shooting between the rails. Leaving this little band to protect them right, the main line, which had come up on the left, leaped the fence at the south edge of the corn-field and charged across the open at the enemy in front. But the concentrated fire of artillery and musketry was more than they could bear. Men fell by scores and hundreds, and the thinned lines gave way and ran for the shelter of the corn. They were rallied in the hollow on the north side of the field. The enemy had rapidly extended his left under cover of the West Wood, and now made a dash at the right flank and at Gibbon's exposed guns. His men on the right faced by that flank and followed him bravely, though with little order, in a dash at the Confederates, who were swarming out of the wood. The gunners double-charged the cannon with canister, and under a terrible fire of both artillery and rifles the enemy broke and sought shelter.

Patrick's brigade had come up in support of Gibbon, and was sent across the turnpike into the West Wood to cover that flank. They pushed forward, the enemy retiring, until they were in advance of the principal fine in the cornfield, upon which the Confederates were now advancing. Patrick faced his men to the left, parallel to the edge of the wood and to the turnpike, and poured his fire into the flank of the enemy, following it by a charge through the field and up to the fence along the road. Again, the Confederates were driven back, but only to push in again by way of these woods, forcing Patrick to resume his original fine of front and to retire to the cover of a ledge at right angles to the road near Gibbon's guns.

Farther to the left Phelps's and Hofmann's brigades had had similar experience, pushing forward nearly to the Confederate fines, and being driven back with great loss when they charged over open ground against the enemy. Ricketts's division entered the edge of the East Wood; but here, at the salient angle, where D. H. Hill and Lawton joined, the enemy held the position stubbornly, and the repulse of Doubleday's division made Ricketts glad to hold even the edge of the East Wood, as the right of the line was driven back.

It was now about 7 o'clock, and Mansfield's corps (the Twelfth) was approaching, for that officer had called his men to arms at the first sound of Hooker's battle and had marched to his support. The corps consisted of two divisions, Williams's and Greene's. It contained a number of new and undrilled regiments, and in hastening to the field in columns of battalions in mass, proper intervals for deployment had not been preserved, and time was necessarily lost before the troops could be put in line. General Mansfield fell mortally wounded before the deployment was complete, and the command devolved on General Williams. Williams had only time to take the most general directions from Hooker, when the latter also was wounded.

★★★★★★

Of the early morning fight in the cornfield, General Hooker says in his report:

> We had not proceeded far before I discovered that a heavy force of the enemy had taken possession of a cornfield (I have since learned about a thirty-acre field), in my immediate front, and from the sun's rays falling on their bayonets projecting above the corn could see that the field was filled with the enemy, with arms in their hands, standing apparently at 'support arms.' Instructions were immediately given for the assemblage of all of my spare batteries near at hand, of which I think there were five or six, to spring into battery on the right of this field, and to open with canister at once. In the time, I am writing every stalk of corn in the northern and greater part of the field was cut as closely as could have been done with a knife, and the slain lay in rows precisely as they had stood in their ranks a few moments before.
>
> It was never my fortune to witness a more bloody, dismal battlefield. Those that escaped fled in the opposite direction from our advance, and sought refuge behind the trees, fences, and stone ledges nearly on a line with the Dunker Church, etc., as there was no resisting this torrent of death-dealing missives. . . . The whole morning had been one of unusual animation to me and fraught with the grandest events. The conduct of my troops was sublime, and the occasion almost lifted me to the skies, and its memories will ever remain near me. My command followed the fugitives closely until we had passed the cornfield a quarter of a mile or more, when I was re-

moved from my saddle in the act of falling out of it from loss of blood, having previously been struck without my knowledge.

★★★★★★

The Twelfth Corps attack seems to have been made obliquely to that of Hooker, and facing more to the westward, for General Williams speaks of the post- and rail-fences along the turnpike being a great obstruction in their front. Greene's division, on his left, moved along the ridge leading to the East Wood, taking as the guide for his extreme left the line of the burning house of Mumma, which had been set on fire by D. H. Hill's men. Doubleday, in his report, notices this change of direction of Williams's division, which had relieved him, and says Williams's brigades were swept away by a fire from their left and front, from behind rocky ledges they could not see. (Both in the West and East Wood and on the ground south of the East Wood the Confederates were protected by outcroppings of rocks, which served as natural breastworks).

★★★★★★

General Mansfield was mortally wounded early in the action. In the *History of the 1st, 10th, 29th Maine Regiments*, Major John M. Gould, who was Adjutant of the 10th Maine regiment, at Antietam, in Crawford's First Brigade, of A. S. Williams's First Division, of Mansfield's Twelfth Corps, gives the following circumstantial account of this event:

> The Confederate force in our front showed no colours. They appeared to be somewhat detached from and in advance of the main rebel line, and were about where the left of General Duryea's brigade might be supposed to have retreated. To General Mansfield we appeared to be firing into Duryea's troops; therefore, he beckoned to us to cease firing, and as this was the very last thing we proposed to do, the few who saw him did not understand what his motions meant, and so no attention was paid to him.
>
> He now rode down the hill from the 128th Pennsylvania, and passing quickly through H, A, K, E, I, G, and D (of the 10th Maine), ordering them to cease firing, he halted in front of C, at the earnest remonstrances of Captain Jordan and Sergeant Burnham, who asked him to see the gray coats of the enemy, and pointed out par-

ticular men of them who were then aiming their rifles at us and at him. The general was convinced, and remarked 'Yes, yes, you are right,' and was almost instantly hit. He turned and attempted to put his horse over the rails, but the animal had also been severely wounded and could not go over. Thereupon the general dismounted, and a gust of wind blowing open his coat we saw that he was wounded in the body. Sergeant Joe Merritt, Storer Knight, and I took the general to the rear, assisted for a while by a negro cook from Hooker's corps. We put the general into an ambulance in the woods in front of which we had deployed, and noticed that General Gordon was just at that moment posting the 107th New York in their front edge.

Colonel Jacob Higgins, 125th Pennsylvania regiment, commanding the brigade after Crawford was wounded, reports that some of his men carried General Mansfield "off the field on their muskets until a blanket was procured." General George H, Gordon, commanding the Third Brigade of this division, which formed on Crawford's left, reports that "General Mansfield had been mortally wounded . . . while making a bold reconnoissance of the woods through which we had just dashed."

★★★★★★

Our officers were deceived in part as to the extent and direction of the enemy's line by the fact that the Confederate cavalry commander, Stuart, had occupied a commanding hill west of the pike and beyond our right flank, and from this position, which, in fact, was considerably detached from the Confederate line, he used his batteries with such effect as to produce the belief that a continuous line extended from this point to the Dunker Church. (Stuart says he had batteries from all parts of Jackson's command, and mentions Poague's, Pegram's, and Carrington's, besides Pelham's which was attached to the cavalry.

He also says he was supported part of the time by Early's brigade; afterward by one regiment of it, the 13th Virginia). Our true lines of attack were convergent ones, the right sweeping southward along the pike and through the narrow strip of the West Wood, while the division which drove the enemy from the East Wood should move upon the commanding ground around the church. This error of direction was repeated with disastrous effect a little later, when Sumner came on the ground with Sedgwick's corps.

Major-General Joseph K. F. Mansfield

When Mansfield's corps came on the field, Meade, who succeeded Hooker, (the order assigning Meade to command is dated 1:25 p. m.), withdrew the First Corps to the ridge north of Poffenberger's, where it had bivouacked the night before. It had suffered severely, having lost 2470 in killed and wounded, but it was still further depleted by straggling, so that Meade reported less than 7000 men with the colours that evening. Its organisation was preserved, however, and the story that it was utterly dispersed was a mistake.

Greene's division, on the left of the Twelfth Corps, profited by the hard fighting of those who had preceded it, and was able to drive the enemy quite out of the East Wood and across the open fields between it and the Dunker Church. Greene even succeeded, about the time of Sumner's advance, in getting a foothold about the Dunker Church itself, which he held for some time. (Until he was driven out, about 1:30, according to Generals Williams and Greene). But the fighting of Hooker's and Mansfield's men, though lacking unity of force and of purpose, had cost the enemy dear. J. R. Jones, who commanded Jackson's division, had been wounded; Starke, who succeeded Jones, was killed; Lawton, who followed Starke, was wounded.

Ewell's division, commanded by Early, had suffered hardly less. Hood was sent back into the fight to relieve Lawton, and had been reenforced by the brigades of Ripley, Colquitt, and McRae (Garland's), from D. H. Hill's division. When Greene reached the Dunker Church, therefore, the Confederates on that wing had suffered more fearfully than our own men. Nearly half their numbers were killed and wounded, and Jackson's famous "Stonewall" division was so completely disorganised that only a handful of men under Colonels Grigsby and Stafford remained and attached themselves to Early's command.

Of the division under Early, his own brigade was all that retained much strength, and this, posted among the rocks in the West Wood and vigorously supported by Stuart's horse artillery on the flank, was all that covered the left of Lee's army. Could Hooker and Mansfield have attacked together,—or, still better, could Sumner's Second Corps have marched before day and united with the first onset,—Lee's left must inevitably have been crushed long before the Confederate divisions, of McLaws, Walker, and A. P. Hill could have reached the field. It is this failure to carry out any intelligible plan which the historian must regard as the unpardonable military fault on the National side. To account for the hours between 4 and 8 on that morning, is the most serious responsibility of the National commander.

SUMNER'S ADVANCE.—FRENCH'S DIVISION CLOSING IN UPON ROULETTE'S BARNS AND HOUSE— RICHARDSON'S DIVISION CONTINUING THE LINE FAR TO THE LEFT. FROM A SKETCH MADE AT THE TIME.

Sumner's Second Corps was now approaching the scene of action, or rather two divisions of it—Sedgwick's and French's—Richardson's being still delayed till his place could be filled by Porter's troops, the strange tardiness in sending orders being noticeable in regard to every part of the army. (Sumner says Richardson came about an hour later. Howard, who succeeded Sedgwick, says his division moved "about 7." French says he followed "about 7:30." Hancock, who succeeded Richardson, says that officer received his orders "about 9:30.")

Sumner met Hooker, who was being carried from the field, and the few words he could exchange with the wounded general were enough to make him feel the need of haste, but not sufficient to give him any clear idea of the position.

Both Sedgwick and French marched their divisions by the right flank, in three columns, a brigade in each column, Sedgwick leading. They crossed the Antietam by Hooker's route, but did not march as far to the north-west as Hooker had done. When the centre of the corps

SCENE AT THE RUINS OF MUMMA'S HOUSE AND BARNS. FROM A SKETCH MADE AT THE TIME.

These buildings were fired early in the morning by D. H. Hill's men, who feared they would become a point of vantage to the Union forces. The sketch was made after the advance of French to the sunken road. Presumably, the battery firing upon the Confederate line to the right of that road is the First Rhode Island Light Artillery; for Captain John A. Tompkins, of Battery A, says, in his report, that he placed his pieces on a knoll "directly in front of some burning ruins," and opened fire upon a battery in front. "At 9:30," he continues, "the enemy appeared upon my right front with a large column, apparently designing to charge the battery. I was not aware of their approach until the head of the column gained the brow of a hill about sixty yards from the right gun of the battery. The pieces were immediately obliqued to the right and a sharp fire of canister opened upon them, causing them to retire in confusion, leaving the ground covered with their dead and wounded, and abandoning one of their battle-flags, which was secured by a regiment which came up on my right after the enemy had retreated. The enemy now opened a fire upon us from a battery in front, and also from one on the right near the white school-house (Dunker Church). Two guns were directed to reply to the battery on the right, while the fire of the rest was directed upon the guns in front, which were silenced in about twenty minutes, and one of their caissons blown up." At noon, Tompkins was relieved by Battery G.

was opposite the Dunker Church, and nearly east of it, the change of direction was given; the troops faced to then.' proper front and advanced in line of battle in three lines, fully deployed, and 60 or 70 yards apart, Sumner himself being in rear of Sedgwick's first line, and near its left.

When they approached the position held by Greene's division at Dunker Church, French kept on so as to form on Greene's left, while Sedgwick, under Sumner's immediate lead, diverged somewhat to the right, passing through the East Wood, crossing the turnpike on the right of Greene and of the Dunker Church, and plunged into the West Wood. At this point, there were absolutely no Confederate troops in front of them. Early was farther to the right, opposing Williams's division of the Twelfth Corps, and now made haste under cover of the woods to pass around Sedgwick's right and to get in front of him to oppose his progress. This led to a lively skirmishing fight in which Early was making as great a demonstration as possible, hut with no chance of solid success. At this very moment, however, McLaws's and Walker's divisions came upon the field, marching rapidly from Harper's Ferry.

Walker charged headlong upon the left flank of Sedgwick's lines, which were soon thrown into confusion, and McLaws, passing by Walker's left, also threw his division diagonally upon the already broken and retreating lines of Sumner. Taken at such a disadvantage, these had never a chance; and in spite of the heroic bravery of Sumner and Sedgwick, with most of their officers (Sedgwick being severely wounded), the division was driven off to the north with terrible losses, carrying along in the rout part of Williams's men of the Twelfth Corps, who had been holding Early at bay. All these troops were rallied at the ridge on the Poffenberger farm, where Hooker's corps had already taken position. Here some thirty batteries of both corps were concentrated, and, supported by the organised parts of all three of the corps which had fought upon this part of the field, easily repulsed all efforts of Jackson and Stuart to resume the aggressive or to pass between them and the Potomac.

Sumner himself did not accompany the routed troops to this position, but as soon as it was plain that the division could not be rallied, he galloped off to put himself in communication. with French and with the headquarters of the army and try to retrieve the misfortune. From the flag-station east of the East Wood he signalled to McClellan:

"Re-enforcements are badly wanted. Our troops are giving way."

179

MAJOR-GENERAL ISRAEL B. RICHARDSON.

Referring in his report to the incidents accompanying General Richardson's fall, General Caldwell says: "The enemy made one more effort to break my line, and this time the attack was made in the center. Colonel Barlow (General Francis C.), hearing firing to his left, on our old front, immediately moved to the left and formed in line with the rest of the brigade. The whole brigade then moved forward in line, driving the enemy entirely out of the corn-field (see E on the map) and through the orchard beyond, the enemy firing grape and canister from two brass pieces in the orchard to our front, and shell and spherical-case-shot from a battery on our right. While leading his men forward under the fire, Colonel Barlow fell dangerously wounded by a grape-shot in the groin. By command of General Richardson I halted the brigade, and, drawing back the line, re-formed it near the edge of the corn-field. It was now 1 o'clock P M. Here we lay exposed to a heavy artillery fire, by which General Richardson was severely wounded. The fall of General Richardson (General Meagher having been previously borne from the field) left me in command of the division, which I formed in line, awaiting the enemy's attack. Not long after, I was relieved of the command by General Hancock, who had been assigned to the command of the division by General McClellan." General Richardson was carried to Pry's house, McClellan's headquarters, where he died November 3d.

It was between 9 and 10 o'clock when Sumner entered the West Wood, and in fifteen minutes, or a little more, the one-sided combat was over.

★★★★★★

Sumner's principal attack was made, as I have already indicated, at right angles to that of Hooker. He had thus crossed the line of Hooker's movement both in the latter's advance and retreat. Greene's division was the only part of the Twelfth Corps troops he saw, and he led Sedgwick's men to the right of these. Ignorant, as he necessarily was, of what had occurred before, he assumed that he formed on the extreme right of the Twelfth Corps, and that he fronted in the same direction as Hooker had done. This misconception of the situation led him into another error. He had seen only a few stragglers and wounded men of Hooker's corps on the line of his own advance, and hence concluded that the First Corps was completely dispersed and its division and brigade organisations broken up.

He not only gave this report to McClellan at the time, but reiterated it later in his statement before the Committee on the Conduct of the War. The truth was that he had marched westward more than half a mile south of the Poffenberger hill, where Meade was with the sadly diminished but still organised First Corps, and half that distance south of the Miller farm buildings, near which Williams's division of the Twelfth Corps held the ground along the turnpike till they were carried away in the disordered retreat of Sedgwick's men toward the right. Sedgwick had gone in, therefore, between Greene and Williams, of the Twelfth Corps, and the four divisions of the two corps alternated in their order from left to right, thus: French, Greene, Sedgwick, Williams.—J. D. C.

★★★★★★

The enemy now concentrated upon Greene at the Dunker Church, and after a stubborn resistance he too was driven back across the turnpike and the open ground to the edge of the East Wood. Here, by the aid of several batteries gallantly handled, he defeated the subsequent effort to dislodge him. French had come up on his left, and both his batteries and the numerous ones on the Poffenberger hill swept the open ground and the cornfield over which Hooker had fought, and he was able to make good his position. The enemy was content to regain the high ground near the church, and French's attack upon D.

181

H. Hill was now attracting their attention.

The battle on the extreme right was thus ended before 10 o'clock in the morning, and there was no more serious fighting north of the Dunker Church. French advanced on Greene's left, over the open farm lands, and after a fierce combat about the Roulette and Clipp farm buildings, drove D. H. Hill's division from them. Richardson's division came up on French's left soon after, and foot by foot, field by field, from hill to hill and from fence to fence, the enemy was pressed back, till after several hours of fighting the sunken road, since known as "Bloody Lane," was in our hands, piled full of the Confederate dead who had defended it with their lives. Richardson had been mortally wounded, and Hancock had been sent from Franklin's corps to command the division. Barlow had been conspicuous in the thickest of the fight, and after a series of brilliant actions was carried off desperately wounded.

On the Confederate side, equal courage had been shown and a magnificent tenacity exhibited. But it is not my purpose to describe the battle in detail. I limit myself to such an outline as may make clear my interpretation of the larger features of the engagement and its essential plan.

The head of Franklin's corps (the Sixth) had arrived about 10 o'clock and taken the position near the Sharpsburg Bridge which Sumner had occupied. Before noon Smith's and Slocum's divisions were ordered to Sumner's assistance, and early in the afternoon Irwin and Brooks, of Smith, advanced to the charge and relieved Greene's division and part of French's, holding the line from Bloody Lane by the Clipp, Roulette, and Mumma houses to the East Wood and the ridge in front. Here Smith and Slocum remained till Lee retreated. Smith's division repelling a sharp attack. French and Richardson's battle may be considered as ended at 1 or 2 o'clock.

It seems to me very clear that about 10 o'clock in the morning was the great crisis in this battle. The sudden and complete rout of Sedgwick's division was not easily accounted for, and with McClellan's theory of the enormous superiority of Lee's numbers, it looked as if the Confederate general had massed overwhelming forces on our right. Sumner's notion that Hooker's corps was utterly dispersed was naturally accepted, and McClellan limited his hopes to holding on at the East Wood and the Poffenberger hill where Sedgwick's batteries were massed and supported by the troops that had been rallied there.

Franklin's corps as it came on the field was detained to support the threatened right centre, and McClellan determined to help it further by a demonstration upon the extreme left by the Ninth Corps. At this time, therefore (10 a. m.), he gave his order to Burnside to try to cross the Antietam and attack the enemy, thus creating a diversion in favour of our hard-pressed right.

✶✶✶✶✶✶

Here, in regard to the time at which Sumner was ordered to march to Hooker's support, is a disputed question of fact. In his official report, McClellan says he ordered Burnside to make this attack at 8 o'clock, and from the day that the latter relieved McClellan in command of the army, and especially after the Battle of Fredericksburg, a hot partisan effort was made to hold Burnside responsible for the lack of complete success at Antietam as well as for the repulse upon the Rappahannock. I think I understand the limitations of Burnside's abilities as a general, but I have had, ever since the battle itself, a profound conviction that the current criticisms upon him in relation to the Battle of Antietam. were unjust.

Burnside's official report declares that he received the order to advance at 10 o'clock. This report was dated on the 30th of September, within two weeks of the battle, and at a time when public discussion of the incomplete results of the battle was animated. It was made after he had in his hands my own report as his immediate subordinate, in which I had given about 9 o'clock as my remembrance of the time.

As I directed the details of the action at the bridge in obedience to this order, it would have been easy for him to have accepted the hour named by me, for I should have been answerable for any delay in execution after that time. But he believed he knew the time at which the order came to him upon the hill-top overlooking the field, and no officer in the whole army has a better established reputation for candour and freedom from any wish to avoid full personal responsibility for his acts.

It was not till quite lately that I saw a copy of his report or learned its contents, although I enjoyed his personal friendship down to the time of his death. He was content to have stated the fact as he knew it, and did not feel the need of debating it. Several circumstances have satisfied me that his accuracy in giving the hour was greater than my own. McClellan's preliminary report (dated October 16th, 1862) explicitly states that

183

CHARGE OF IRWIN'S BRIGADE (SMITH'S DIVISION) AT THE DUNKER CHURCH. FROM A SKETCH MADE AT THE TIME.

General Wm. F. Smith, commanding the Second Division of Franklin's corps, went to the assistance of French. On getting into position, for the most part to the right of French, General Smith, in his report, says: "Finding that the enemy were advancing, I ordered forward the Third Brigade (Colonel Irwin's), who, passing through the regular battery then commanded by Lieutenant Thomas (Fourth Artillery), charged upon the enemy and drove them gallantly until abreast the little church at the point of woods, the possession of which had been so fiercely contested. At this point a severe flank fire from the woods was received." The brigade rallied behind the crest of a slope, and remained in an advanced position until the next day.

the order to Burnside to attack was "communicated to him at 10 o'clock a. m." This exact agreement with General Burnside would ordinarily be conclusive in itself.—J. D. C.

★★★★★★

Facts within my own recollection strongly sustain this view that the hour was 10 a. m. I have mentioned the hill above the Burnside Bridge where Burnside took his position, and to which I went after the preliminary orders for the day had been issued. There I remained until the order of attack came, anxiously watching what we could see at the light, and noting the effect of the fire of the heavy guns of Benjamin's battery.

From that point we could see nothing that occurred beyond the Dunker Church, for the East and West Woods, with farmhouses and orchards between, made an impenetrable screen. But as the morning wore on we saw lines of troops advancing from our right upon the other side of the Antietam, and engaging the enemy between us and the East Wood. The Confederate lines facing them now rose into view. From our position we looked, as it were, down between the opposing lines as if they had been the sides of a street, and as the fire opened we saw wounded men carried to the rear and stragglers making off.

Our lines halted, and we were tortured with anxiety as we speculated whether our men would charge or retreat. The enemy occupied lines of fences and stone-walls, and their batteries made gaps in the National ranks. Our long-range guns were immediately turned in that direction, and we cheered every well-aimed shot. One of our shells blew up a caisson close to the Confederate line. This contest was going on, and it was yet uncertain which would succeed, when one of McClellan's staff, (Colonel D. B. Sackett, who says he got the order from McClellan about 9 o'clock), rode up with an order to Burnside. The latter turned to me, saying we were ordered to make our attack.

I left the hill-top at once to give personal supervision to the movement ordered, and did not return to it, and my knowledge by actual vision of what occurred on the right ceased. The manner in which we had waited, the free discussion of what was occurring under our eyes and of our relation to it, the public receipt of the order by Burnside in the usual and business-like form, all forbid the supposition that this was any reiteration of a former order. It was immediately transmitted to me without delay or discussion, further than to inform us that things were not going altogether well on the right, and that it was hoped our attack would be of assistance to that wing.

185

GENERAL McCLELLAN RIDING THE LINE OF BATTLE AT ANTIETAM. FROM A SKETCH MADE AT THE TIME.

The troops were Hooker's and Sedgwick's, and the time about 11 A. M. of September 17th. General McClellan rode his black horse, "Daniel Webster," which, on account of the difficulty of keeping pace with him, was better known to the staff as "that devil Dan.".

If then we can determine whose troops we saw engaged, we shall know something of the time of day; for there has been a general agreement reached as to the hours of movement during the forenoon on the right. The official map settles this. No lines of our troops were engaged in the direction of Bloody Lane and the Roulette farmhouse, and between the latter and our station on the hill, till French's division made its attack. We saw them distinctly on the hither side of the farm buildings, upon the open ground, considerably nearer to us than the Dunker Church or the East Wood. In number, we took them to be a corps.

The place, the circumstances, all fix it beyond controversy that they were French's men, or French's and Richardson's. No others fought on that part of the field until Franklin went to their assistance at noon or later. The incident of their advance and the explosion of the caisson was illustrated by the pencil of the artist, Forbes, on the spot, and placed by him at the time Franklin's head of column was approaching from Rohrersville, which was about 10 o'clock.

★★★★★★

It will not be wondered at, therefore, if to my mind the story of the 8 o'clock order is an instance of the way in which an erroneous memory is based upon the desire to make the facts accord with a theory. The actual time must have been as much later than 9 o'clock as the period during which, with absorbed attention, we had been watching the battle on the right,—a period, it is safe to say, much longer than it seemed to us. The Judgment of the hour, 9 o'clock, which I gave in my report, was merely my impression from passing events, for I hastened at once to my own duties without thinking to look at my watch, while the cumulative evidence seems to prove conclusively that the time stated by Burnside, and by McClellan himself in his original report, is correct.—J. D. C.

★★★★★★

McClellan truly said, in his original report, that the task of carrying the bridge in front of Burnside was a difficult one. The depth of the valley and the shape of its curve made it impossible to reach the enemy's position at the bridge by artillery fire from the hill-tops on our side. Not so from the enemy's position, for the curve of the valley was such that it was perfectly enfiladed near the bridge by the Confederate batteries at the position now occupied by the national cemetery. (See map). The Confederate defence of the passage was intrusted to D. E. Jones's division of four brigades, which was the one Longstreet himself had disciplined and led till he was assigned to a larger command.

Toombs's brigade was placed in advance, occupying the defences of the bridge itself and the wooded slopes above, while the other brigades supported him, covered by the ridges which looked down upon the valley. The division batteries were supplemented by others from the reserve, and the valley, the bridge, and the ford below were under the direct and powerful fire of shot and shell from the Confederate cannon. Toombs speaks in his report in a characteristic way of his brigade holding hack Burnside's corps; but his force, thus strongly supported, was as large as could be disposed of at the head of the bridge, and abundantly large for resistance to any that could be brought against it. Our advance upon the bridge could only be made by a narrow column, showing a front of eight men at most. But the front which Toombs deployed behind his defences was three or four hundred yards both above and below the bridge. He himself says in his report:

> From the nature of the ground on the other side, the enemy were compelled to approach mainly by the road which led up the river for near three hundred paces parallel with my line of battle and distant therefrom from fifty to a hundred and fifty feet, thus exposing his flank to a destructive fire the most of that distance.

Under such circumstances, I do not hesitate to affirm that the Confederate position was virtually impregnable to a direct attack over the bridge, for the column approaching it was not only exposed at pistol-range to the perfectly covered infantry of the enemy and to two batteries which were assigned to the special duty of supporting Toombs, and which had the exact range of the little valley with their shrapnel, but if it should succeed in reaching the bridge its charge across it must be made under a fire ploughing through its length, the head of the column melting away as it advanced, so that, as every soldier knows, it could show no front strong enough to make an impression upon the enemy's breastworks, even if it should reach the other side.

As a desperate sort of diversion in favour of the right wing, it might be justifiable; but I believe that no officer or man who knew the actual situation at that bridge thinks a serious attack upon it was any part of McClellan's original plan. Yet, in his detailed official report, instead of speaking of it as the difficult task the original report had called it, he treats it as little different from a parade or march across, which might have been done in half an hour.

BRIGADIER-GENERAL ISAAC P. RODMAN,
MORTALLY WOUNDED AT ANTIETAM

Burnside's view of the matter was that the front attack at the bridge was so difficult that the passage by the ford below must be an important factor in the task; for if Rodman's division should succeed in getting across there, at the bend in the Antietam, he would come up in rear of Toombs, and either the whole of D. E. Jones's division would have to advance to meet Rodman, or Toombs must abandon the bridge. In this I certainly concurred, and Rodman was ordered to push rapidly for the ford. It is important to remember, however, that Walker's Confederate division had been posted during the earlier morning to hold that part of the Antietam line, and it was probably from him that Rodman suffered the first casualties which occurred in his ranks.

But, as we have seen, Walker had been called away by Lee only an hour before, and had made the hasty march by the rear of Sharpsburg, to fall upon Sedgwick. If, therefore, Rodman had been sent to cross at 8 o'clock, it is safe to say that his column fording the stream in the face of Walker's deployed division would never have reached the farther bank,—a contingency that McClellan did not consider when arguing long afterward the favourable results that might have followed an earlier attack. As Rodman died upon the field, no full report for his division was made, and we only know that he met with some resistance from both infantry and artillery; that the winding of the stream made his march longer than he anticipated, and that, in fact, he only approached the rear of Toombs's position from that direction about the time when our last and successful charge upon the bridge was made, between noon and 1 o'clock.

The attacks at Burnside's Bridge were made under my own eye. Sturgis's division occupied the centre of our line, with Crook's brigade of the Kanawha Division on his right front, and Willcox's division in reserve, as I have already stated. Crook's position was somewhat above the bridge, but it was thought that by advancing part of Sturgis's men to the brow of the hill they could cover the advance of Crook, and that the latter could make a straight dash down the hill to our end of the bridge. The orders were accordingly given, and Crook advanced, covered by the 11th Connecticut (of Rodman), under Colonel Kingsbury, deployed as skirmishers. In passing over the spurs of the hills, Crook came out on the bank of the stream above the bridge and found himself under a heavy fire. He faced the enemy and returned the fire, getting such cover for his men as he could and trying to drive off or silence his opponents.

The engagement was one in which the Antietam prevented the combatants from coming to close quarters, but it was none the less vigorously continued with musketry fire. Crook reported that his hands were full, and that he could not approach closer to the bridge. But later in the contest, and about the time that the successful charge at the bridge was made, he got five companies of the 28th Ohio over by a ford above. Sturgis ordered forward an attacking column from Nagle's brigade, supported and covered by Ferrero's brigade, which took position in a field of corn on one of the lower slopes of the hill opposite the head of the bridge. The whole front was carefully covered with skirmishers, and our batteries on the heights overhead were ordered to keep down the fire of the enemy's artillery.

Nagle's effort was gallantly made, but it failed, and his men were forced to seek cover behind the spur of the hill from which they had advanced. We were constantly hoping to hear something from Rodman's advance by the ford, and would gladly have waited for some more certain knowledge of his progress, but at this time McClellan's sense of the necessity of relieving the right was such that he was sending reiterated orders to push the assault. Not only were these forwarded to me, but to give added weight to my instructions Burnside sent direct to Sturgis urgent messages to carry the bridge at all hazards.

I directed Sturgis to take two regiments from Ferrero's brigade, which had not been engaged, and make a column by moving them by the flank, the one left in front and the other right in front, side by side, so that when they passed the bridge they could turn to left and right,

THE CHARGE ACROSS THE BURNSIDE BRIDGE. FROM A SKETCH MADE AT THE TIME.

In his report General Sturgis describes as follows the charge across the bridge:

"Orders arrived from General Burnside to carry the bridge at all hazards. I then selected the Fifty-first New York and the Fifty-first Pennsylvania from the Second Brigade, and directed them to charge with the bayonet. They started on their mission of death full of enthusiasm, and, taking a route less exposed than the regiments [Second Maryland and Sixth New Hampshire] which had made the effort before them, rushed at a double-quick over the slope leading to the bridge and over the bridge itself, with an impetuosity which the enemy could not resist; and the Stars and Stripes were planted on the opposite bank at 1 o'clock P. M., amid the most enthusiastic cheering from every part of the field from where they could be seen."

forming line as they advanced on the run. He chose the 51st New York, Colonel Robert B. Potter, and the 51st Pennsylvania, Colonel John P. Hartranft (both names afterward greatly distinguished), and both officers and men were made to feel the necessity of success.

At the same time Crook succeeded in bringing a light howitzer of Simmonds's mixed battery down from the hill-tops, and placed it where it had a point-blank fire on the farther end of the bridge. The howitzer was one we had captured in West Virginia, and had been added to the battery, which was partly made up of heavy rifled Parrott guns. When everything was ready, a heavy skirmishing fire was opened all along the bank, the howitzer threw in double charges of canister, the two regiments charged np the road in column with fixed bayonets, and in scarcely more time than it takes to tell it, the bridge was passed and Toombs's brigade fled through the woods and over the top of the hill.

The charging regiments were advanced in line to the crest above the bridge as soon as they were deployed, and the rest of Sturgis's division, with Crook's brigade, were immediately brought over to strengthen the line. These were soon joined by Rodman's division with Scammon's brigade, which had crossed at the ford, and whose presence on that side of the stream had no doubt made the final struggle of Toombs's men less obstinate than it would otherwise have been, the fear of being taken in rear having always a strong moral effect upon even the best of troops. It was now about 1 o'clock, and nearly three hours had been spent in a bitter and bloody contest across the narrow stream.

The successive efforts to carry the bridge had been made as closely following each other as possible. Each had been a fierce combat, in which the men, with wonderful courage, had not easily accepted defeat, and even when not able to cross the bridge had made use of the walls at the end, the fences, and every tree and stone as cover, while they strove to reach with their fire their well-protected and nearly concealed opponents. The lulls in the fighting had been short, and only to prepare new efforts. The severity of the work was attested by our losses, which, before the crossing was won, exceeded five hundred men and included some of our best officers, such as Colonel Kingsbury, of the 11th Connecticut; Lieutenant-Colonel Bell, of the 51st Pennsylvania, and Lieutenant-Colonel Coleman, of the 11th Ohio, two of them commanding regiments. The proportion of casualties to the number engaged was much greater than common, for the nature of the task required that comparatively few troops should be exposed at once, the others remaining under cover.

Our first task was to prepare to hold the height we had gained against the return assault of the enemy which we expected, and to reply to the destructive fire from the enemy's abundant artillery. The light batteries were brought over and distributed in the line. The men were made to lie down behind the crest to save them from the concentrated artillery fire which the enemy opened upon us as soon as Toombs's regiments succeeded in reaching their main line. But McClellan's anticipation of an overwhelming attack upon his right was so strong that he determined still to press our advance, and sent orders accordingly.

The ammunition of Sturgis's and Crook's men had been nearly exhausted, and it was imperative that they should be freshly supplied before entering into another engagement. Sturgis also reported his men so exhausted by their efforts as to be unfit for an immediate advance. On this I sent to Burnside the request that Willcox's division be sent over, with an ammunition train, and that Sturgis's division be replaced by the fresh troops, remaining, however, on the west side of the stream as support to the others. This was done as rapidly as was practicable, where everything had to pass down the steep hill road and through so narrow a defile as the bridge.

Still, it was 3 o'clock before these changes and further preparations could be made. Burnside had personally striven to hasten them, and had come over to the west bank to consult and to hurry matters, and took his share of personal peril, for he came at a time when the ammunition wagons were delivering cartridges, and the road where they were, at the end of the bridge, was in the range of the enemy's constant and accurate fire. It is proper to mention this because it has been said that he did not cross the stream.

The criticisms made by McClellan as to the time occupied in these changes and movements will not seem forcible, if one will compare them with any similar movements on the field; such as Mansfield's to support Hooker, or Sumner's or Franklin's to reach the scene of action. About this, however, there is fair room for difference of opinion; what I personally know is that it would have been folly to advance again before Willcox had relieved Sturgis, and that as soon as the fresh troops reported and could be put in line, the order to advance was given. McClellan is in accord with all other witnesses in declaring that when the movement began, the conduct of the troops was gallant

193

BURNSIDE'S ATTACK UPON SHARPSBURG.   FROM A SKETCH MADE AT THE TIME.

In this attack Willcox's division (the right of the line) charged into the village. Colonel Fairchild, commanding a brigade in Rodman's division, on the left of the line (which included Hawkins's Zouaves, seen at the stone-wall in the picture), describes as follows in his report the advance upon Sharpsburg after the hill above the bridge had been gained: "We continued to advance to the opposite hill under a tremendous fire from the enemy's batteries, up steep embankments. Arriving near a stone fence, the enemy — a brigade composed of South Carolina and Georgia regiments — opened on us with musketry. After returning their fire I immediately ordered a charge, which the whole brigade gallantly responded to, moving with alacrity and steadiness. Arriving at the fence, behind which the enemy were awaiting us, receiving their fire, losing large numbers of our men, we charged over the fence, dislodging them and driving them from their positions down the hill toward the village, a stand of regimental colors belonging to a South Carolina regiment being taken by Private Thomas Hare, Company D, 89th New York Volunteers, who was afterward killed. We continued to pursue the enemy down the hill. Discovering that they were massing fresh troops on our left, I went back and requested General Rodman to bring up rapidly the Second Brigade to our support, which he did, they engaging the enemy, he soon afterward falling badly wounded. . . . The large force advancing on our left flank compelled us to retire from the position, which we could have held had we been properly supported."

beyond criticism.

Willcox's division formed the right, Christ's brigade being north and Welsh's brigade south of the road leading from the bridge to Sharpsburg. Crook's brigade of the Kanawha Division supported Willcox. Rodman's division formed on the left, Harland's brigade having the position on the flank, and Fairchild's uniting with Willcox at the centre. Scammon's brigade of the Kanawha Division was the reserve for Rodman on the extreme left. Sturgis's division remained and held the crest of the hill above the bridge. About half the batteries of the divisions accompanied the movement, the rest being in position on the hill-tops east of the Antietam. The advance necessarily followed the high ground toward Sharpsburg, and as the enemy made strongest resistance toward our right, the movement curved in that direction, the six brigades of D. R. Jones's Confederate division being deployed diagonally across our front, holding the stone fences and crests of the cross ridges and aided by abundant artillery, in which arm the enemy was particularly strong.

The battle was a fierce one from the moment Willcox's men showed themselves on the open ground. Christ's brigade, taking advantage of all the cover the trees and inequalities of surface gave them, pushed on along the depression in which the road ran, a section of artillery keeping pace with them in the road. The direction of movement brought all the brigades of the first line in echelon, but Welsh soon fought his way up beside Christ, and they, together, drove the enemy successively from the fields and farmyards till they reached the edge of the village. Upon the elevation on the right of the road was an orchard in which the shattered and diminished force of Jones made a final stand, but Willcox concentrated his artillery fire upon it, and his infantry was able to push forward and occupy it.

They now partly occupied the town of Sharpsburg, and held the high ground commanding it on the south-east, where the national cemetery now is. The struggle had been long and bloody. It was half-past 4 in the afternoon, and ammunition had again run low, for the wagons had not been able to accompany the movement. Willcox paused for his men to take breath again, and to fetch up some cartridges; but meanwhile affairs were taking a serious turn on the left. As Rodman's division went forward, he found the enemy before him seemingly detached from Willcox's opponents, and occupying ridges upon his left front, so that he was not able to keep his own connection with Willcox in the swinging movement to the right. Still, he made good progress in the face of stubborn resistance, though finding the enemy constantly developing more to his left, and the interval between him and Willcox widening. In fact, his movement became practically by column of brigades.

The view of the field to the south was now obstructed by fields of tall Indian corn, and under this cover Confederate troops approached the flank in line of battle. Scammon's officer's in the reserve saw them as soon as Rodman's brigades echeloned, as these were toward the front and right. This hostile force proved to be A. P. Hill's division of six brigades, the last of Jackson's force to leave Harper's Ferry, and which had reached Sharpsburg since noon. Those first seen by Scammon's men were dressed in the National blue uniforms which they had captured at Harper's Ferry, and it was assumed that they were part of our own forces till they began to fire.

Scammon quickly changed front to the left, drove back the enemy before him, and occupied a line of stone fences, which he held until he was withdrawn from it. Harland's brigade was partly moving in the corn-fields. One of his regiments was new, having been organised only three weeks, and the brigade had somewhat lost its order and connection when the sudden attack came. Rodman directed Colonel Harland to lead the right of the brigade, while he himself attempted to bring the left into position. In performing this duty, he fell mortally wounded, and the brigade broke in confusion after a brief effort of its right wing to hold on. Fairchild, also, now received the fire on his left, and was forced to fall back and change front.

Being at the centre when this break occurred on the left, I saw that it would be impossible to continue the movement to the right, and sent instant orders to Willcox and Crook to retire the left of their line, and to Sturgis to come forward into the gap made in Rodman's. The troops on the right swung back in perfect order; Scammon's brigade hung on at its stone-wall with unflinching tenacity till Sturgis had formed on the curving hill in rear of them, and Rodman's had found refuge behind. Willcox's left, then united with Sturgis and Scammon, was withdrawn to a new position on the left flank of the whole line.

That these manoeuvres on the field were really performed in good order is demonstrated by the fact that, although the break in Rodman's line was a bad one, the enemy was not able to capture many prisoners, the whole number of missing, out of the 2340 casualties which the Ninth Corps suffered in the battle, being 115, which includes wounded men unable to leave the field. The enemy were not lacking in bold efforts to take advantage of the check we had received, but were repulsed with severe punishment, and as the day declined were content to entrench themselves along the line of the road leading from Sharpsburg to the Potomac at the mouth of the Antietam, half a mile in our front.

The men of the Ninth Corps lay that night upon their arms, the line being one which rested with both flanks near the Antietam, and curved outward upon the rolling hill-tops which covered the bridge and commanded the plateau between us and the enemy. With my staff, I lay upon the ground behind the troops, holding our horses by the bridles as we rested, for our orderlies were so exhausted that we could not deny them the same chance for a little broken slumber.

The conduct of the battle on the left has given rise to several criticisms, among which the most prominent has been that Porter's corps, which lay in reserve, was not put in at the same time with the Ninth Corps.

★★★★★★

General Thomas M, Anderson, in 1886 Lieutenant-Colonel of the 9th Infantry, U. S. A., wrote to the editors in that year:

> At the Battle of Antietam, I commanded one of the battalions of Sykes's division of regulars, held in reserve on the north of Antietam creek near the stone bridge. Three of our battalions were on the south side of the creek, deployed as skirmishers in front of Sharpsburg. At the time A. P. Hill began to force Burnside back upon the left, I was talking with Colonel Buchanan, our brigade commander, when an orderly brought him a note from Captain (now Colonel) Blunt, who was the senior officer with the battalions of our brigade beyond the creek. The note, as I remember, stated in effect that Captain Dryer, commanding the 4th Infantry, had ridden into the enemy's lines, and upon returning had reported that there were but one Confederate battery and two regiments in front of Sharpsburg, connecting the wings of Lee's army.

(General Fitz John Porter writes to say that no such note as "Captain Dryer's report" was seen by him, and that no such discussion as to the opportunity for using the "reserve" took place between him and General McClellan. General Porter says that nearly all of his Fifth Corps—according to McClellan's report,

12,900 strong—instead of being idle at that critical hour, had been sent to re-enforce the right and left wings, leaving of the Fifth Corps to defend the centre a force "not then four thousand strong," according to General Porter's report.)

Dryer was one of the coolest and bravest officers in our service, and on his report Blunt asked instructions. We learned afterward that Dryer proposed that he, Blunt, and Brown, commanding the 4th, 12th, and 14th Infantries, should charge the enemy in Sharpsburg instanter. But Blunt preferred asking for orders. Colonel Buchanan sent the note to Sykes, who was at the time talking with General McClellan and Fitz John Porter, about a hundred and fifty yards from us. They were sitting on their horses between Taft's and Weed's batteries a little to our left. I saw the note passed from one to the other in the group, but could not, of course, hear what was said.

We received no orders to advance, however, although the advance of a single brigade at the time (sunset) would have cut Lee's army in two.

After the war, I asked General Sykes why our reserves did not advance upon receiving Dryer's report. He answered that he remembered the circumstance very well and that he thought McClellan was inclined to order In the Fifth Corps, but that when he spoke of doing so Fitz John Porter said: 'Remember, General! I command the last reserve of the last Army of the Republic.'

★★★★★★

McClellan answered this by saying that he did not think it prudent to divest the centre of all reserve troops. (At this time Sykes and Griffin, of Porter's corps, had been advanced, and part of their troops were actively engaged.) No doubt a single strong division marching beyond the left flank of the Ninth Corps would have so occupied A. P. Hill's division that our movement into Sharpsburg could not have been checked, and, assisted by the advance of Sumner and Franklin on the right, apparently would have made certain the complete rout of Lee. As troops are put in reserve, not to diminish the army, but to be used in a pinch,

I am deeply convinced that McClellan's refusal to use them on the left was the result of his continued conviction through all the day after Sedgwick's defeat, that Lee was overwhelmingly superior in force, and

PRESIDENT LINCOLN IN GENERAL MCCLELLAN'S TENT
AT ANTIETAM AFTER THE BATTLE.

was preparing to return a crushing blow upon our right flank. He was keeping something in hand to cover a retreat, if that wing should be driven back. Except in this way, also, I am at a loss to account for the inaction of our right during the whole of our engagement on the left. Looking at our part of the battle as only a strong diversion to prevent or delay Lee's following up his success against Hooker and the rest, it is intelligible.

I certainly so understood it at the time, as my report witnesses, and McClellan's preliminary report supports this view. If he had been impatient to have our attack delivered earlier, he had reason for double impatience that Franklin's fresh troops should assail Lee's left simultaneously with ours, unless he regarded action there as hopeless, and looked upon our movement as a sort of forlorn-hope to keep Lee from following up his advantages.

But even these are not all the troublesome questions requiring an answer. Couch's division had been left north-east of Maryland Heights to observe Jackson's command, supposed still to be in Harper's Ferry. Why could it not have come up on our left as well as A. P. Hill's division, which was the last of the Confederate troops to leave the Ferry, there being nothing to observe after it was gone? Couch's division, coming with equal pace with Hill's on the other side of the river, would have answered our needs as well as one from Porter's corps. Hill came, but Couch did not.

Yet even then, a regiment of horse watching that flank and scouring the country as we swung it forward would have developed Hill's presence and enabled the commanding general either to stop our movement or to take the available means to support it; but the cavalry was put to no such use; it occupied the centre of the whole line, only its artillery being engaged during the day. It would have been invaluable to Hooker in the morning as it would have been to us in the afternoon. McClellan had marched from Frederick City with the information that Lee's army was divided, Jackson being detached with a large force to take Harper's Ferry. He had put Lee's strength at 120,000 men.

Assuming that there was still danger that Jackson might come upon our left with a large force, and that Lee had proven strong enough without Jackson to repulse three corps on our right and right centre, McClellan might have regarded his own army as divided also for the purpose of meeting both opponents, and his cavalry would have been upon the flank of the part with which he was attacking Lee; Porter would have been in position to help either part in an extremity, or to cover a retreat, and Burnside would have been the only subordinate available to check Lee's apparent success. Will any other hypothesis intelligibly account for McClellan's dispositions and orders? The error in the above assumption would be that McClellan estimated Lee's troops at nearly double their actual numbers, and that what was taken for proof of Lee's superiority in force on the field was a series of partial reverses which resulted directly from the piecemeal and disjointed way in which McClellan's morning attacks had been made.

The same explanation is the most satisfactory one that I can give for the inaction of Thursday, the 18th of September. Could McClellan have known the desperate condition of most of Lee's brigades he would have known that his own were in much better case, badly as they had suffered. I do not doubt that most of his subordinates discouraged the resumption of the attack, for the rooted belief in Lee's preponderance of numbers had been chronic in the army during the whole year. That belief was based upon the inconceivably mistaken reports of the secret service organisation, accepted at headquarters, given to the War Department at Washington as a reason for incessant demands of re-enforcements, and permeating downward through the whole organisation till the error was accepted as truth by officers and men, and became a factor in their morale which can hardly be over-estimated.

The result was that Lee retreated unmolested on the night of the 18th, and that what might have been a real and decisive success was a drawn battle in which our chief claim to victory was the possession of the field.

The Ninth Corps occupied its position on the heights west of the Antietam without further molestation, except an irritating picket firing, till the Confederate army retreated. But the position was one in which no shelter from the weather could be had; nor could any cooking be done; and the troops were short of rations. Late in the afternoon of Thursday, Morell's division of Porter's corps was ordered to report to Burnside to relieve the picket line and some of the regiments in the most exposed position. One brigade was sent over the Antietam for this purpose, and a few of the Ninth Corps regiments were enabled to withdraw far enough to cook some rations of which they had been in need for twenty-four hours. (Porter in his report says that Morell took the place of the whole Ninth Corps. In this he is entirely mistaken, as the reports from Morell's division show.—J. D. C.) Harland's brigade of Edman's division had been taken to the east side of the stream on the evening of the 17th to be reorganised.

GENERAL McCLELLAN AND PRESIDENT LINCOLN AT ANTIETAM.

The Proclamation of Emancipation was published September 22d, three days after the withdrawal of Lee to Virginia, and was communicated to the army officially on September 24th.

On October 1st President Lincoln visited the army to see for himself if it was in no condition to pursue Lee into Virginia. General McClellan says in his general report: "His Excellency the President honored the Army of the Potomac with a visit, and remained several days, during which he went through the different encampments, reviewed the troops, and went over the battle-fields of South Mountain and Antietam. I had the opportunity during this visit to describe to him the operations of the army since the time it left Washington, and gave him my reasons for not following the enemy after he crossed the Potomac." In "McClellan's Own Story" he says that the President "more than once assured me that he was fully satisfied with my whole course from the beginning; that the only fault he could possibly find was, that I was too prone to be sure that everything was ready before acting, but that my actions were all right when I started. I said to him that I thought a few experiments with those who acted before they were ready would probably convince him that in the end I consumed less time than they did."

After the President's return to Washington, October 5th, Halleck telegraphed to McClellan under date of October 6th: "The President directs that you cross the Potomac and give battle to the enemy or drive him south," etc.

On October 7th McClellan, in "General Orders No. 163," referred to the Proclamation of Emancipation. He warned the army of the danger to military discipline of heated political discussions, and reminded them that the "remedy for political errors, if any are committed, is to be found only in the action of the people at the polls." On October 5th General McClellan had said, in a letter to his wife [see "McClellan's Own Story," p. 655], "Mr. Aspinwall [W. H., of New York] is decidedly of the opinion that it is my duty to submit to the President's proclamation and quietly continue doing my duty as a soldier. I presume he is right, and am at least sure that he is honest in his opinion. I shall surely give his views full consideration."

With Burnside at Antietam

By David L. Thompson, Co. G, 9th N.Y. Vols.

At Antietam our corps the Ninth, under Burnside—was on the extreme left, opposite the stone bridge. Our brigade stole into position about half-past 10 o'clock on the night of the 16th. No lights were permitted, and all conversation was carried on in whispers. As the regiment was moving past the 103rd New York to get to its place, there occurred, on a small scale and without serious results, one of those unaccountable panics often noticed in crowds, by which each man, however brave individually, merges his individuality for the moment, and surrenders to an utterly causeless fear. When everything was at its darkest and stealthiest one of the 103rd stumbled over the regimental dog, and, in trying to avoid treading on it, staggered against a stack of muskets and knocked them over.

The giving way of the two or three men upon whom they fell was communicated to others in a sort of wave movement of constantly increasing magnitude, re-enforced by the ever-present apprehension of attack, till two regiments were in confusion. In a few seconds order was restored, and we went on to our place in the line—a field of thin corn sloping toward the creek, where we sat down on the ploughed ground and watched for a while the dull glare on the sky of the Confederate campfires behind the hills. We were hungry, of course, but, as no fires were allowed, we could only mix our ground coffee and sugar in our hands and eat them dry. I think we were the more easily inclined to this crude disposal of our rations from a feeling that for many of us the need of drawing them would cease forever with the following day.

All through the evening the shifting and placing had gone on, the moving masses being dimly descried in the strange half lights of earth and sky. There was something weirdly impressive yet unreal in the gradual drawing together of those whispering armies under cover of the night—something of awe and dread, as always in the secret preparation for momentous deeds. By 11 o'clock the whole line, four miles or more in length, was sleeping, each corps apprised of its appointed task, each battery in place.

It is astonishing how soon, and by what slight causes, regularity of formation and movement are lost in actual battle. Disintegration begins with the first shot. To the book-soldier all order seems destroyed, months of drill apparently going for nothing in a few minutes. Next after the most powerful factor in this derangement—the enemy—come natural obstacles and the inequalities of the ground. One of the commonest is a patch of trees. An advancing line lags there inevitably, the rest of the line swinging around insensibly, with the view of keeping the alignment, and so losing direction. The struggle for the possession of such a point is sure to be persistent. Wounded men crawl to a wood for shelter, broken troops reform behind it, a battery planted in its edge will stick there after other parts of the line have given way. Often a slight rise of ground in an open field, not noticeable a thousand yards away, becomes, in the keep of a stubborn regiment, a powerful head-land against which the waves of battle roll and break, requiring new dispositions and much time to clear it. A stronger fortress than a casual railroad embankment often proves, it would be difficult to find; and as for a sunken road, what possibilities of victory or disaster lie in that obstruction, let Waterloo and Fredericksburg bear witness.

ON THE LINE OF A SCATTERED FENCE
AT ANTIETAM.

At Antietam it was a low, rocky ledge, prefaced by a corn-field. There were woods, too, and knolls, and there were other cornfields; but the student of that battle knows one cornfield only—the corn-field, now historic, lying a quarter of a mile north of Dunker Church, and east of and bordering the Hagerstown road. About it and across it, to and fro, the waves of battle swung almost from the first, till by 10 o'clock in the morning, when the struggle was over, hundreds of men lay dead among its peaceful blades.

While these things were happening on the right, the left was not without its excitement. A Confederate battery discovered our position in our corn-field, as soon as it was light enough to see, and began to shell us. As the range became better we were moved back and ordered to boil coffee in the protection of a hollow. The general plan of battle appears to have been to break through the Confederate left, following up the advantage with a constantly increasing force, sweep him away from the fords, and so crowd his whole army down into the narrow peninsula formed by the Potomac and Antietam Creek.

Even the non-military eye, however, can see that the tendency of such a plan would be to bring the two armies upon concentric arcs, the inner and shorter of which must be held by the enemy, affording him the opportunity for re-enforcement by interior lines—an im-mense advantage only to be counteracted by the utmost activity on our part, who must attack vigorously where attacking at all, and where not, imminently threaten. Certainly, there was no imminence in the threat of our centre or left—none whatever of the left, only a vague consciousness of whose existence even seems to have been in the en-emy's mind, for he flouted us all the morning with hardly more than a meagre skirmish line, while his coming troops, as fast as they arrived upon the ground, were sent off to the Dunker Church.

So, the morning wore away, and the fighting on the right ceased entirely. That was fresh anxiety—the scales were turning perhaps, but which way? About noon the battle began afresh. This must have been Franklin's men of the Sixth Corps, for the firing was nearer, and they came up behind the centre. Suddenly a stir beginning far up on the right, and running like a wave along the line, brought the regiment to its feet. A silence fell on every one at once, for each felt that the mo-mentous "now" had come. Just as we started I saw, with a little shock, a line-officer take out his watch to note the hour, as though the affair beyond the creek were a business appointment which he was going to keep.

When we reached the brow of the hill the fringe of trees along the creek screened the fighting entirely, and we were deployed as skirmishers under their cover. We sat there two hours. All that time the rest of the corps had been moving over the stone bridge and going into position on the other side of the creek. Then we were ordered over at a ford which had been found below the bridge, Where the water was waist-deep. One man was shot in mid-stream. At the foot of the slope on the opposite side the line was formed and we moved up through the thin woods. Reaching the level, we lay down behind a battery which seemed to have been disabled. There, if anywhere, I should have remembered that I was soaking wet from my waist down. So great was the excitement, however, that I have never been able to recall it. Here some of the men, going to the rear for water, discovered in the ashes of some hay-ricks which had been fired by our shells the charred remains of several Confederates. After long waiting it became noised along the line that we were to take a battery that was at work several hundred yards ahead on the top of a hill. This narrowed the field and brought us to consider the work before us more attentively.

Right across our front, two hundred feet or so away, ran a country road bordered on each side by a snake fence. Beyond this road stretched a ploughed field several hundred feet in length, sloping up to the battery, which was hidden in a cornfield. A stone fence, breast-high, enclosed the field on the left, and behind it lay a regiment of Confederates, who would be directly on our flank if we should attempt the slope. The prospect was far from encouraging, but the order came to get ready for the attempt.

Our knapsacks were left on the ground behind us. At the word, a rush was made for the fences. The line was so disordered by the time the second fence was passed that we hurried forward to a shallow undulation a few feet ahead, and lay down among the furrows to re-form, doing so by crawling up into line. A hundred feet or so ahead was a similar undulation to which we ran for a second shelter. The battery, which at first had not seemed to notice us, now, apprised of its danger, opened fire upon us. We were getting ready now for the charge proper, but were still lying on our faces. Lieutenant-Colonel Kimball was ramping up and down the line. The discreet regiment behind the fence was silent. Now and then a bullet from them cut the air over our heads, but generally they were reserving their fire for that better shot which they knew they would get in a few minutes.

The battery, however, whose shots at first went over our heads, had depressed its guns so as to shave the surface of the ground. Its fire was beginning to tell. I remember looking behind and seeing an officer riding diagonally across the field—a most inviting target—instinctively bending his head down over his horse's neck, as though he were riding through driving rain. While my eye was on him I saw, between me and him, a rolled overcoat with its straps on bound into the air and fall among the furrows.

One of the enemy's grape-shot had ploughed a groove in the skull of a young fellow and had cut his overcoat from his shoulders. He never stirred from his position, but lay there face downward—a dreadful spectacle. A moment after, I heard a man cursing a comrade for lying on him heavily. He was cursing a dying man. As the range grew better, the firing became more rapid, the situation desperate and exasperating to the last degree. Human nature was on the rack, and there burst forth from it the most vehement, terrible swearing I have ever heard. Certainly, the joy of conflict was not ours that day. The suspense was only for a moment, however, for the order to charge came just after. Whether the regiment was thrown into disorder or not, I never knew. I only remember that as we rose and started all the fire that had been held back so long was loosed.

In a second the air was full of the hiss of bullets and the hurtle of grape-shot. The mental strain was so great that I saw at that moment the singular effect mentioned, I think, in the life of Goethe on a similar occasions—the whole landscape for an instant turned slightly red. I

MAJOR-GENERAL JOHN G. WALKER, C. S. A.

see again, as I saw it then in a flash, a man just in front of me drop his musket and throw up his hands, stung into vigorous swearing by a bullet behind the ear. Many men fell going up the hill, but it seemed to be all over in a moment, and I found myself passing a hollow where a dozen wounded men lay—among them our sergeant-major, who was calling me to come down. He had caught sight of the blanket rolled across my back, and called me to unroll it and help to carry from the field one of our wounded lieutenants.

When I returned from obeying this summons the regiment (?) was not to be seen. It had gone in on the run, what there was left of it, and had disappeared in the cornfield about the battery. There was nothing to do but lie there and await developments. Nearly all the men in the hollow were wounded, one man—a recruit named Devlin, I think—frightfully so, his arm being cut short off. He lived a few minutes only. All were calling for water, of course, but none was to be had. We lay there till dusk,—perhaps an hour, when the fighting ceased. During that hour, while the bullets snipped the leaves from a young locust-tree growing at the edge of the hollow and powdered us with the fragments, we had time to speculate on many things—among others, on the impatience with which men clamour, in dull times, to be led into a fight.

We heard all through the war that the army "was eager to be led against the enemy." It must have been so, for truthful correspondents said so, and editors confirmed it. But when you came to hunt for this particular itch, it was always the next regiment that had it. The truth is, when bullets are whacking against tree-trunks and solid shot are cracking skulls like egg-shells, the consuming passion in the breast of the average man is to get out of the way. Between the physical fear of going forward and the moral fear of turning back, there is a predicament of exceptional awkwardness from which a hidden hole in the ground would be a wonderfully welcome outlet.

Night fell, preventing further struggle. Of 600 men of the regiment who crossed the creek at 3 o'clock that afternoon, 45 were killed and 176 wounded. The Confederates held possession of that part of the field over which we had moved, and just after dusk they sent out detachments to collect arms and bring in prisoners. When they came to our hollow all the unwounded and slightly wounded there were marched to the rear—prisoners of the 15th Georgia. We slept on the ground that night without protection of any kind; for, with a recklessness quite common throughout the war, we had thrown away

208

every incumbrance on going into the fight. The weather, however, was warm and pleasant, and there was little discomfort.

The next morning, we were marched—about six hundred of us, fragments of a dozen different commands—to the Potomac, passing through Sharpsburg. We crossed the Potomac by the Shepherdstown ford, and bivouacked in the yard of a house near the river, remaining there all day. The next morning (the 19th) shells began to come from over the river, and we were started on the road to Richmond with a mixed guard of cavalry and infantry. When we reached Winchester, we were quartered for a night in the court-house yard, where we were beset by a motley crew who were eager to exchange the produce of the region for greenbacks.

On the road between Shepherdstown and Winchester we fell in with the Maryland Battalion—a meeting I have always remembered with pleasure. They were marching to the front by companies, spaced apart about 300 or 400 feet. We were an ungainly, draggled lot, about as far removed as well could be from any claim to ceremonious courtesy; yet each company, as it passed, gave us the military salute of shouldered arms. They were noticeable, at that early stage of the war, as the only organisation we saw that wore the regulation Confederate gray, all other troops having assumed a sort of revised regulation uniform of homespun butternut—a significant witness, we thought, to the efficacy of the blockade.

From Winchester, we were marched to Staunton, where we were put on board cattle-cars and forwarded at night, by way of Gordonsville, to Richmond, where we entered Libby Prison. We were not treated with special severity, for Libby was not at that time the hissing it afterward became. Our time there, also, was not long. Only nine days after we entered it we were sent away, going by steamer to Camp Parole, at Annapolis. From that place, I went home without ceremony, reporting my address to my company officers. Three weeks afterward they advised me that I was exchanged—which meant that I was again, legally and technically, food for powder.

The Invasion of Maryland

By James Longstreet, Lieutenant-General, C. S. A.

When the Second Bull Run campaign closed we had the most brilliant prospects the Confederates ever had. We then possessed an army which, had it been kept together, the Federals would never have dared attack. With such a splendid victory behind us, and such bright prospects ahead, the question arose as to whether or not we should go into Maryland. General Lee, on account of our short supplies, hesitated a little, but I reminded him of my experience in Mexico, where sometimes we were obliged to live two or three days on green corn. I told him we could not starve at that season of the year so long as the fields were loaded with "roasting ear's."

Finally, he determined to go on, and accordingly crossed the river and went to Frederick City. On the 6th of September some of our cavalry, moving toward Harper's Ferry, became engaged with some of the Federal artillery near there. General Lee proposed that I should organise a force, and surround the garrison and capture it. I objected, and urged that our troops were worn with marching and were on short rations, and that it would be a bad idea to divide our forces while we were in the enemy's country, where he could get information, in six or eight hours, of any movement we might make. The Federal Army, though beaten at the Second Manassas, was not disorganised, and it would certainly come out to look for us, and we should guard against being caught in such a condition.

Our army consisted of a superior quality of soldiers, but it was in no condition to divide in the enemy's country. I urged that we should keep it well in hand, recruit our strength, and get up supplies, and then we could do anything we pleased. General Lee made no reply to this, and I supposed the Harper's Ferry scheme was abandoned. A day or two after we had reached Frederick City, I went up to General

Lee's tent and found the front walls closed. I inquired for the general, and he, recognising my voice, asked me to come in. I went in and found Jackson there. The two were discussing the move against Harper's Ferry, both heartily approving it. They had gone so far that it seemed useless for me to offer any further opposition, and I only suggested that Lee should use his entire army in the move instead of sending off a large portion of it to Hagerstown as he intended to do. General Lee so far changed the wording of his order as to require me to halt at Boonsboro' with General D. H. Hill; Jackson being ordered to Harper's Ferry *via* Bolivar Heights, on the south side; McLaws by the Maryland Heights on the north, and Walker, *via* Loudoun Heights, from the south-east. This was afterward changed, and I was sent on to Hagerstown, leaving D. H. Hill alone at South Mountain.

The movement against Harper's Ferry began on the 10th. Jackson made a wide, sweeping march around the Ferry, passing the Potomac at Williamsport, and moving from there on toward Martinsburg, and turning thence upon Harper's Ferry to make his attack by Bolivar Heights. McLaws made a hurried march to reach Maryland Heights before Jakobson could get in position, and succeeded in doing so. With Maryland Heights in our possession the Federals could not hold their position there. McLaws put 200 or 300 men to each piece of his artillery and carried it up the heights, and was in position when Jackson came on the heights opposite. Simultaneously Walker appeared upon Loudoun Heights, south of the Potomac and east of the Shenandoah, thus completing the combination against the Federal garrison. The surrender of the Ferry and the twelve thousand Federal troops there was a matter of only a short time.

If the Confederates had been able to stop with that, they might have been well contented with their month's campaign. They had had a series of successes and no defeats; but the division of the army to make this attack on Harper's Ferry was a fatal error, as the subsequent events showed.

While a part of the army had gone toward Harper's Ferry I had moved up to Hagerstown. In the meantime, Pope had been relieved and McClellan was in command of the army, and with ninety thousand refreshed troops was marching forth to avenge the Second Manassas. The situation was a very serious one for us. McClellan was close upon us. As we moved out of Frederick he came on and occupied that place, and there he came across a lost copy of the order assigning position to the several commands in the Harper's Ferry move.

This "lost order" has been the subject of much severe comment by Virginians who have written of the war. It was addressed to D. H. Hill, and they charged that its loss was due to him, and that the failure of the campaign was the result of the lost order. As General Hill has proved that he never received the order at his headquarters it must have been lost by someone else.

★★★★★★

See General Hill's statement and General Colgrove's. The following is the text of the "lost order" as quoted by General McClellan in his official report;

Special Orders, No. 191.

Headquarters, Army of Northern Virginia,
September 9th, 1862.

The army will resume its march tomorrow, taking the Hagerstown road. General Jackson's command will form the advance, and after passing Middletown, with such portions as he may select, take the route toward Sharpsburg, cross the Potomac at the most convenient point, and by Friday night take possession of the Baltimore and Ohio Railroad, capture such of the enemy as may be at Martinsburg, and intercept such as may attempt to escape from Harper's Ferry.

General Longstreet's command will pursue the same road as far as Boonsboro', where it will halt with the reserve, supply, and baggage trains of the army.

General McLaws, with his own division and that of General R. H. Anderson, will follow General Longstreet; on reaching Middletown he will take the route to Harper's Ferry, and by Friday morning possess himself of the Maryland Heights and endeavour to capture the enemy at Harper's Ferry and vicinity.

General Walker, with his division after accomplishing the object in which he is now engaged, will cross the Potomac at Cheek's ford, ascend its right bank to Lovettsville, take possession of Loudoun Heights, if practicable, by Friday morning, Keyes's ford on his left, and the road between the end of the mountain and the Potomac on his right. He will, as far as practicable, cooperate with General McLaws and General Jackson in intercepting the retreat of the enemy.

General D. H. Hill's division will form the rear-guard of the army, pursuing the road taken by the main body. The reserve artillery, ordnance, and supply trains, etc., will precede General Hill.

General Stuart will detach a squadron of cavalry to accompany the commands of Generals Longstreet, Jackson, and McLaws, and, with the main body of the cavalry, will cover the route of the army and bring up all stragglers that may have been left behind.

The commands of Generals Jackson, McLaws, and Walker, after accomplishing the objects for which they have been detached, will join the main body of the army at Boonsboro' or Hagerstown.

Each regiment on the march will habitually carry its axes in the regimental ordnance-wagons, for use of the men at their encampments, to procure wood, etc.

By command of General R. E. Lee.

R. H. Chilton, Assistant Adjutant-General.

Major-General D. H. Hill, Commanding Division.

Comparison of the above with the copy of the order as printed among the Confederate Correspondence (*Official Records* Volume XIX., Part II., p. 603) shows that the latter contains two paragraphs, omitted above. In the first paragraph, the officers and men of Lee's army are prohibited from visiting Fredericktown except on written permission; and in the second paragraph directions are given for the transportation of the sick and disabled to Winchester.

★★★★★★

Ordinarily, upon getting possession of such an order, the adversary would take it as a *ruse de guerre,* but it seems that General McClellan gave it his confidence, and made his dispositions accordingly. He planned his attack upon D. H. Hill under the impression that I was there with 12 brigades, 9 of which were really at Hagerstown, while R. H. Anderson's division was on Maryland Heights with General McLaws. Had McClellan exercised due diligence in seeking information from his own resources, he would have known better the situation at South Mountain and could have enveloped General D. H. Hill's division on the afternoon of the 13th, or early on the morning of the 14th, and then turned upon McLaws at Maryland Heights, before I could have reached either point. As it was, McClellan, af-

THE OLD LUTHERAN CHURCH, SHARPSBURG.

The church stands at the east end of the village, on Main street, and was a Federal hospital after the battle. Burnside's skirmishers gained a hold in the first cross-street below the church, where there was considerable fighting. On the hill in the extreme distance Main street becomes the Shepherdstown road, by which the Confederates retreated.

ter finding the order, moved with more confidence on toward South Mountain, where D. H. Hill was stationed as a Confederate rear-guard with five thousand men under his command.

As I have stated, my command was at Hagerstown, thirteen miles farther on. General Lee was with me, and on the night of the 13th we received information that McClellan was at the foot of South Mountain with his great army. General Lee ordered me to march back to the mountain early the next morning. I suggested that, instead of meeting McClellan there, we withdraw Hill and unite my forces and Hill's at Sharpsburg, at the same time explaining that Sharpsburg was a strong defensive position from which we could strike the flank or rear of any force that might be sent to the relief of Harper's Ferry.

I endeavoured to show him that by making a forced march to Hill my troops would be in an exhausted condition and could not make a proper battle. Lee listened patiently enough, but did not change his plans, and directed that I should go back the next day and make a stand at the mountain. After lying down, my mind was still on the battle of the next day, and I was so impressed with the thought that it would be impossible for us to do anything at South Mountain with

LEE'S HEADQUARTERS IN SHARPSBURG.

This house, which was the residence of Jacob H. Grove, is noted in Sharpsburg as the place where Lee held a conference with Longstreet and D. H. Hill. But Lee's headquarters tents were pitched in a small grove on the right of the Shepherdstown road, just outside the town.

the fragments of a worn and exhausted army, that I rose and, striking a light, wrote a note to General Lee, urging him to order Hill away and concentrate at Sharpsburg. To that note I got no answer, and the next morning I marched as directed, leaving General Toombs, as ordered by General Lee, at Hagerstown to guard our trains and supplies.

We marched as hurriedly as we could over a hot and dusty road, and reached the mountain about 3 o'clock in the afternoon, with the troops much scattered and worn. In riding up the mountain to join General Hill I discovered that everything was in such disjointed condition that it would be impossible for my troops and Hill's to hold the mountain against such forces as McClellan had there, and wrote a note to General Lee, in which I stated that fact, and cautioned him to make his arrangements to retire that night. We got as many troops up as we could, and by putting in detachments here and there managed to hold McClellan in check until night, when Lee ordered the withdrawal to Sharpsburg.

On the afternoon of the 15th of September my command and Hill's crossed the Antietam Creek, and took position in front of Sharpsburg, my command filing into position on the right of the Sharpsburg and Boonsboro' turnpike, and D. H. Hill's division on the left. Soon after getting into position we found our left, at Dunker Church, the weak point, and Hood, with two brigades, was changed from my right to guard this point, leaving General D. H. Hill between the parts of my command.

That night, after we heard of the fall of Harper's Ferry, General Lee ordered Stonewall Jackson to march to Sharpsburg as rapidly as he could come. Then it was that we should have retired from Sharpsburg and gone to the Virginia side of the Potomac.

The moral effect of our move into Maryland had been lost by our discomfiture at South Mountain, and it was then evident we could not hope to concentrate in time to do more than make a respectable retreat, whereas by retiring before the battle we could have claimed a very successful campaign.

On the forenoon of the 15th, the blue uniforms of the Federals appeared among the trees that crowned the heights on the eastern bank of the Antietam. The number increased, and larger and larger grew the field of blue until it seemed to stretch as far as the eye could see, and from the tops of the mountains down to the edges of the stream gathered the great army of McClellan. It was an awe-inspiring spectacle as this grand force settled down in sight of the Confederates, then shattered by battles and scattered by long and tiresome marches. On the 16th Jackson came and took position with part of his command on my left. Before night the Federals attacked my left and gave us a severe fight, principally against Hood's division, but we drove them back, holding well our ground.

After nightfall Hood was relieved from the position on the left, ordered to replenish his ammunition, and be ready to resume his first position on my right in the morning. General Jackson's forces, who relieved Hood, were extended to our left, reaching well back toward the Potomac, where most of our cavalry was. Toombs had joined us with two of his regiments, and was placed as guard on the bridge on my right. Hooker, who had thrown his corps against my left in the afternoon, was re-enforced by the corps of Sumner and Mansfield. Sykes's division was also drawn into position for the impending battle. Burnside was over against my right, threatening the passage of the Antietam at that point. On the morning of the 17th the Federals were in good position along the Antietam, stretching up and down and across it to our left for three miles. They had a good position for their guns, which were of the most approved make and metal. Our position over-crowned theirs a little, but our guns were inferior and our ammunition was very imperfect.

Back of McClellan's line was a high ridge upon which was his signal station overlooking every point of our field. D. R. Jones's brigades of my command deployed on the right of the Sharpsburg pike, while Hood's brigades awaited orders. D. H. Hill was on the left extending toward the Hagerstown-Sharpsburg pike, and Jackson extended out from Hill's left toward the Potomac. The battle opened heavily with the attacks of the corps of Hooker, Mansfield, and Sumner against our left centre, which consisted of Jackson's right and D. H. Hill's left. So severe and persistent were these attacks that I was obliged to send Hood to support our centre.

The Federals forced us back a little, however, and held this part of our position to the end of the day's work. With new troops and renewed efforts McClellan continued his attacks upon this point from time to time, while he brought his forces to bear against other points. The line swayed forward and back like a rope exposed to rushing currents. A force too heavy to be withstood would strike and drive in a weak point till we could collect a few fragments, and in turn force back the advance till our lost ground was recovered. A heroic effort was made by D. H. Hill, who collected some fragments and led

SOUTH-EASTERN STRETCH OF THE SUNKEN ROAD, OR "BLOODY LANE." SEE MAP

THE SUNKEN ROAD, OR "BLOODY LANE."
FROM A PHOTOGRAPH TAKEN SINCE THE WAR.

This view is from the second bend in the lane, looking toward the Hagerstown pike, the Dunker Church wood appearing in the background. In the foreground Richardson crossed to the left into the cornfield near Piper's house. The house in the middle-ground, erected since the war, marks the scene of French's hard fight after passing Roulette's house.

a charge to drive back and recover our lost ground at the centre. He soon found that his little band was too much exposed on its left flank and was obliged to abandon the attempt. Thus, the battle ebbed and flowed with terrific slaughter on both sides.

The Federals fought with wonderful bravery and the Confederates clung to their ground with heroic courage as hour after hour they were mown down like grass. The fresh troops of McClellan literally tore into shreds the already ragged army of Lee, but the Confederates never gave back.

I remember at one time they were surging up against us with fearful numbers. I was occupying the left over by Hood, whose ammunition gave out. He retired to get a fresh supply. Soon after the Federals moved up against us in great masses.

We were under the crest of a hill occupying a position that ought to have been held by from four to six brigades. The only troops there were Cooke's regiment of North Carolina infantry, and they were without a cartridge. As I rode along the line with my staff I saw two pieces of the Washington Artillery (Miller's battery), but there were not enough men to man them. The gunners had been either killed or wounded.

This was a fearful situation for the Confederate centre. I put my staff officers to the guns while I held their horses. It was easy to see that if the Federals broke through our line there, the Confederate army would be cut in two and probably destroyed, for we were already badly whipped and were only holding our ground by sheer force of desperation. Cooke sent me word that his ammunition was out. I replied that he must hold his position as long as he had a man left. He responded that he would show his colours as long as there was a man alive to hold them up. We loaded up our little guns with canister and sent a rattle of hail into the Federals as they came up over the crest of the hill.

That little battery shot harder and faster, with a sort of human energy, as though it realised that it was to hold the thousands of Federals at bay or the battle was lost. So warm was the reception we gave them that they dodged back behind the crest of the hill. We sought to make them believe we had many batteries before them. As the Federals would come up they would see the colours of the North Carolina regiment waving placidly and then would receive a shower of canister. We made it lively while it lasted.

In the meantime, General Chilton, General Lee's chief of staff,

THE SUNKEN ROAD, LOOKING EAST FROM ROULETTE'S
LANE. FROM A PHOTOGRAPH TAKEN IN 1885.

CONFEDERATE DEAD (OF D. H. HILL'S DIVISION) IN THE SUNKEN ROAD.

made his way to me and asked, "Where are the troops you are holding your line with?"

I pointed to my two pieces and to Cooke's regiment, and replied, "There they are; but that regiment hasn't a cartridge."

Chilton's eyes popped as though they would come out of his head; he struck spurs to his horse and away he went to General Lee. I suppose he made some remarkable report, although I did not see General Lee again until night. After a little a shot came across the Federal front, ploughing the ground in a parallel line. Another and another, each nearer and nearer their line. This enfilade fire, so distressing to soldiers, was from a battery on D. H. Hill's line, and it soon beat back the attacking column.

Meanwhile, R. H. Anderson and Hood came to our support and gave us more confidence. It was a little while only until another assault was made against D. H. Hill, far over and extending toward our left, where McLaws and Walker were supporting Jackson. In this desperate effort, the lines seemed to swing back and forth for many minutes, but at last they settled down to their respective positions, the Confederates holding with a desperation which seemed to say, "We are here to die."

Meantime General Lee was over toward our right, where Burnside was trying to cross to the attack. Toombs, who had been assigned as guard at that point, did handsome service. His troops were footsore and worn from marching, and he had only four hundred men to meet the Ninth Corps. The little band fought bravely, but the Federals were pressing them slowly back. The delay that Toombs caused saved that part of the battle, however, for at the last moment A. P. Hill came in to re-enforce him, and D. H. Hill discovered a good place for a battery and opened with it. Thus, the Confederates were enabled to drive the Federals back, and when night settled down the army of Lee was still in possession of the field. But it was dearly bought, for thousands of brave soldiers were dead on the field and many gallant commands were torn as a forest in a cyclone. It was heart-rending to see how Lee's army had been slashed by the day's fighting.

Nearly one-fourth of the troops who went into the battle were killed or wounded. We were so badly crushed that at the close of the day ten thousand fresh troops could have come in and taken Lee's army and everything it had. But McClellan did not know it, and (apparently) feared, when Burnside was pressed back, that Sharpsburg was a Confederate victory, and that he would have to retire. As it was, when night settled down both armies were content to stay where they were.

ROULETTE'S FARM.

1.—View of William Roulette's farm-house. 2.—Roulette's spring-house, in which Confederate prisoners were confined during the battle. 3.—Roulette's spring, a copious fountain which refreshed many thirsty soldiers of both armies.

AFTER THE BATTLE — POSITION OF THE CONFEDERATE
BATTERIES IN FRONT OF DUNKER CHURCH.

During the progress of the Battle of Sharpsburg General Lee and I were riding along my line and D. H. Hill's, when we received a report of movements of the enemy and started up the ridge to make a reconnoissance. General Lee and I dismounted, but Hill declined to do so. I said to Hill, "If you insist on riding up there and drawing the fire, give us a little interval so that we may not be in the line of the fire when they open upon you." General Lee and I stood on the top of the crest with our glasses, looking at the movements of the Federals on the rear left. After a moment I turned my glass to the right—the Federal left. As I did so, I noticed a puff of white smoke from the mouth of a cannon.

"There is a shot for you," I said to General Hill. The gunner was a mile away, and the cannon-shot came whisking through the air for three or four seconds and took off the front legs of the horse that Hill sat on and let the animal down upon his stumps. The horse's head was so low and his croup so high that Hill was in a most ludicrous position. With one foot in the stirrup he made several efforts to get the other leg over the croup, but failed. Finally, we prevailed upon him to try the other end of the horse, and he got down. He had a third horse shot under him before the close of the battle. That shot at Hill was the second best shot I ever saw. The best was at Yorktown. There a Federal officer came out in front of our line, and sitting down to his little platting table began to make a map. One of our officers carefully sighted a gun, touched it off, and dropped a shell into the hands of the man at the little table.

★★★★★★

Major Alfred A. Woodhull, Surgeon, U. S. A., wrote from David's Island, N.Y., July 16th, 1886:

General Longstreet's 'best shot' was undoubtedly the shell that shattered the plane table that First Lieutenant Orlando G. Wagner, Topographical Engineer, was using in front of Yorktown, when he was mortally wounded, precisely as described, He died April 2lst, 1862.

Early on the morning of September 17th, 1862 (about 8 or 2 o'clock), I was standing near the guns of Captain Stephen H. Weed, 5th Artillery, when a small group came in sight, directly in our front, about a mile away. There was no firing of any importance at that time on our left, and Captain Weed, who was a superb artillerist himself, aimed and fired at the single mounted man and struck the horse.

I witnessed the shot, and have no doubt it was the one General Longstreet commemorates as the 'second best.' My recollection is that the horse was gray, and I had the impression that the party was somewhat to the left (south) of the turnpike. General Longstreet kindly writes me that he cannot now recall the hour, but that there was little firing at the time, and that the place 'was about twenty feet from the Boonsboro'pike, north.'

★★★★★★

When the battle was over and night was gathering, I started to Lee's headquarters to make my report. In going through the town, I passed a house that had been set afire and was still burning. The family was in great distress, and I stopped to do what I could for them. By that I was detained until after the other officers had reached headquarters and made their reports. My delay caused some apprehension on the part of General Lee that I had been hurt; in fact, such a report had been sent him. When I rode up and dismounted he seemed much relieved, and, coming to me very hurriedly for one of his dignified manner, threw his arms upon my shoulders and said:

"Here is my old war-horse at last."

When all the reports were in, General Lee decided that he would not be prepared the next day for offensive battle, and would prepare only for defence, as we had been doing.

The next day (the 18th) the Federals failed to advance and both armies remained in position. During the day, some of the Federals came

FIELD-HOSPITALS OF FRENCH'S DIVISION AT ANTIETAM.

These pictures, according to a letter received by the editors from Dr. Samuel Sexton (8th Ohio), represent two field-hospitals established for the use of French's division at Antietam. The upper one was in charge of Dr. Sexton, who sent back the wounded men under his care at the front to this place during the battle, and afterward organized a hospital for all of the wounded soldiers found there,—utilizing for that purpose two or three barns, and erecting, besides, a number of shelters (shown in the cut) out of Virginia split-rails, set up on end in two parallel rows, meeting at the top, where they were secured. The sheds thus made were afterward thatched with straw, and could accommodate about 10 or 15 men each.

The lower picture shows an adjacent hospital for wounded Confederate prisoners, which was in charge of Dr. Anson Hurd of the 14th Indiana, who is seen standing on the right.

over under a flag of truce to look after their dead and wounded. The following night we withdrew, passing the Potomac with our entire army. After we had crossed, the Federals made a show of pursuit, and a force of about fifteen hundred crossed the river and gave a considerable amount of trouble to the command under Pendleton. A. P. Hill was sent back with his division, and attacked the Federals who had crossed the river in pursuit of us. His lines extended beyond theirs, and he drove them back in great confusion. Some sprang over the bluffs of the river and were killed; some were drowned and others were shot.

★★★★★★

Major Alfred A. Woodhull, Surgeon, U. S. A., wrote from David's Island, K Y., July 21st, 1886, concerning this movement: Early Saturday, September 20th, Major Charles S. Lovell, 10th Infantry, crossed to reconnoiter with the Second Brigade (regulars), of Sykes's division, and other troops followed. On our ascent to the plateau we passed some abandoned artillery, but met with no opposition until nearly a mile from the bank, where a long infantry line was confronted unexpectedly. Major Lovell had been informed that cavalry was to cross before us at daylight, but we were then found to be in advance, and the cavalry which was to feel the way was in our rear, and being useless was at once withdrawn.

The overlapping size of the advancing force in front, its manifest effort to envelop our left flank as well, and the probability of its extension beyond our right, compelled an immediate return, which was effected with steadiness, while skirmishing. Infantry re-enforcements that had crossed the river were simultaneously withdrawn, but on the right the 118th Pennsylvania, known as the "Corn Exchange" regiment, suffered severely, especially in one wing, where it was said at the time that there was a misapprehension of orders. When our men were in the stream there were dropping shots, but there was no direct infantry fire of importance. A fierce Union artillery fire was kept up to cover the retreat of our right, which indeed lost heavily.

But there was no such slaughter as the Confederate reports announced (I think A. P, Hill put it at 3000, and said the Potomac was blue with the Yankee dead). Had the cavalry really been in advance, the reconnoissance could have been accomplished with comparative ease. I was a medical officer attached to the infantry, and, acting as an *aide* for Major Lovell, had opportunity

BLACKFORD'S, OR BOTELER'S, FORD, FROM THE MARYLAND SIDE. FROM A RECENT PHOTOGRAPH.

This picture, taken from the tow-path of the Chesapeake and Ohio Canal, shows the ford below Shepherdstown by which Lee's army retreated after Antietam, the cliff on the Virginia side being the scene of the disaster to the 118th Pennsylvania, or Corn Exchange, regiment. When Porter's corps arrived at the Potomac in pursuit, on September 19th, Confederate artillery on the cliffs disputed the passage. A small Union force, under General Griffin, moved across the river in face of a warm fire, and, scaling the heights, captured several pieces of artillery. This attacking party was recalled during the night. Next morning, the 20th, two brigades of Sykes's division crossed and gained the heights on the left by the cement mill, while one brigade of Morell's division advanced to the right toward Shepherdstown and ascended the heights by way of the ravine. The 118th Pennsylvania formed beyond the crest and abreast of the dam. Soon the Confederates attacked with spirit. The Union forces were withdrawn without much loss, except to the 118th Pennsylvania, which was a new regiment, numbering 737 men, and had been armed, as it proved, with defective rifles. They made a stout resistance, until ordered to retreat, when most of the men fled down the precipitous face of the bluff and thence across the river, some crossing on the dam, the top of which was then dry. They were also under fire in crossing; and out of 361 in killed, wounded, and captured at this place, the 118th Pennsylvania lost 269.

to witness what is here stated.

✶✶✶✶✶✶

Proceeding on our march, we went to Bunker Hill, where we remained for several days. A report was made of a Federal advance, but it turned out to be only a party of cavalry and amounted to nothing. As soon as the cavalry retired we moved back and camped around Winchester, where we remained until sometime in October. Our stragglers continued to come in until November, which shows how many we had lost by severe marches.

The great mistake of the campaign was the division of Lee's army. If General Lee had kept his forces together, he could not have suffered defeat. At Sharpsburg, he had hardly 37,000 men, who were in poor condition for battle, while McClellan had about 87,000, who were fresh and strong.

✶✶✶✶✶✶

This was Lee's estimate as stated to me at the time. It is much above the estimate of those who have since written of this campaign. Colonel Charles Marshall, in his evidence in the Fitz John Porter case, gives our forces at the Second Manassas on August 29th as 50,000, not including artillery or cavalry. R, H. Anderson Joined me on the night of August 29th, with over 4000.—J. L.

(Lee says officially that "Antietam was fought with less than 40,000 men on our side.")

✶✶✶✶✶✶

The next year, when on our way to Gettysburg, there was the same situation of affairs at Harper's Ferry, but we let it alone.

General Lee was not satisfied with the result of the Maryland campaign, and seemed inclined to attribute the failure to the Lost Dispatch; though I believe he was more inclined to attribute the loss of the dispatch to the fault of a courier or to other negligence than that of the officer to whom it was directed.

Our men came in so rapidly after the battle that renewed hope of gathering his army in great strength soon caused Lee to look for other and new prospects, and to lose sight of the lost campaign. But at Sharpsburg was sprung the keystone of the arch upon which the Confederate cause rested. Jackson was quite satisfied with the campaign, as the Virginia papers made him the hero of Harper's Ferry, although the greater danger was with McLaws, whose service was the severer and more important. Lee lost nearly 20,000 by straggling in this cam-

229

paign,—almost twice as many as were captured at Harper's Ferry.

The battle casualties of Jackson's command from the Rappahannock to the Potomac, according to the *Official Records*, were 4629, while mine, including those of R. H. Anderson's division, were 4725, making in all, 9354. That taken from the army of 55,000 at the Second Manassas left a force of 45,646 moving across the Potomac. To that number must be added the forces that joined us; namely, D. H. Hill with 5000, McLaws with 4000, and Walker with 2000. Thus, Lee's army on entering Maryland was made up of nearly 57,000 men, exclusive of artillery and cavalry. As we had but 37,000 at Sharpsburg, our losses in the several engagements after we crossed the Potomac, *including stragglers*, reached nearly 20,000.

Our casualties in the affairs of the Maryland campaign, including Sharpsburg, were 13,964. Estimating the casualties in the Maryland campaign preceding Sharpsburg at 2000, it will be seen that we lost at Sharpsburg 11,000 to 12,000. Only a glance at these figures is necessary to impress one with the number of those who were unable to stand the long and rapid marches, and fell by the wayside, *viz.*, 8000 to 9000. The Virginians who have written of the war have often charged the loss of the Maryland campaign to "laggards." It is unkind to apply such a term to our soldiers, who were as patient, courageous, and chivalrous as any ever marshalled into *phalanx*. Many were just out of the hospitals, and many more were crippled by injuries received in battle. They were marching without sufficient food or clothing, with their muskets, ammunition, provisions, and in fact their all, packed upon their backs. They struggled along with bleeding feet, tramping rugged mountain roads through a heated season. Such soldiers should not be called "laggards" by their countrymen. Let them have their well-earned honours though the fame of others suffer thereby.

RALLYING BEHIND THE TURNPIKE FENCE.

Sharpsburg

By John G. Walker, Major-Genbral, C. S. A.

A little past the hour of noon on the 16th of September, 1862, General "Stonewall" Jackson and myself reached General Lee's headquarters at Sharpsburg and reported the arrival of our commands. I am thus particular in noting the hour of the arrival of my division for the reason that some writers have fallen into the error of mentioning my arrival as coincident with that of McLaws's division, which was some twenty-two hours later.

The thought of General Lee's perilous situation, with the Potomac River in his rear, confronting, with his small force, McClellan's vast army, had haunted me through the long hours of the night's march, and I expected to find General Lee anxious and careworn. Anxious enough, no doubt, he was; but there was nothing in his look or manner to indicate it. On the contrary, he was calm, dignified, and even cheerful. If he had had a well-equipped army of a hundred thousand veterans at his back, he could not have appeared more composed and confident. On shaking hands with us, he simply expressed his satisfaction with the result of our operations at Harper's Ferry, and with our timely arrival at Sharpsburg; adding that with our re-enforeement he felt confident of being able to hold his ground until the arrival of the divisions of R. H. Anderson, McLaws, and A. P. Hill, which were still behind, and which did not arrive until the next day.

At four in the afternoon I received an order from General Lee to move at 3 o'clock the next morning, and take position with my division on the extreme right of his line of battle, so as to cover a ford of the Antietam, and to lend a hand, in case of necessity, to General Toombs, whose brigade was guarding the bridge over the Antietam called by Federal writers "Burnside's Bridge."

At daybreak on the 17th I took the position assigned me, form-

BURNSIDE'S BRIDGE — 1.

This picture, after a photograph taken in 1887, is a view of the Confederate position from the slope of the hill occupied by the Union batteries before a crossing was effected. At the time of the battle the buildings had not been erected, and the Confederate hill-side was covered with trees. A Confederate battery on the left enfiladed the crossing. Union sharp-shooters took advantage of the stone-wall on the right of the approach to the bridge. The continuation of the road to Sharpsburg is seen on the right across the bridge.

ing my line of battle on the crest of a ridge in front of the ford just mentioned. The ground, from my position to the creek, distant about five hundred yards, sloped gradually down to the crossing, just below which there was a wooded, bluff-like hill commanding the approach to the ford from the east. (The ford by which Rodman crossed after Walker's forces were withdrawn). Here I posted a battalion of skirmishers.

While these dispositions, after a careful reconnoissance of the ground on both sides of the Antietam, were being made, the booming of artillery, at some distance on my left, warned us that the battle had begun. As the morning wore on the firing grew heavier and heavier, until Elk Mountain, to the eastward, gave back an incessant echo.

About 9 o'clock an order was brought by a staff-officer of General Lee, directing me to hurry to the left to re-enforce Jackson, who was being hard pressed. Hastily recalling my skirmishers, I hurried forward, left in front, along the rear of the whole Confederate line of battle. As I passed what is now known as Cemetery Hill, I saw General Lee standing erect and calm, with a field-glass to his eye, his fine

BURNSIDE'S BRIDGE — II.

This picture, after a photograph taken in 1885, is a view of the Union position from the hill where Confederate artillery was planted to enfilade the bridge. From a point below, the 2d Maryland and the 6th New Hampshire charged up the road, but they were swept by such a murderous fire that only a few reached the bridge and sought shelter behind the stone-wall above. Subsequently, the bridge was carried by the 51st Pennsylvania and the 51st New York, charging from the pines on the hill-side

form sharply outlined against the sky, and I thought I had never seen a nobler figure. He seemed quite unconscious that the enemy's shells were exploding around and beyond him.

To those who have not been witnesses of a great battle like this, where more than a hundred thousand men, armed with all the appliances of modern science and skill, are engaged in the work of slaughtering each other, it is impossible by the power of words to convey an adequate idea of its terrible sublimity. The constant booming of cannon, the ceaseless rattle and roar of musketry, the glimpses of galloping horsemen and marching infantry, now seen, now lost in the smoke, adding weirdness to terror, all together make up a combination of sights and sounds wholly indescribable.

Opposite the rear of Longstreet's position, I overtook General Ripley, of D. H. Hill's division, who, after having had dressed a serious wound in the neck, was returning to the command of his brigade, then hotly engaged. From him I obtained some information of the progress of the battle in the centre.

Hurrying on, I was soon met by a staff-officer, who informed me

BRIGADIER-GENERAL ROSWELL S. RIPLEY, C.S.A.

that it was General Jackson's wish that I should go to the assistance of Hood, who was hard pressed and almost out of ammunition, adding that if I found the Federals in possession of the wood on the Hagerstown road, I must drive them out, as it was the key of the battlefield.

He further explained that there was between the wood, just referred to, and the left of D. H. Hill's position, a gap of at least a third of a mile, and that I must leave a part of my command to fill it, and to support the reserve batteries under Colonel Stephen D. Lee which would also occupy the gap.

For this purpose, I detached the 27th North Carolina and the 3rd Arkansas of Manning's brigade, and placed them under the orders of Colonel John R. Cooke, of the former regiment.

★★★★★★

These are the troops spoken of in General D. H. Hill's report as "Walker's," who assisted in the repulse of Federal General French, later in the day. As the main body of my division was some distance to the left of the cornfields where Cooke's regiments were posted, General Palfrey (in his volume *The Antietam and Fredericksburg*) expresses some uncertainty as to General Hill's meaning.—J.G.W.

See also General Longstreet's report previous.

★★★★★★

Moving forward, we soon reached the rear of Hood's position, and there, forming line of battle with Ransom on the left, we moved forward to Hood's relief, supported by McLaws's division, which at that moment (10:30 a. m.) arrived from Harper's Ferry. By this time the Federals (under Sedgwick) had forced Hood's men out of the wood, and were in possession of the key of the battle-field. To regain this position and restore our line was now the task before us. This we soon accomplished, but only after perhaps the severest struggle of the day.

The Federals contended for every foot of the ground, but, driven from rock to rock, from tree to tree, of the "West Wood," after a bloody struggle of some thirty minutes, Sedgwick's forces were pressed back into the open fields beyond, and, being there exposed to the fire of S. D. Lee's artillery, broke and fled in great disorder back to the cover of the "East Wood," beyond the Hagerstown road.

My loss in this attack was heavy, including the gallant Colonel Van H. Manning, commanding Walker's brigade, who fell severely wounded. The regiment which suffered most was the 30th Virginia. In the ardour of their pursuit of the enemy through the wood, the Virginians followed three hundred yards into the open, where they were fearfully cut up by the Federal batteries; they only saved themselves from annihilation by a timely retreat to the cover of the wood.

This ended the attempt of the Federals to drive Jackson from his position by infantry attacks. Their artillery, however, continued throughout the day to pour a heavy fire upon him, but with little effect. Our position was a most advantageous one. The space between it and the "East Wood," occupied by the Federals, consisted of meadows and corn-fields, intersected by fences, and in passing over the ground their attacking columns were exposed to the fire of our batteries. Sev-

CONFEDERATE DEAD ON THE WEST SIDE OF THE HAGERSTOWN ROAD
OPPOSITE THE CORNFIELD.

235

enty or eighty yards in front of our position, and parallel with it, was a ridge, which, although slight, was sufficient to cover our men as they lay down among the trees and bowlders which covered the ground. The projectiles from the Federal batteries, striking this ridge, passed harmlessly over our heads, shattering the branches of the trees and tumbling them down in showers upon our men. Occasionally a shell would explode above us and send its hissing fragments in the midst of us, but our loss from this cause was surprisingly small.

The Federal infantry assaults having ceased, about half-past twelve I sought Jackson to report that from the front of my position in the wood I thought I had observed a movement of the enemy, as if to pass through the gap where I had posted Colonel Cooke's two regiments. I found Jackson in rear of Barksdale's brigade, under an apple-tree, sitting on his horse, with one leg thrown carelessly over the pommel of his saddle, plucking and eating the fruit. Without making any reply to my report, he asked me abruptly: "Can you spare me a regiment and a battery?"

I replied that Colonel Hill's 49th North Carolina, a very strong regiment, was in reserve, and could be spared, and that I could also give him both French's and Branch's batteries, but that they were without long-range ammunition, which had been exhausted at Harper's Ferry.

Jackson then went on to say that, owing to the nature of the ground, General Stuart's cavalry could take no part in the battle and were in the rear, but that Stuart himself had reported for such duty as he could perform.

Jackson added that he wished to make up, from the different commands on our left, a force of four or five thousand men, and give them to Stuart, with orders to turn the enemy's right, and attack him in the rear; that I must give orders to my division to advance to the front, and attack the enemy as soon as I should hear Stuart's guns—and that our whole left wing would move to the attack at the same time. Then, replacing his foot in the stirrup, he said with great emphasis: "We'll drive McClellan into the Potomac."

After giving orders for the regiment and batteries to report to Stuart, I galloped down the line where I had posted Cooke, but found that General Longstreet, having observed the danger from General French's formidable attack, had ordered Cooke forward, and that (together with D. H. Hill's division) he was then closely engaged. Soon returning to my command, I repeated General Jackson's order to my brigade commanders and directed them to listen for the sound of

NORTH-WEST ANGLE OF THE "EAST WOOD" AND THE CORN-FIELD.
FROM A SKETCH MADE AT THE TIME.

When the artist sketched this scene he was told that the guns in the corn-field belonged to a Maryland battery (Union), which was firing into the Dunker Church wood beyond. Most of the dead and wounded in this angle of the "East Wood" were Confederates. One of them, under the large tree at the left, had bound his shattered leg with corn-stalks and leaves to stop the flow of blood. He asked for water, of which there was none, and then begged the artist to remove his dead comrade, who was lying partly upon him, which was done. He wanted to be carried out of the woods, because he expected his friends to return and fight for them again. At the right was a tall young Georgian with a shattered ankle, sitting at the feet of one of the dead, who, he said, was his father.

Stuart's guns. We all confidently expected to hear the welcome sound by 2 o'clock, at least, and as that hour approached every ear was on the alert. Napoleon at Waterloo did not listen more intently for the sound of Grouchy's fire than did we for Stuart's. Two o'clock came, hut nothing was heard of Stuart. Half-past two and then three, and still Stuart made no sign.

About half-past three a staff-officer of General Longstreet brought me an order from that general to advance and attack the enemy in my front. As the execution of this order would materially interfere with Jackson's plans, I thought it my duty before beginning the movement to communicate with General Longstreet personally. I found him in rear of the position in which I had posted Cooke in the morning, and upon informing him of Jackson's intentions, he withdrew his order.

While we were discussing this subject, Jackson himself joined us with the information of Stuart's failure to turn the Federal right, for the reason that he had found it securely *posted on the Potomac.* Upon my expressing surprise at this statement, Jackson replied that he also had been surprised, as he had supposed the Potomac much farther away; but he remarked that Stuart had an excellent eye for topography, and it must be as he represented. He added: "It is a great pity,—we should have driven McClellan into the Potomac."

By this time, with staff-officers, couriers, etc., we were a mounted group of some ten or a dozen persons, presenting so tempting a target that a Federal battery, at a distance of five hundred yards, opened fire upon us, but with no other result, strange to say, than the slaughter of the horse of one of my couriers.

The attempt of the Federals to penetrate our centre, and its repulse by D. H. Hill, materially assisted by Colonel John R. Cooke's two regiments of my division, ended infantry operations on our portion of the field for the day.

★★★★★★

The gallant conduct of Colonel Cooke on this occasion deservedly won for him promotion to the grade of brigadier-general. His losses in this engagement were terrible. In his own regiment, the 27th North Carolina, out of 26 commissioned officers who went into action, 18 were killed or wounded. In the 3rd Arkansas the losses were equally great.—J. G. W.

★★★★★★

The batteries, however, continued to pound away at each other until dark.

Late in the afternoon the direction of the firing on our extreme right was most alarming,—indicating, as it did, that the Federal left had forced a crossing of the Antietam, and that it must be perilously near our only line of retreat to the Potomac, at Shepherdstown. Could it be that A. P. Hill had come up and had been repulsed? If so, we had lost the day.

We hoped that A. P. Hill was still behind, but within striking distance. Soon the sound of musketry, which had almost ceased, roared out again with increased volume, indicating that fresh troops had been brought up, on one side or the other. For thirty minutes, the sound of the firing came steadily from the same direction; then it seemed to recede eastward, and finally to die away almost entirely. We knew then that Hill *was* up; that the Federals had been driven back, and that the Confederate Army had narrowly escaped defeat.

As night closed down, the firing along the whole line ceased; one of the bloodiest and most hotly contested battles of the war had been fought. The men of my division—worn out by a week's incessant marching and fighting by day and night—dropped down where they were, and could with difficulty be roused, even to take their cooked rations, brought up from our camp in the rear.

But there was little sleep for the ambulance corps; and all night long their lanterns could be seen flashing about the battlefield while they were searching for and bringing in the wounded, of friend and foe alike. In company with General Barksdale of Mississippi, whose brigade was on my left, I rode over that part of the battlefield where our own troops had been engaged, to see that none of the wounded had been overlooked. While passing along a worm fence, in the darkness, we heard a feeble voice almost under our horses' feet: "Don't let your horses t-r-e-a-d on m-e!" We at once pulled up, and peering over the pommels of our saddles into the darkness, we could distinguish the dim outlines of a human form extended across our path.

"Who are you?" we inquired.

"I belong to the 20th Mas-sa-chu-setts rig-i-ment," answered the voice; "I can't move—I think my back's broken."

We sent for an ambulance and gave orders to care for the poor fellow, who was one of Sedgwick's men. This was but one of the very many instances of human suffering we encountered that night.

During the whole of the 18th the two armies rested in the positions which they had occupied at the close of the battle. There was a tacit truce, and Federal and Confederate burying-parties passed freely between the lines.

We had fought an indecisive battle, and although we were, perhaps, in as good a condition to renew the struggle as the enemy were, General Lee recognised the fact that his ulterior plans had been thwarted by this premature engagement, and after a consultation with his corps commanders he determined to withdraw from Maryland. At dark on the night of the 18th the rearward movement began; and a little after sunrise of the next morning the entire Confederate army had safely recrossed the Potomac at Shepherdstown.

Detained in superintending the removal of a number of the wounded of my division, I was among the last to cross the Potomac. As I rode into the river I passed General Lee, sitting on his horse in the stream, watching the crossing of the wagons and artillery. Returning my greeting, he inquired as to what was still behind. There was nothing but the wagons containing my wounded, and a battery of artillery, all of which were near at hand, and I told him so. "Thank God!" I heard him say as I rode on.

UNION BURIAL PARTY AT ANTIETAM

Antietam Scenes

By Charles Carleton Coffin

The cannon were thundering when at early morn, September 17th, 1862, I mounted my horse at Hagerstown, where I had arrived the preceding day, as an army correspondent, upon its evacuation by the Confederates. The people of the town, aroused by the cannonade, were at the windows of the houses or in the streets, standing in groups, listening to the reverberations rolling along the valley. The wind was south-west, the clouds hanging low and sweeping the tree-tops on South Mountain.

The cannonade, reverberating from cloud to mountain and from mountain to cloud, became a continuous roar, like the unbroken roll of a thunderstorm. The breeze, being in our direction, made the battle seem much nearer than it was. I was fully seven miles from Hooker's battlefield, I turned down the Hagerstown and Sharpsburg turnpike at a brisk gallop, although I knew that Lee's army was in possession of the thoroughfare by the toll-gate which then stood about two miles north of Sharpsburg. A citizen who had left his home, to be beyond harm during the battle, had given me the information. The thought upper-most in my mind was to gain the left flank of the Confederate Army, mingle with the citizens, and so witness the battle from the Confederate side. It would be a grand accomplishment if successful. It would give me a splendid opportunity to see the make-up of the Confederate Army. It would be like going behind the scenes of a theatre. I was in citizen's dress; splashed with mud, and wore a dilapidated hat.

While wondering what would be the outcome of the venture, I came upon a group of farmers, who were listening with dazed coun-tenances to the uproar momentarily increasing in volume. It was no longer alone the boom of the batteries, but a rattle of musketry—at first like pattering drops upon a roof; then a roll, crash, roar, and rush, like a mighty ocean billow upon the shore, chafing the pebbles, wave on wave,—with deep and heavy explosions of the batteries, like the crashing of thunderbolts. I think the currents of air must have had something to do with the effect of sound. The farmers were walking about nervously, undecided, evidently, whether to flee or to remain.

"I wouldn't go down the pike if I were you," said one, addressing me. "You will ride right into the Rebs."

"That is just where I would like to go."

"You can't pass yourself off for a Reb; they'll see, the instant they set eyes on you, that you are a Yank, They'll gobble you up and take you to Richmond," said the second.

No doubt I acted wisely in leaving the turnpike and riding to gain the right flank of the Union line. A short distance and I came upon a Confederate soldier lying beneath a tree. He doubtless supposed that I was a cavalryman, and raised his hand as if to implore me not to shoot him. His face was pale and haggard, and he had dropped from the ranks through sheer exhaustion. I left the poor fellow with the conviction that he never again would see his Southern home.

A mile farther on and I came upon the driftwood of McClellan's army. Every army has its driftwood soldiers—valiant at the mess-table, brave in the story around the bivouac fire, but faint of heart when battle begins. Some of them were old skulkers, others fresh recruits, with bright uniforms, who had volunteered under the pressure of enthusiasm. This was their first battle and was not what they had pictured a battle to be.

"Where does this road lead to?" asked one with white lips.

"To Hagerstown. But where are you going?"

"Oh, our division has been ordered to Hagerstown," was the reply as they hastened on.

Ammunition trains were winding up the hill from the road leading to Keedysville. Striking across the fields, I soon came upon the grounds on Hoffman's farm selected for the field-hospitals. Even at that hour of the morning it was an appalling sight. The wounded were lying in rows awaiting their turn at the surgeons' tables. The hospital stewards had a corps of men distributing straw over the field for their comfort.

Turning from the scenes of the hospital, I ascended the hill and came upon the men who had been the first to sweep across the Hagerstown pike, past the toll-gate, and into the Dunker Church woods, only to be hurled back by Jackson, who had established his line in a strong position behind outcropping limestone ledges.

"There are not many of us left," was the mournful remark of an officer.

I learned the story of the morning's engagement, and then rode to the line of batteries on the ridge by the house of J. Poffenberger; if my memory serves me there were thirty guns in position there pointing south-west. There was a lull in the strife. All was quiet in the woods along the turnpike, and in the corn-field beyond D. R. Miller's house,—so quiet that I thought I would ride on to the front line, not knowing that the brigade lying upon the ground near the cannon was the advanced line of the army. I rode through Poffenberger's door-yard, and noticed that a Confederate cannon-shot had ripped through the building; another had upset a hive of bees, and the angry insects had taken their revenge on the soldiers. I walked my horse down the pike past the toll-gate.

"Hold on!" It was the peremptory hail of a Union soldier crouching under the fence by the roadside. "Where are you going?"

"I thought I would go out to the front!"

"The front! you have passed it. This is the picket line. If you know what is good for yourself, you'll skedaddle mighty quick. The Rebs are in the corn right out there."

I acted upon the timely advice and retreated to a more respectful distance; and none too soon, for a moment later the uproar began again—solid shot tearing through the woods and crashing among the trees, and shells exploding in unexpected places. I recall a round shot that came ricocheting over the ground, cutting little furrows, tossing the earth into the air, as the plough of the locomotive turns its white furrow after a snowstorm. Its speed gradually diminished and a soldier was about to catch it, as if he were at a game of baseball, but a united yell of "Look out!" "Don't!" "Take care!" "Hold on!" caused him to desist. Had he attempted it, he would have been knocked over instantly.

Turning from the conflict on the right, I rode down the line, toward the centre, forded the Antietam and ascended the hill east of it to the large square mansion of Mr. Pry, where General McClellan had established his headquarters. The general was sitting in an armchair in front of the house. His staff were about him; their horses, saddled and bridled, were hitched to the trees and fences. Stakes had been driven in the earth in front of the house, to which were strapped the headquarters telescopes, through which a view of the operations and movements of the two armies could be obtained.

It was a commanding situation. The panorama included fully two-thirds of the battlefield, from the woods by the Dunker Church southward to the hills below Sharpsburg.

The Fifth Corps, under Fitz John Porter, was behind the ridge extending south toward the bridge, where the artillery of the Ninth Corps was thundering. Porter, I remember, was with McClellan, watching the movements of the troops across the Antietam—French's and Richardson's divisions, which were forming in the fields east of Roulette's and Mumma's houses. What a splendid sight it was! How beautifully the lines deployed! The clouds which had hung low all the morning had lifted, and the sun was shining through the rifts, its bright beams falling on the flags and glinting from gun-barrel and bayonet. Upon the crest of the hill south of the Dunker Church, I could see Confederates on horseback, galloping, evidently with orders; for, a few moments later, there was another gleam in the sunshine from the bayonets of their troops, who were apparently getting into position to resist the threatened movement of French and Richardson.

Memory recalls the advance of the line of men in blue across the meadow east of Roulette's. They reach the spacious barn, which divides the line of men as a rock parts the current of a river, flowing around it, but uniting beyond. The orchard around the house screens the movement in part. I see the blue uniforms beneath the apple-trees. The line halts for alignment. The skirmishers are in advance. There are isolated puffs of smoke, and then the Confederate skirmishers scamper up the hill and disappear. Up the slope moves the line to the top of a knoll. Ah! what a crash! A white cloud, gleams of lightning, a yell, a hurrah, and then up in the corn-field a great commotion, men firing into each other's faces, the Confederate line breaking, the ground strewn with prostrate forms. The Confederate line in "Bloody Lane" has been annihilated, the centre pierced.

Just here McClellan lost a great opportunity. It was the plain dictate of common sense that then was the time when Porter's eleven thousand should have been sent across the Antietam and thrown like a thunderbolt upon the enemy. It was so plain that the rank and file saw it. "Now is the time" was the universal comment. But not a soldier stirred from his position. McClellan saw it, but issued no order. All through the day most of the Fifth Corps remained in reserve.

The battle was in the main fought by divisions—one after another. There was no concerted action, no hammering all along the line at the same time. Heavy blows were given, but they were not followed up. It has been said that McClellan's excuse for not throwing in Porter's corps at that moment was the reason given by Napoleon at Borodino when asked why he did not at a certain moment put in the Imperial Guard:

If I am defeated today, where is my army for tomorrow?

There was no parallel between Antietam and Borodino. The moment had come for dividing Lee's army at its centre and crushing it back upon the Potomac in utter rout. A. P. Hill, on his way from Harper's Ferry to join Lee, was at that moment fording the Potomac at Shepherdstown. This General McClellan did not know, but the fact was before him that French and Richardson had pierced the Confederate centre.

With the falling back of the Confederates I went up past Roulette's house to the sunken road. The hillside was dotted with prostrate forms of men in blue, but in the sunken road, what a ghastly spectacle! The Confederates had gone down as the grass falls before the scythe. Words are inadequate to portray the scene. Resolution and energy still lingered in the pallid cheeks, in the set teeth, in the gripping hand. I recall a soldier with the cartridge between his thumb and finger, the end of the cartridge bitten off, and the paper between his teeth when the bullet had pierced his heart, and the machinery of life—all the muscles and nerves—had come to a standstill. A young lieutenant had fallen while trying to rally his men; his hand was still firmly grasping his sword, and determination was visible in every line of his face. I counted fourteen bodies lying together, literally in a heap, amid the corn rows on the hillside. The broad, green leaves were sprinkled and stained with blood.

The close of the battle presented a magnificent spectacle as the artillery of both armies came into play. The arrival of A. P. Hill had a stimulating effect upon Lee's veterans, while the carrying off the bridge and the work accomplished by French's and Richardson's divisions in the centre gave great encouragement to the Union army. It was plain that Lee was economical in the use of artillery ammunition. In fact, he had a short supply. The engagements at Gainesville, Groveton, Bull Run, Chantilly, Harper's Ferry, and South Mountain had depleted his ammunition-chests, and supply trains had not reached him from the west side of the Potomac.

Far up on the Union right, as well as in the centre, the Union batteries were pounding. I recall a remarkable scene. The sun was going down,—its disc red and large as seen through the murky battle-cloud. One of Sumner's batteries was directly in line toward the sun, on the crest of the ridge north of the smoking ruins of Mumma's house and barn, and there was one piece of which the gunners, as they rammed home the cartridge, seemed to be standing in the sun. Beyond, hid from view by the distance and the low-hanging branches of the oaks by the Dunker Church, the Confederate guns were flashing. Immediately north of Sharpsburg, and along the hill in front, now the National Cemetery, Longstreet's cannon were in play. Halfway up the hill were Burnside's men sending out a continuous flame, with A. P. Hill's veterans confronting them.

All the country was flaming and smoking; shells were bursting above the contending lines; Burnside was asking for re-enforcements. How quickly Porter's eleven thousand could have rushed across Antietam bridge with no Confederates to oppose them, swept up the hillside and forced themselves like a wedge between Longstreet and A. P. Hill!—but McClellan had only Miller's battery to send him! The sun went down; the thunder died away, the musketry ceased, bivouac fires gleamed out as if a great city had lighted its lamps.

When the soldiers are seeking rest, the work of the army correspondent begins. All through the day eyes and ears have been open. The note-book, is scrawled with characters intelligible to him if read at once, but wholly meaningless a few hours later. He must grope his way along the lines in the darkness, visit the hospitals, hear the narratives of all, eliminate error, get at the probable truth, keeping ever in mind that each general thinks his brigade, each colonel his regiment, every captain his company, did most of the fighting. While thus visiting the lines, I heard a song rising on the night air sweet and plaintive:

Do they miss me at home, do they miss me?
'Twould be an assurance most dear
To know that this moment some lov'd one
Were saying, 'I wish he were here';
To feel that the group at the fireside
Were thinking of me, as I roam.
Oh, yes, 'twould be joy beyond measure
To know that they miss me at home.

Both before and after a battle, sad and solemn thoughts come to the soldier. Before the conflict they are of apprehension; after the strife there is a sense of relief; but the thinned ranks, the knowledge that the comrade who stood by your side in the morning never will stand there again, bring inexpressible sadness. The soldiers, with thoughts far away, were apprehensive that the conflict of the day was but a prelude to another struggle more fierce and bloody in the morning. They were in position and lying on their arms, ready to renew the battle at daylight; but day dawned and the cannon were silent. The troops were in line, yet there was no order to advance. I could hear now and then the isolated shots of the pickets. I could see that Lee had contracted his line between Dunker Church and Sharpsburg. His cannon were in position, his troops in line. Everybody knew that Franklin's corps was comparatively fresh; that McClellan had 29,000 men who either had as yet not fired a musket or had been only slightly engaged. Why did he not attack? No one could tell.

Riding up to the right, I found that hostilities had ceased; that the ambulance corps of both armies were gathering up the wounded in the field near the Dunker Church.

★★★★★★

Surgeon Jonathan Letterman, Medical Director, Army of the Potomac, reports as follows upon the work of his department on the field:

> Immediately after the retreat of the enemy from the field of Antietam, measures were taken to have all the Confederate wounded gathered in from the field, over which they lay scattered in all directions, and from the houses and barns in the rear of their lines, and placed under such circumstances as would permit of their being properly attended to, and at such points as would enable their removal to be effected to Frederick, and thence to Baltimore and Fortress Monroe to their own lines.
>
> They were removed as rapidly as their recovery would permit. . . . There were many cases both on our right and left whose wounds were so serious that their lives would be endangered by their removal; and to have every opportunity afforded them for recovery, the Antietam hospital, consisting of hospital tents and capable of comfortably accommodating nearly six hundred cases, was established at a place called Smoketown, near Keedysville, for those who were wounded on our right, and a similar hospital, but not so capacious,—the Locust

Spring hospital,—was established in the rear of the Fifth Corps for those cases which occurred on our left. To one or other of these hospitals all the wounded were carried whose wounds were of such a character as to forbid their removal to Frederick or elsewhere. . . . Immediately after the battle a great many citizens came within our lines in order to remove their relatives or friends who had been injured, and in a great many instances when the life of the man depended upon his remaining at rest.

It was impossible to make them understand that they were better where they were, and that a removal would probably be done only with the sacrifice of life. Their minds seemed bent on having them in a house. If that could be accomplished, all would, in their opinion, be well. No greater mistake could exist, and the results of that battle only added additional evidence of the absolute necessity of a full supply of pure air, constantly renewed—a supply which cannot be obtained in the most perfectly constructed building.

Within a few yards a marked contrast could be seen between the wounded in houses and barns and in the open air. Those in houses progressed less favourably than those in the barns, those in barns less favourably than those in the open air, although all were in other respects treated alike. The capacious barns, abundantly provided with hay and straw, the delightful weather with which we were favoured, and the kindness exhibited by the people afforded increased facilities to the medical department for taking care of the wounded thrown upon it by that battle. . . . . .

★★★★★★

Going out over the ground where the tides had ebbed and flowed, I found it thickly strewn with dead. I recall a Union soldier lying near the Dunker Church with his face turned upward, and his pocket Bible open upon his breast. I lifted the volume and read the words:

Though I walk through the valley of the shadow of death, I will fear no evil; for Thou art with me. Thy rod and Thy staff, they comfort me.

Upon the fly-leaf were the words:

We hope and pray that you may be permitted by a kind Providence, after the war is over, to return.

Nearby stood a wounded battery-horse and a shattered caisson belonging to one of Hood's batteries. The animal had eaten every blade of grass within reach. No human being ever looked more imploringly for help than that dumb animal, wounded beyond the possibility of moving, yet resolutely standing, as if knowing that lying down would be the end.

The assumed armistice came to an end, the pickets stood in hostile attitude once more, but the day wore away and no orders were issued for a renewal of the attack. Another morning, and Lee was beyond the Potomac. I galloped along the lines where his army had stood, and saw the wreck and ruin of battle. I recall the body of a Confederate sharpshooter, lying in the forks of a tree by the roadside, between the Dunker Church and Sharpsburg. Shells had exploded in the streets of Sharpsburg. The horses of a Confederate battery had gone down in a heap in the public square.

Porter's corps was passing through the town. McClellan and his staff came galloping up the hill. Porter's men swung their hats and gave a cheer; but few hurrahs came from the other corps—none from Hooker's. A change had come over the army. The complacent look which I had seen upon McClellan's countenance on the 17th, as if all were going well, had disappeared. There was a troubled look instead— a manifest awakening to the fact that his great opportunity had gone by. Lee had slipped through his fingers.

IN THE WAKE OF BATTLE.

1. SHEPHERDSTOWN, FROM
   THE MARYLAND SIDE.
2. BELOW SHEPHERDSTOWN
   —THE POTOMAC TO THE
   FORD BY WHICH LEE RE-
   TREATED (SHOWN WHERE
   THE RIVER NARROWS).

A Woman's Recollections of Antietam

By Mary Bedinger Mitchell

September, 1862, was in the skies of the almanac, but August still reigned in ours; it was hot and dusty. The railroads in the Shenandoah Valley had been torn up, the bridges had been destroyed, communication had been made difficult, and Shepherdstown, cornered by the bend of the Potomac, lay as if forgotten in the bottom of somebody's pocket. We were without news or knowledge, except when some chance traveller would repeat the last wild and uncertain rumour that he had heard. We had passed an exciting Sumner. Winchester had changed hands more than once; we had been "in the Confederacy" and out of it again, and were now waiting, in an exasperating state of ignorance and suspense, for the next move in the great game.

It was a saying with us that Shepherdstown was just nine miles from everywhere. It was, in fact, about that distance from Martinsburg and Harper's Ferry—-oft-mentioned names—and from Williamsport, where the armies so often crossed, both to and from Maryland. It was off the direct road between those places and lay, as I said, at the foot of a great sweep in the river, and five miles from the nearest station on the Baltimore and Ohio railroad. As no trains were running now, this was of little consequence; what was more important was that a turnpike road—unusually fine for that region of stiff, red clay—led in almost a straight line for thirty miles to Winchester on the south, and stretched northward, beyond the Potomac, twenty miles to Hagerstown.

Two years later it was the scene of "Sheridan's ride." Before the days of steam this had been part of the old posting-road between the Valley towns and Pennsylvania, and we had boasted a very substantial

251

bridge. This had been burned early in the war, and only the massive stone piers remained; but a mile and a half down the Potomac was the ford, and the road that led to it lay partly above and partly along the face of rocky and precipitous cliffs. It was narrow and stony, and especially in one place, around the foot of "Mount Misery," was very steep and difficult for vehicles.

It was, moreover, entirely commanded by the hills on the Maryland side, hut it was the ford over which some part of the Confederate army passed every year, and in 1863 was used by the main body of infantry on the way to Gettysburg. Beyond the river were the Cumberland Canal and its willow-fringed tow-path, from which rose the soft and rounded outlines of the hills that from their farther slopes looked down upon the battle-field of Antietam. On clear days, we could see the fort at Harper's Ferry without a glass, and the flag flying over it, a mere speck against the sky, and we could hear the gun that was fired every evening at sunset.

Shepherdstown's only access to the river was through a narrow gorge, the bed of a small tributary of the Potomac, that was made to do much duty as it slipped cheerily over its rocks and furnished power for several mills and factories, most of them at that time silent. Here were also three or four stone warehouses, huge empty structures, testifying mutely that the town had once had a business. The road to the bridge led through this cleft, down an indescribably steep street skirting the stream's ravine to whose sides the mills and factories clung in most extraordinary fashion; but it was always a marvel how anything heavier than a wheelbarrow could be pulled up its tedious length, or how any vehicle could be driven down without plunging into the water at the bottom.

In this odd little borough, then, we were waiting "developments," hearing first that "our men" were coming, and then that they were not coming, when suddenly, on Saturday, the 13th of September, early in the morning, we found ourselves surrounded by a hungry horde of lean and dusty tatterdemalions, who seemed to rise from the ground at our feet. I did not know where they came from, or to whose command they belonged; I have since been informed that General Jackson recrossed into Virginia at Williamsport, and hastened to Harper's Ferry by the shortest roads. These would take him some four miles south of us, and our haggard apparitions were perhaps a part of his force. They were stragglers, at all events,—professional, some of them, but some worn out by the incessant strain of that Sumner.

When I say that they were hungry, I convey no impression of the gaunt starvation that looked from their cavernous eyes. All day they crowded to the doors of our houses, with always the same drawling complaint:

"I've been a-marchin' an' a-fightin' for six weeks stiddy, and I ain't had n-a-r-thin' to eat 'cept green apples an' green cawn, an' I wish you'd please to gimme a bite to eat."

Their looks bore out their statements, and when they told us they had "clean gin out," we believed them, and went to get what we had. They could be seen afterward asleep in every fence corner, and under every tree, but after a night's rest they "pulled themselves together" somehow and disappeared as suddenly as they had come. Possibly they went back to their commands, possibly they only moved on to repeat the same tale elsewhere. I know nothing of numbers, nor what force was or was not engaged in any battle, but I saw the troops march past us every Sumner for four years, and I know something of the appearance of a marching army, both Union and Southern. There are always stragglers, of course, but never before or after did I see anything comparable to the demoralized state of the Confederates at this time. Never were want and exhaustion more visibly put before my eyes, and that they could march or fight at all seemed incredible.

As I remember, the next morning—it was Sunday, September 14th—we were awakened by heavy firing at two points on the mountains. We were expecting the bombardment of Harper's Ferry, and knew that Jackson was before it. Many of our friends were with him, and our interest there was so intense that we sat watching the bellowing and smoking Heights, for a long time, before we became aware that the same phenomena were to be noticed in the north. From our windows both points could be observed, and we could not tell which to watch more keenly. We knew—almost nothing except that there was fighting, that it must be very heavy, and that our friends were surely in it somewhere, but whether at South Mountain or Harper's Ferry we had no means of discovering. I remember how the day wore on, how we staid at the windows until we could not endure the suspense; how we walked about and came back to them; and how finally, when night fell, it seemed cruel and preposterous to go to bed still ignorant of the result.

Monday afternoon, about 2 or 3 o'clock, when we were sitting about in disconsolate fashion, distracted by the contradictory rumours, our negro cook rushed into the room with eyes shining and face working with excitement. She had been down in "de ten-acre lot to pick a few years ob cawn," and she had seen a long train of wagons coming up from the ford, and "dey is full ob wounded men, and de blood runnin' outen dem dat deep," measuring on her out-stretched arm to the shoulder. This horrible picture sent us flying to town, where we found the streets already crowded, the people all astir, and the foremost wagons, of what seemed an endless line, discharging their piteous burdens. The scene speedily became ghastly, but fortu-nately we could not stay to look at it. There were no preparations, no accommodations—the men could not be left in the street—what was to be done!

A Federal soldier once said to me, "I was always sorry for your wounded; they never seemed to get any care." The remark was ex-treme, but there was much justice in it. There was little mitigation of hardship to our unfortunate armies. We were fond of calling them Spartans, and they were but too truly called upon to endure a Spartan system of neglect and privation. They were generally ill-fed and ill-cared for. It would have been possible at this time, one would think, to send a courier back to inform the town and bespeak what comforts it could provide for the approaching wounded; but here they were, unannounced, on the brick pavements, and the first thing was to find roofs to cover them.

Men ran for keys and opened the shops, long empty, and the unused rooms; other people got brooms and stirred up the dust of ages; then swarms of children began to appear with bundles of hay and straw, taken from anybody's stable. These were hastily disposed in heaps, and covered with blankets—the soldiers' own, or blankets begged or bor-rowed. On these improvised beds the sufferers were placed, and the next question was how properly to dress their wounds. No surgeons were to be seen. A few men, detailed as nurses, had come, but they were incompetent, of course. Our women set bravely to work and washed away the blood or stanched it as well as they could, where the jolting of the long rough ride had disarranged the hasty binding done upon the battlefield.

But what did they know of wounds beyond a cut finger, or a boil? Yet they bandaged and bathed, with a devotion that went far to make up for their inexperience. Then there was the hunt for band-ages. Every housekeeper ransacked her stores and brought forth things new and old. I saw one girl, in despair for a strip of cloth, look about helplessly, and then rip off the hem of her white petticoat. The doctors

254

came up, by and by, or I suppose they did, for some amputating was done—rough surgery, you may be sure. The women helped, holding the instruments and the basins, and trying to soothe or strengthen. They stood to their work nobly; the emergency brought out all their strength to meet it.

One girl who had been working very hard helping the men on the sidewalks, and dressing wounds afterward in a close, hot room, told me that at one time the sights and smells (these last were fearful) so overcame her that she could only stagger to the staircase, where she hung, half conscious, over the banisters, saying to herself, "Oh, I hope if I faint someone will kick me into a corner and let me lie there!" She did not faint, but went back to her work in a few moments, and through the whole of what followed was one of the most indefatigable and useful. She was one of many; even children did their part.

It became a grave question how to feed so many unexpected guests. The news spread rapidly, and the people from the country neighbourhoods came pouring in to help, expecting to stay with friends who had already given up every spare bed and every inch of room where beds could be put up. Virginia houses are very elastic, but ours were strained to their utmost. Fortunately, some of the farmers' wives had been thoughtful enough to bring supplies of linen, and some bread and fruit, and when our wants became better known other contributions flowed in; but when all was done it was not enough.

We worked far into the night that Monday, went to bed late, and rose early next morning. Tuesday brought fresh wagon-loads of wounded, and would have brought despair, except that they were accompanied by an apology for a commissariat. Soon more reliable sources of supply were organised among our country friends. Some doctors also arrived, who—with, a few honourable exceptions—might as well have staid away. The remembrance of that worthless body of officials stirs me to wrath.

Two or three worked conscientiously and hard, and they did all the medical work, except what was done by our own town physicians. In strong contrast was the conduct of the common men detailed as nurses. They were as gentle as they knew how to be, and very obliging and untiring. Of course, they were uncouth and often rough, but with the wounded dying about us every day, and with the necessity that we were under for the first few days, of removing those who died at once that others not yet quite dead might take their places, there was no time to be fastidious; it required all our efforts to be simply decent, and we sometimes failed in that.

We fed our men as well as we could from every available source, and often had some difficulty in feeding ourselves. The townspeople were very hospitable, and we were invited here and there, but could not always go, or hesitated, knowing every house was full. I remember once, that having breakfasted upon a single roll and having worked hard among sickening details, about 4 o'clock I turned wolfishly ravenous and ran to a friend's house down the street. When I got there, I was almost too faint to speak, but my friend looked at me and disappeared in silence, coming back in a moment with a plate of hot soup. What luxury! I sat down then and there on the front doorstep and devoured the soup as if I had been without food for a week.

It was known on Tuesday that Harper's Ferry had been taken, but it was growing evident that South Mountain had not been a victory. We had heard from some of our friends, but not from all, and what we did hear was often most unsatisfactory and tantalizing. For instance, we would be told that someone whom we loved had been seen standing with his battery, had left his gun an instant to shake hands and send a message, and had then stepped hack to position, while our civilian informant had come away for safety, and the smoke of conflict had hidden battery and all from view. As night drew nearer, whispers of a great battle to be fought the next day grew louder, and we shuddered at the prospect, for battles had come to mean to us, as they never had before, blood, wounds, and death.

On the 17th of September, cloudy skies looked down upon the two armies facing each other on the fields of Maryland. It seems to me now that the roar of that day began with the light, and all through its long and dragging hours its thunder formed a background to our pain and terror. If we had been in doubt as to our friends' whereabouts on Sunday, there was no room for doubt now. There was no sitting at the windows now and counting discharges of guns, or watching the curling smoke. We went about our work with pale faces and trembling hands, yet trying to appear composed for the sake of our patients, who were much excited.

We could hear the incessant explosions of artillery, the shrieking whistles of the shells, and the sharper, deadlier, more thrilling roll of musketry; while every now and then the echo of some charging cheer would come, borne by the wind, and as the human voice pierced that demoniacal clangour we would catch our breath and listen, and try not to sob, and turn back to the forlorn hospitals, to the suffering at our feet and before our eyes, while imagination fainted at thought of those other scenes hidden from us beyond the Potomac.

On our side of the river there were noise, confusion, dust; throngs of stragglers; horsemen galloping about; wagons blocking each other, and teamsters wrangling; and a continued din of shouting, swearing, and rumbling, in the midst of which men were dying, fresh wounded arriving, surgeons amputating limbs and dressing wounds, women going in and out with bandages, lint, medicines, food. An ever-present sense of anguish, dread, pity, and, I fear, hatred—these are my recollections of Antietam.

When night came we could still hear the sullen guns and hoarse, indefinite murmurs that succeeded the day's turmoil. That night was dark and lowering and the air heavy and dull. Across the river innumerable camp-fires were blazing, and we could but too well imagine the scenes that they were lighting. We sat in silence, looking into each other's tired faces. There were no impatient words, few tears; only silence, and a drawing close together, as if for comfort. We were almost hopeless, yet clung with desperation to the thought that we were hoping. But in our hearts, we could not believe that anything human could have escaped from that appalling fire.

On Thursday, the two armies lay idly facing each other, but we could not be idle. The wounded continued to arrive until the town was quite unable to hold all the disabled and suffering. They filled every building and overflowed into the country round, into farmhouses, barns, corn-cribs, cabins,—wherever four walls and a roof were found together. Those able to travel were sent on to Winchester and other towns back from the river, but their departure seemed to make no appreciable difference. There were six churches, and they were all full; the Odd Fellows' Hall, the Freemasons', the little Town Council room, the barn-like place known as the Drill Room, all the private houses after their capacity, the shops and empty buildings, the school-houses,—every inch of space, and yet the cry was for room.

The unfinished Town Hall had stood in naked ugliness for many along day. Somebody threw a few rough boards across the beams, placed piles of straw over them, laid down single planks to walk upon, and lo, it was a hospital at once. The stone warehouses down in the ravine and by the river had been passed by, because low and damp and undesirable as sanatoriums, but now their doors and windows were thrown wide, and, with barely time allowed to sweep them, they were all occupied,—even the " old blue factory," an antiquated, crazy, dismal building of blue stucco that peeled off in great blotches, which had been shut up for years, and was in the last stages of dilapidation.

On Thursday night, we heard more than usual sounds of disturbance and movement, and in the morning, we found the Confederate Army in full retreat. General Lee crossed the Potomac under cover of the darkness, and when the day broke the greater part of his force—or the more orderly portion of it—had gone on toward Kearneysville and Leetown. General McClellan followed to the river, and without crossing got a battery in position on Douglas's Hill, and began to shell the retreating army and, in consequence, the town. What before was confusion grew worse; the retreat became a stampede. The battery may not have done a very great deal of execution, but it made a fearful noise. It is curous how much louder guns sound when they are pointed at you than when turned the other way! And the shell, with its long-drawn screeching, though no doubt less terrifying than the singing minie-ball, has a way of making one's hair stand on end. Then, too, everyone who has had any experience in such things, knows how infectious fear is, how it grows when yielded to, and how, when you once begin to run, it soon seems impossible to run fast enough; whereas, if you can manage to stand your ground, the alarm lessens and sometimes disappears.

Someone suggested that yellow was the hospital colour, and immediately everybody who could lay hands upon a yellow rag hoisted it over the house. The whole town was a hospital; there was scarcely a building that could not with truth seek protection under that plea, and the fantastic little strips were soon flaunting their ineffectual remonstrance from every roof-tree and chimney. When this specific failed the excitement became wild and ungovernable. It would have been ludicrous had it not produced so much suffering. The danger was less than it seemed, for McClellan, after all, was not bombarding the town, but the army, and most of the shells flew over us and exploded in the fields; but aim cannot be always sure, and enough shells fell short to convince the terrified citizens that their homes were about to be battered down over their ears.

The better people kept some outward coolness, with perhaps a feeling of "*nobelesse oblige*"; but the poorer classes acted as if the town were already in a blaze, and rushed from their houses with their families and household goods to make their way into the country. The road was thronged, the streets blocked; men were vociferating, women crying, children screaming; wagons, ambulances, guns, caissons, horsemen, footmen, all mingled—nay, even wedged and jammed together—in one struggling, shouting mass. The negroes were the worst, and with faces of a ghastly ash-colour, and staring eyes, they swarmed into the fields, carrying their babies, their clothes, their pots and kettles, fleeing from the wrath behind them. The comparison to a hornet's nest attacked by boys is not a good one, for there was no "fight" shown; but a disturbed ant-hill is altogether inadequate. They fled widely and camped out of range, nor would they venture back for days.

Had this been all, we could afford to laugh now, but there was another side to the picture that lent it an intensely painful aspect. It was the hurrying crowds of wounded. Ah me! those maimed and bleeding fugitives! When the firing commenced the hospitals began to empty. All who were able to pull one foot after another, or could bribe or beg comrades to carry them, left in haste. In vain we implored them to stay; in vain we showed thein the folly, the suicide, of the attempt; in vain we argued, cajoled, threatened, ridiculed; pointed out that we were remaining and that there was less danger here than on the road. There is no sense or reason in a panic.

The cannon were bellowing upon Douglas's Hill, the shells whistling and shrieking, the air rail of shouts and cries; we had to scream to make ourselves heard. The men replied that the "Yankees" were crossing; that the town was to be burned; that *we* could not be made prisoners, but they could; that, anyhow, they were going as far as they could walk, or be carried. And go they did. Men with cloths about their heads went hatless in the sun, men with cloths about their feet limped shoeless on the stony road; men with arms in slings, without arms, with one leg, with bandaged sides and backs; men in ambulances, wagons, carts, wheelbarrows, men carried on stretchers or supported on the shoulder of some self-denying comrade—all who could crawl went, and went to almost certain death. They could not go far, they dropped off into the country houses, where they were received with as much kindness as it was possible to ask for; but their wounds had become inflamed, their frames were weakened by fright and over-exertion: erysipelas, mortification, gangrene set in; and long rows of nameless graves still bear witness to the results.

Our hospitals did not remain empty. It was but a portion who could get off in any manner, and their places were soon taken by others, who had remained nearer the battlefield, had attempted to follow the retreat, but, having reached Shepherdstown, could go no farther. We had plenty to do, but all that day we went about with hearts bursting with rage and shame, and breaking with pity and grief for the needless, needless waste of life. The amateur nurses all stood firm, and managed to be cheerful for the sake of keeping their men quiet, but they could not be without fear.

One who had no thought of leaving her post desired to send her sister—a mere child—out of harm's way. She, therefore, told her to go to their home, about half a mile distant, and ask their mother for some yellow cloth that was in the house, thinking, of course, that the mother would never permit the girl to come back into the town. But she miscalculated. The child accepted the commission as a sacred trust, forced her way out over the crowded road, where the danger was more real than in the town itself, reached home, and made her request. The house had its own flag flying, for it was directly in range and full of wounded. Perhaps for this reason the mother was less anxious to keep her daughter with her; perhaps in the hurry and excitement she allowed herself to be persuaded that it was really necessary to get that strip of yellow flannel into Shepherdstown as soon as possible.

At all events, she made no difficulty, but with streaming tears kissed the girl, and saw her set out to go alone, half a mile through a panic-stricken rabble, under the fire of a battery and into a town whose escape from conflagration was at best not assured. To come out had been comparatively easy, for she was going with the stream. The return was a different matter. The turbulent tide had now to be stemmed. Yet she managed to work her way along, now in the road, now in the field, slipping between the wagon wheels, and once, at least, crawling under a stretcher.

No one had noticed her coming out, she was but one of the crowd; and now most were too busy with their own safety to pay much heed to anything else. Still, as her face seemed alone set toward the town, she attracted some attention. One or two spoke to her. Now it was, "Look-a here, little gal! don't you know you're a-goin' the wrong way?" One man looked at the yellow thing she had slung across her shoulder and said, with an approving nod:

"That's right, that's right; save the wounded if ye kin." She meant to do it, and finally reached her sister, breathless but triumphant, with as proud a sense of duty done as if her futile errand had been the deliverance of a city.

I have said that there was less danger than appeared, but it must not be supposed that there was none. A friend who worked chiefly in the old blue factory had asked me to bring her a bowl of gruel that someone had promised to make for one of her patients. I had just taken it to her, and she was walking across the floor with the bowl in her hands, when a shell crashed through a corner of the wall and passed out at the opposite end of the building, shaking the rookery to its foundations, filling the room with dust and plaster, and throwing her upon her knees to the floor. The wounded screamed, and had they not been entirely unable to move, not a man would have been left in the building. But it was found that no one was hurt, and things proceeded as before.

I asked her afterward if she was frightened. She said yes, when it was over, but her chief thought at the time was to save the gruel, for the man needed it, and it had been very hard to find any one composed enough to make it. I am glad to be able to say that he got his gruel in spite of bombs. That factory was struck twice. A schoolhouse, full of wounded, and one or two other buildings were hit, but I believe no serious damage was done.

On Saturday morning, there was a fight at the ford. The negroes were still encamped in the fields, though some, finding that the town was yet standing, ventured back on various errands during the day. What we feared were the stragglers and hangers-on and nondescripts that circle round an army like the great buzzards we shuddered to see wheeling silently over us. The people were still excited, anticipating the Federal crossing and dreading a repetition of the bombardment or an encounter in the streets. Some parties of Confederate cavalry rode through, and it is possible that a body of infantry remained drawn up in readiness on one of the hills during the morning, but I remember no large force of troops at any time on that day.

About noon, or a little after, we were told that General McClellan's advance bad been cheeked, and that it was not believed he would attempt to cross the river at once—a surmise that proved to be correct. The country grew more composed. General Lee lay near Leetown, some seven miles south of us, and General McClellan rested quietly in Maryland. On Sunday, we were able to have some short church services for our wounded, cut still shorter, I regret to say, by reports that the "Yankees" were crossing. Such reports continued to harass us, especially as we feared the capture of our friends, who would often ride down to see us during the day, but who seldom ventured to spend a night so near the river. We presently passed into debatable land, when we were in the Confederacy in the morning, in the Union after dinner, and on neutral ground at night. We lived through a disturbed and eventful autumn, subject to continual "alarms and excursions," but when this Saturday came to an end, the most trying and tempestuous week of the war for Shepherdstown was over.

CONFEDERATE MONUMENT AT SHEPHERDSTOWN. FROM A PHOTOGRAPH TAKEN IN 1885.